e Crux delivers. Rumelt is at the top of his game, masterfully breaking down v to think about strategy, diagnose challenges, and put coherent solutions) action. I experienced firsthand how his concept of 'addressable strategic llenge' was invaluable for the Defense Intelligence Agency."

—Lieutenant General (ret.) Robert P. Ashley Jr., director, Defense Intelligence Agency (2017–2020)

midst all the vacuous talk of business purpose, Rumelt gets to the crux. other triumph from the most insightful—and entertaining—commentator strategy writing today."

—Sir John Kay, London School of Economics, author of *Other People's Money* and *Obliquity*

ssential reading if you want to cut through the fog of what it takes to build d drive a successful business. The deep insight of *The Crux* lays out a road ap of first getting to a deep and clear diagnosis of your situation, then [build-g] a clear approach and direction to be followed by a set of actions. *The Crux* your guide to become a successful leader and strategist with impact."

—Essa Al-Saleh, CEO, Volta Trucks

ew have been as successful at integrating strategic management scholarship nd practice as Richard Rumelt. In this book, he develops insights and ideas oout strategy that are at once inspiring and actionable. He challenges many f our established assumptions about strategy, but also gives us a path forward) help identify and address the central strategic challenges facing real firms."

—Jay B. Barney, former editor in chief, Academy of Management Review, and presidential professor of strategic management, Eccles School of Business, the University of Utah

The Crux dissipates fog around what strategy is all about and establishes clar-ty. It forces strategists to reflect deeply on the issues that really matter and vhere strategic thinking and resources need to be deployed to succeed. In an ncreasingly complex world and an overflow of not-always-pertinent informa-tion that at times can be confusing, *The Crux* is refreshing and challenging. A must-read."

—Francesco Starace, CEO and general manager, Enel Group

"The German poet Friedrich Hölderlin once said, 'but where the danger grows, also grows the saving power.' This is what Richard Rumelt invites us to discover in this inspirational book. On the way to the summit, the crux is the point at which we either collapse and give up, or...a tipping point that will lead us to the next challenge. And this is about strategy, an ongoing process of identifying critical challenges and deciding what actions to take. Richard Rumelt's book is both a provocation and an invitation to find the crux and take decisive action accordingly."

—Tobias Martinez Gimeno, CEO, Cellnex Telecom

Praise for

The Crux

"*The Crux* shows why Richard Rumelt is a global authority on book takes you into real strategy situations ranging from Netfli ness to the US military's development of battle doctrine to a det of a three-day 'strategy foundry.' An immensely readable guide difficult subjects: how to create a way forward when facing kno

—Andy D. Bryant, chairman, Board Intel Corporat

"In his powerful new book, Rumelt tells us 'strategy is not mag does manage to cast a spell. As a reader, I was drawn into th drums and 'a-ha' or 'uh-oh' moments in each story. As a strate felt challenged and inspired to push myself to a higher level of ing us away from rote frameworks and feel-good prescriptions us into the company of great strategists where curiosity, creativ confront 'gnarly' situations by getting to the bottom of the r leveraging our power to crack it. For any leader looking to de of strategic thinking—and put it into practice—this book full tion and practical ideas will accelerate your progress."

—Chris Bradley, senior partner,
coauthor of *Strategy Beyond*

"Richard Rumelt is the thinker with the biggest impact on my companies I have been with, making my work more enjoyable the creation of wealth which is nothing short of astonishing. triumph, a big step forward in how to approach this most vital concept of the crux now makes it much easier to come up with th able, strategy. This is the book I will press into the hands of my best way to make them strategists."

—Simon Galbraith, CEO and cofou

"In this powerful and practical book, Rumelt reminds us that rea a process of setting financial goals—it's an in-depth, no-holds-bar tion about the real challenges facing the firm and the creativity re transformative solutions. Drawing on a range of intriguing exam shows us both how this can be done and the enormous benefits of

—Rebecca Henderson, John and Natt
University Professor, Harvard University, a
Reimagining Capitalism in a

"Strategy was a meaningless concept for our business until we eng ard Rumelt. He helped us turn away from empty goals and ficti of an unknown future and instead turn towards figuring out the issue so that we could focus on the right set of actions. This is the you'll need as a strategist if you are determined to build a focused ar strategy for your business."

—Dawn Farrell, president and CEO, TransAlta Corp. (2

The Crux

How Leaders Become Strategists

Richard P. Rumelt

PUBLICAFFAIRS
NEW YORK

Cover design by Pete Garceau
Cover illustrations © iStock/Getty Images

PublicAffairs
Hachette Book Group
1290 Avenue of the Americas, New York, NY 10104
www.publicaffairsbooks.com
@Public_Affairs

Printed in the United States of America

First Edition: May 2022

Published by PublicAffairs, an imprint of Perseus Books, LLC, a subsidiary of Hachette Book Group, Inc. The PublicAffairs name and logo is a trademark of the Hachette Book Group.

Print book interior design by Trish Wilkinson

Library of Congress Cataloging-in-Publication Data has been applied for.

ISBNs: 9781541701243 (hardcover), 9781541701267 (ebook)

LSC-C

Printing 1, 2022

For my Kate,
who is the best thing that ever happened to me

CONTENTS

Introduction

The Roof of the Dog's Ass

When I lived in Fontainebleau, France, I would go for noon walks in the nearby forest. Old and deep, it was the hunting grounds of French kings for five hundred years. Perhaps a hundred square miles in extent, it is now crossed by paths frequented by hikers, runners, and bicyclers. Most of the students from INSEAD, the graduate business school located in Fontainebleau, walk or picnic in the forest, but few seem to know it contains rock outcroppings that attract the best boulder climbers from all over the world.

On my walks I would sometimes pass the boulder route known as Le Toit du Cul de Chien (The Roof of the Dog's Ass). It is one of the finest sandstone boulder problems in the world. Standing at its base, I see a smooth twelve-foot face capped by a horizontal roof that extends out over me for about four feet. Above the roof is another vertical section leading to the top. I try a tiny foothold, then another, then slide down two feet to the ground.[1]

On a summer day I see two climbers preparing to try Le Toit du Cul de Chien. They climb without ropes, spotting each other in case of a fall. One, a German, tells me that he has been practicing by doing one-hand squeeze-grip pull-ups on a high door frame. Nevertheless, neither he nor his partner can make it up, each falling as they try to navigate the overhang. They each solve the first problem of advancing on very tiny footholds to a small dent that can hold one finger from the right hand. But they fail to get any farther, each falling down to the sand below. I admire their strength, ambition, and tenacity.

Climbers call such boulders "problems" and describe the toughest part as "the crux." In the case of the Cul de Chien, you cannot get up with just strength or ambition. You have to solve the puzzle of the crux and have the courage to make delicate moves almost two stories above the ground.

Sometime later, I see a talented climber work through the crux. To get off the ground, she toe-dances up about three feet and presses a finger of her right hand into that small dent. Using that amazingly poor hold, she swings her left heel over her left arm to cam on a tiny ledge, gaining support from the muscular tension in her body between her right finger and left leg. She arches her back to match the angle of the roof and extends her left hand to a small indent on the edge of the roof, large enough for one finger. (Figure 1 shows Asya Grechka successfully making that reach.) This is where most people fall off. Pulling straight up will put her chest against the lip of the overhang and push her fingers off the tiny grips.[2]

For the next move, hanging by a finger or two on each arm, she swings a bit in and then out . . . then snaps upward into space, clearing the edge, and slapping her left hand onto a round hold the size and shape of a half cantaloupe. Hanging onto the smooth round hold with finger strength and friction, she swings her leg up to press her right toe into a small indentation in the rock and then is finally able to use leg strength to reach a small niche. Another lunge, an invisible toehold, a mantelshelf, and she is on the top. Watching, my palms sweat.

Seeing these and other climbers in the Fontainebleau forest, one cannot help but marvel at this hidden reservoir of pure excellence. Beyond a pair of shoes, it is flesh, muscle, and nerve against stone and gravity. There are no stock options, no teams or owners, no audience but other climbers. No TV cameras or fan clubs. No million-dollar contracts or product endorsements. There are just people pushing

FIGURE 1. Le Toit du Cul de Chien—at the Crux

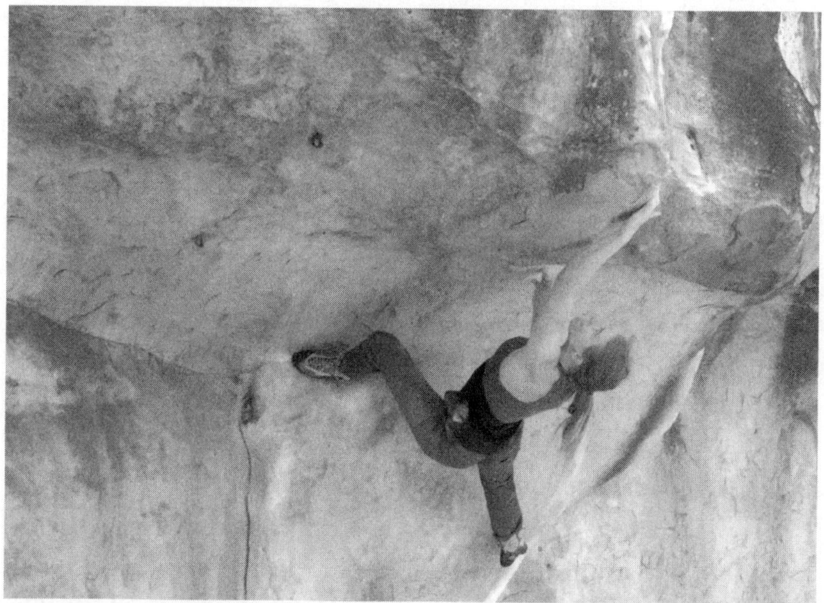

Source: From a video by Konrad Kalisch. See adventureroutine.de and clixmedia.eu.

themselves to their very limits for the private joy of doing something that, to the ordinary person, looks impossible.

Near another boulder I stop to chat with two French climbers who are having lunch. They are from a town in southern France. I ask them why they have driven past the Alps to come climb these boulders in Fontainebleau.

"These are the best boulders in Europe," one replies. "In the Alps," he continues, "I attempt the most interesting climbs where I think I can solve the crux. Here, I can get to a crux move in ten seconds and . . ."

"And fall off five times until you get it!" his partner says, smiling.

In France there are many mountains and boulders, each promising a different mixture of difficulty and reward, whether in terms of height, beauty, significance, or other measures. The first climber said that he chooses the climb having the greatest expected reward and whose crux he believes he can solve. In a flash of insight, I realize this describes the approaches of many of the more effective people I have known and observed. Whether facing problems or opportunities, they focused on the way forward promising the greatest *achievable* progress—the path whose crux was judged to be solvable.

I began to use the term *crux* to denote the outcome of a three-part strategic skill. The first part is judgment about which issues are truly important and which are secondary. The second part is judgment about the difficulties of dealing with these issues. And the third part is the ability to focus, to avoid spreading resources too thinly, not trying to do everything at once. The combination of these three parts lead to a focus on *the crux*—the most important part of a set of challenges that is addressable, having a good chance of being solved by coherent action.

As with climbers, every person, every company, every agency faces both opportunities and obstacles to their progress. Yes, we all need motivation, ambition, and strength. But, by themselves, they are not enough. To deal with a set of challenges, there is power in locating *your crux*—where you can gain the most by designing, discovering, or finding a way to move through and past it.

One of entrepreneur Elon Musk's passions is populating Mars. He imagined promoting this idea by sending a small payload there. In a 2001 visit to Russia, Musk tried to buy an old Russian rocket but was unhappy with the style of bargaining and how the price tripled during the negotiations. He began to look at the problem of why it cost so much to put payloads into orbit.

Studying the challenge, the cost was clearly due to the fact that rockets are not reusable. One payload takes one rocket. Musk came to believe that the *crux* of the cost issue was reentry. How could the rocket avoid the fiery furnace of blasting back through the atmosphere at eighteen thousand miles per hour? To make the old space shuttle reusable, the large wings had thirty-five thousand separate thermal tiles. Each had to perform perfectly, and each had to be inspected after each flight and then fitted back into its unique slot. The shuttle boosters were supposed to be reusable but became too damaged by the fall into the ocean to refurbish. It seemed to be cheaper to throw a rocket away than build it for reuse.

Think of this challenge as having a one-finger and left-heel hold on Cul de Chien with your body arched up to face the roof: What is the trick for letting those fingers go and lunging up to that half-cantaloupe hold? *The concept of a crux narrows attention to a critical issue.* A *strategy* is a mix of policy and action designed to overcome a significant challenge. The *art of strategy* is in defining a crux that can be mastered and in seeing or designing a way through it.

Focusing on the problems of reusability and reentry, Musk had an insight. Fuel was a lot cheaper than vehicles. It might make sense to avoid the huge complexity of super-high-heat reentry by carrying more fuel and using it to slow the rocket's return to Earth. Like many old science fiction stories, Musk imagined a rocket turning around and slowing down by firing its engine, softly landing. No violent reentry furnace, charring the outside of the vehicle. The process could be automated—no necessary human to fly it. The key would be engineering a rocket engine that could reliably start and stop and accurately throttle and direct its power.

For organizations, the usual way through the crux will be via intense focus, bringing many elements of power and knowledge and skill to bear. For the strategist, focus is not just attention. It means bringing a source of power to bear on a selected target. If the power is weak, nothing happens. If it is strong but scattered and diffused across targets, nothing happens. If power is focused on the wrong target, nothing happens. But when power is focused on the right target, breakthroughs occur.

When Musk started SpaceX in 2002, he created focused, coherent policies. SpaceX rockets would be complete redesigns and done in a low-cost, spare manner. They would not be adapted intercontinental ballistic missiles. SpaceX would not be one of thousands of contractors. Its vehicles would not try to satisfy the US Air Force by flying around the globe. There would be no complex of scientists wanting to explore the universe. No fancy R&D (research and development) labs. Musk saw the challenge as engineering, not high science. Unlike NASA, SpaceX would not be charged with the mission to inspire children to study science and math. The first step on the quest would be an intense single-minded focus on getting the cost down.

Many people challenged Musk that a low-cost approach would sacrifice reliability. His answer was pure engineer:

> We've been asked "if you reduce the cost, don't you reduce reliability?" This is completely ridiculous. A Ferrari is a very expensive car. It is not reliable. But I would bet you 1,000-to-1 that if you bought a Honda Civic that that sucker will not break down in the first year of operation. You can have a cheap car that's reliable, and the same applies to rockets.

To get costs down, Musk focused on simplicity in engineering and manufacturing and on limiting the number of subcontractors. The Falcon 9 used an Ethernet data bus rather than a custom design. The in-house machine shop fashioned special shapes for much less than the cost of an aerospace contractor.

Working at big contractors was basically boring because most of the job was running subcontracts and dealing with the government. The engineers at SpaceX were stressed but not bored.

SpaceX's first commercial flight was in 2009, putting a Malaysian observation satellite into orbit. But the revolution began in 2015 with the Falcon 9 being the first rocket to ever gain orbit and then turn around and fire its engines for a slow reentry and a soft landing on its tail. By 2018 the Falcon 9's cost per pound into low-Earth orbit was twenty-three times cheaper than the old space shuttle. Its bigger brother, the Falcon Heavy, cut the Falcon 9's cost per pound in half.

On May 30, 2020, SpaceX carried two NASA astronauts to the International Space Station. In early June, NASA approved SpaceX's plan to reuse its Falcon 9 launch vehicle and its Dragon crew capsule on future missions.

FIGURE 2. Cost into Low-Earth Orbit (2018 dollars per pound)

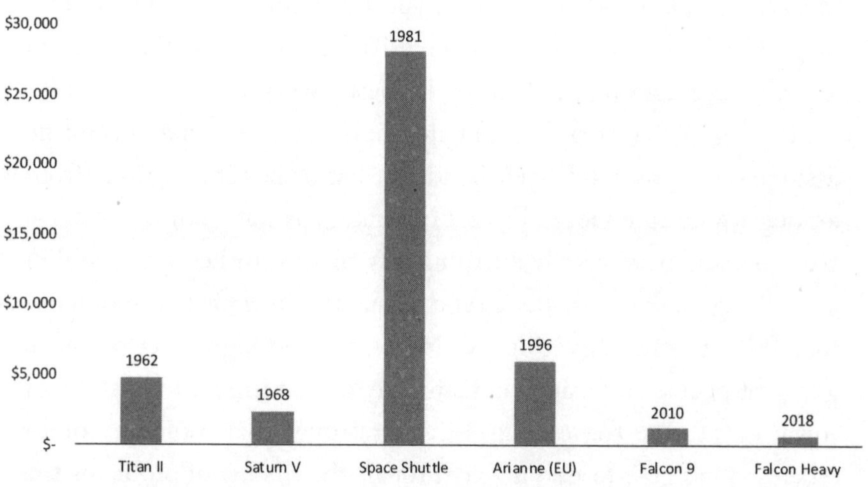

NASA had estimated it would cost $200 billion to go to Mars. Musk estimated $9 billion. The key to such advantage would be more of the same—coherent policies aimed at simplicity, reusability, and cost. If Congress or bureaucrats design the mission, costs will explode, as hundreds of different agendas and payoffs will be tacked on to the project.

I cannot tell you that SpaceX will be a great success in the future. Going into space is risky, and rockets are risky. The current media climate would turn any fatal accident into a circus. Under current norms, there would have never been the development of aircraft during the twentieth century—someone might get hurt. I can tell you that the key to SpaceX's advantage in rocketry arose from Elon Musk's grasp of the crux of the problem and his insight into how to surmount it. Plus, advantage is created by the company's coherent policies, all directed reliably at putting mass into orbit at the lowest cost possible.

Effective people gain *insight through finding and concentrating attention on the crux of a challenge—the part of the tangle of issues that is both very important and addressable (which can be overcome with reasonable surety).* To act effectively, you must fully examine the mix of problems and opportunities, identify the crux, and take actions aimed at overcoming it. Ignoring it doesn't work.

The "art of strategy" is not decision making—that discipline assumes that you have been handed a list of possible actions from among which to choose. The art of strategy is not finding your one true goal and passionately pursuing it with all your heart and soul in everything you do—that is a type of mental illness called monomania. The art of strategy is not setting higher and higher performance goals for people and using charisma, carrots, and sticks to push them toward attaining those goals—that presumes that someone somewhere knows how to find a way through the thicket of problems the organization actually faces.

To be a strategist you will need to embrace the full complex and confusing force of the challenges and opportunities you face.

To be a strategist you will have to develop a sense for the *crux* of the problem—the place where a commitment to action will have the best chance of surmounting the most critical obstacles.

To be a strategist you will need persistence because it is so tempting to grab at the first glimmer of a pathway through the thicket of issues.

To be a strategist you have to take responsibility for external challenges, but also for the health of the organization itself.

To be a strategist you will have to balance a host of issues with your bundle of ambitions—the variety of purposes, values, and beliefs that you and other stakeholders wish to support.

To be a strategist you will have to keep your actions and policies coherent with each other, not nullifying your efforts by having too many different initiatives or conflicting purposes. These facts are rarely written or spoken about with honesty. We are told that strategy is about having an advantage (duh!). That it is about having a long-term vision of where you want to be. We are told that by adopting method *X* or mind-set *Y*, the average business can become as successful as the very best—your consultant has charts comparing you to the very best (and shakes her head at the chasm).

The honest facts are that we do not live in Lake Wobegon and that the majority of businesses, no matter what methods they adopt, cannot be above average. The honest facts are that some situations are irretrievable, that there is not always a clever way out. The honest fact is that organizations cannot change direction on a dime—yes, we would like to be in the Web-services industry instead of trying to sell look-alike Vietnam-made jeans in overbuilt shopping malls, but here we are. The honest facts are that some situations are so locked up with competing political interests that there is not enough executive power anywhere to break the logjam. Strategy is not magic.

What is true is that to meet a challenge, you should first work to comprehend its nature. You cannot improve a failing school system unless you have a clear idea about why it is failing. To supply shoppers with a better shopping experience, you need to know about their wants, habits, and needs, as well as the technologies of selling. Don't start with goals—start by understanding the challenge and finding its crux.

Heraclitus said, "Character is fate." People with character speak plainly. They may gamble and take risks, but they are clear about the nature of the bet. You build trust in your company's longer-term results by having a story—a strategy, a narrative—about how your actions today fit into a plan to create a better future. The logic of the strategy should be sensible to other level-headed people. Saying "We are always increasing sales and cutting costs" is just not convincing. Saying "Our paint company is going to beat all the other paint companies because we are customer focused" doesn't work either. To have someone believe you and trust in your strategy, there has to be a logic and argument, and some evidence, as to how you are dealing with the challenges you face.

THIS BOOK'S IMMEDIATE impetus was a December 2019 fall while skiing the Aspen Mountain black-diamond FIS mogul trail. The resulting back injury kept me from most skiing and hiking over the next several months. Then the COVID-19 virus kept me from traveling. This quiet time allowed the development of ideas and themes that had been brewing within for some time.

The quiet time in 2020 let me write down these ideas and learnings. My own personal experience is that I don't actually know what I know until I work to write it down. The process of writing reveals contradictions, weak arguments, and places where more data is needed to back up an opinion. And it helps sort out the important from the less important. Mentally, it reminds me of combing out the knots and tangles in my eight-year-old daughter's hair.

In this book I tend to use the first-person *I* a great deal. Some readers feel that this sounds a bit self-promoting. It is not. I am uncomfortable with writers who present their ideas as facts and their models as reality. Economists tend to write textbooks about what "the firm" does in certain circumstances. They don't qualify that they are talking about their model of the firm, not actual firms. Business writers often express their opinions as facts. One author writes, "There are two ways to specialize: by selecting a target market segment or by having a limited range of products." Is this a theory? Did this author learn this from experience? Is it taken from some other writer? If the author had expressed this opinion (which is false) in the first person, readers might be more vigilant in comparing it to their own experiences.

I use the first person to explain how I have come to know and believe certain things. These "things" are often not facts or logical arguments. They are conclusions and views I have developed over a lifetime of work. If, for example, the issue is the relationship between strategic goals and strategy itself, I explain and describe the situation that first clarified my thinking on the subject. If the issue is the uncertainty in cash-flow estimates, I recount my personal experiences with executives making such estimates.

I EXPLORE FOUR themes in the pages that follow. First, the best way to deal with strategic issues is by squarely facing the challenge. Too many people start with goals and other visions of a desired end state. Start with the challenge, and diagnose its structure and the forces at work. Once you do that, your sense of purpose and the actions you consider will change. In that diagnosis, find the crux. That is the most critical part of the challenge that you can actually expect to solve. Don't pick a challenge you cannot yet deal with—attack the crux of the situation, build momentum, and then reexamine your position and its possibilities.

Second, understand the sources of power and leverage that are relevant to your situation. To punch through the crux, you will use one or more of them. Willpower is not enough.

Third, avoid the bright, shiny distractions that abound. Don't spend days on mission statements; don't start with goals in strategy work. Don't confuse management tools with strategy, and don't get too caught up in the ninety-day chase around quarterly earnings results.

Fourth, there are multiple pitfalls when executives work in a group, or workshop, to formulate strategy. By starting with the challenge, and avoiding a too rapid convergence on action, a group can define the crux and design coherent actions to overcome it.

I hope that this book can help you understand the power of challenge-based strategy and the power gained by finding the crux of the challenge.

PART I

Challenge-Based Strategy and the Crux

A strategy is a mixture of policy and action designed to surmount a high-stakes challenge. It is not a goal or wished-for end state. It is a form of problem solving, and you cannot solve a problem you do not understand or comprehend. Thus, challenge-based strategy begins with a broad description of the challenges—problems and opportunities—facing the organization. They may be competitive, legal, due to changing social norms, or issues with the organization itself.

As understanding deepens, the strategist seeks the crux—the one challenge that both is critical and appears to be solvable. This narrowing down is the source of much of the strategist's power, as focus remains the cornerstone of strategy.

1

Carolyn's Dilemma

How Do I Create a Strategy?

My 10:00 a.m. appointment is with a student in the UCLA Anderson Fully-Employed MBA program. About thirty-five, she has responsibility for business planning at a health-products company. She works full-time (as do her fellow students), attends classes on Fridays and Saturdays, and is in my fifth-floor office at the Anderson School to talk about a problem at work.

"We have a new CEO," Carolyn begins, explaining that the chief executive officer has asked her to rethink her division's business strategy. He wants a new approach to deliver at least 15 percent annual profit growth. He indicated that her success at this could really influence her trajectory in the company. She says she "likes the strategy course and is getting a lot out of the case discussions . . ." She pauses and then explains that she needs to "jump on some specific tools to create the strategy my boss wants." She is looking for help in filling the gaps between where the company is and where the boss wants to go.

We talk for a bit about her business and about the course concepts. I encourage her to identify what makes her business different, or special, compared to its competitors. I ask her about the particular challenges and opportunities it faces. She replies haltingly at first, in generalities.

"We have good people," Carolyn says. "We try to keep our products up to date." She pauses and then spills out her concern. The company's strategic plans are short documents that describe financial goals and show the milestones for getting there. She is looking for a "simple road map. . . a plan the CEO can take to the board, with steps for achieving the goals."

I nod, but don't say anything.

"There must be some system for creating a logical business strategy," Carolyn finishes.

I get a sudden mental flash—a visual picture of an imaginary "strategy calculator," something like Figure 3. I keep it to myself, as Carolyn is not in the mood for humor.

In truth, Carolyn is in a tough spot. She has put her finger on what has been the great missing piece in the foundation of almost all writings and teachings about strategy. This weakness was well captured more than a decade ago by strategy authority Gary Hamel: "Of course, everyone knows a strategy once they see one—be it Microsoft's, Nucor's, or Virgin Atlantic's. Anyone can recognize a

FIGURE 3. Strategy Calculator

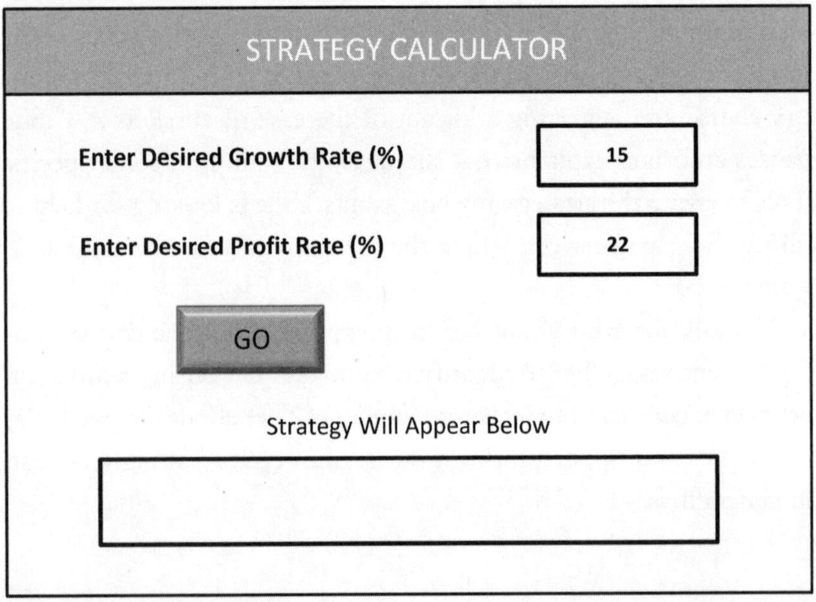

great strategy after the fact. We also understand planning as a 'process.' The only problem is that process doesn't produce strategy—it produces plans. The dirty little secret of the strategy industry is that it doesn't have any theory of strategy creation."[1] (By "strategy industry" Hamel means the cadre of academics and consultants who opine about and are hired to work on strategy.)

Carolyn's problem is that her boss has not wrapped his head around the crux of his situation. He is focused on performance goals and outcomes rather than opportunities and problems.

A STRATEGY WALKTHROUGH FOR NETFLIX

The key steps in dealing with a strategic challenge are a diagnosis of the situation—a comprehension of "what is going on here," finding the crux, and then creating reasonable action responses. To take a closer look at these steps, I am going to look at the situation Netflix faced a few years back, in early 2018. In what follows, I am going to *simulate* the process of diagnosis and the creation of action responses.

Netflix began in 1998 and soon established itself as the leading company in the DVD rent-by-mail business. Its clever Cinematch system for predicting customers' orders and its efficient logistics were broadly admired. Then, starting in 2010, in one of the most dramatic pivots in business strategy, CEO Reed Hastings moved the center of the company's activity to online streaming, gradually leaving the DVD rental business behind. It signed important content deals with Starz, Disney, Lionsgate, MGM, Paramount, and Sony.

In 2013 Netflix offered its first "original" productions, *House of Cards* and *Orange Is the New Black*. These shows were commissioned to be produced solely for Netflix. By the end of 2017, it had distributed twenty-six originals on its streaming service. In addition, Netflix was growing internationally. At the start of 2018 it had fifty-eight million international subscribers compared with fifty-three million in the United States. Revenue was $11.7 billion and was growing at a good pace. On the other hand, the company was burning cash, showing a net cash outflow of negative $1.8 billion in 2017.

As can be seen in the second part of Figure 4, Netflix's monthly cash costs exceeded its revenue per subscriber. The discrepancy between cash profit and accounting profit arose because the company amortized, or spread, its content costs over several years, creating the appearance of an accounting profit as long as it kept growing. Most of this outflow was financed with additional debt. Its expenses were also high due to the company's aggressive marketing campaigns.

FIGURE 4. Netflix Financial Results

	2017	2016
Dollars in Millions		
Revenues	11,693	8,831
Cost of revenues	7,660	6,030
Marketing	1,278	991
Technology and development	1,053	852
General and administrative	864	578
Operating income	839	380
Other income (expense):	(353)	(119)
Income before income taxes	485	261
Provision for income taxes	(74)	74
Net income	559	187
Dollars per Subscriber per Month		
Revenue	9.38	8.64
Production of content	1.51	1.44
Licensed content	5.92	5.73
Marketing	1.20	1.03
Technology	0.80	0.89
General and administrative	0.36	0.60
Other	1.36	1.02
Total cash cost	11.15	10.71
Cash profit	(1.77)	(2.07)

Among paid streaming services, Netflix's market share was about 76 percent, far ahead of Amazon Prime at about 17 percent, Hulu at 4 percent, and HBO's 3 percent.

In 2011 Netflix faced a significant upset. It had been paying $30 million per year to Starz for access to its shows. At contract renewal, Starz asked for an increase to $300 million per year. Netflix had to raise subscription fees by 60 percent, and its stock price took a nosedive.

The Starz moment was a harbinger of things to come. Content suppliers began to ask for higher fees, and some began to pull their content back in the hopes of establishing their own streaming services. In particular, Netflix faced the loss of its two most popular TV series: *Friends* and *The Office*. WarnerMedia was taking *Friends* to its own streaming service (HBO Max), and *The Office* was being recalled by owner NBCUniversal for its planned Peacock streaming service.

Further storm clouds were the rising costs of original productions and the coming entry of new competitors. Disney was merging with 21st Century Fox and was planning an aggressive entry into streaming. It announced that it would remove its content from Netflix in 2019. Importantly, Disney planned to put all its archive and future theatrical releases on a new streaming platform. That would include properties from Lucasfilm, Marvel, Pixar, Fox, ESPN, and its own materials, everything from *Fantasia* to *Dumbo* to *Frozen*. As one observer put it, "Disney has 75 years of cultural capital to bring to the table."[2]

To make matters worse for Netflix, Apple announced it was joining the streaming wars. Its new Apple TV+ service would be priced at five dollars monthly and provide a growing list of titles. And Apple had very deep pockets to pay for new programming.

The Snare of Long-Term Goals

The advice often given to leaders such as Carolyn and her boss struggling to create a strategy is to first clarify your goals. Alice in

Wonderland–like parables are told about Cheshire cats and about how it doesn't matter what you do if you don't know where you are going. And, most likely, you will be advised to first write mission and vision statements before you define your strategic goals. Guidance from the authors of a leading strategy textbook is typical:

> The first element of a coherent strategy is a clear set of long-term goals toward which strategy is directed. These long-term goals typically refer to the market position or status that the firm hopes to achieve through its strategy. For example, long-term goals might be to "dominate the market," to be "the technology leader," or to be "the premium quality firm." By "long term" we mean that these goals are enduring.[3]

Take a moment and reflect on that advice. In this very common framework, strategy is portrayed as a set of actions directed at attaining certain "first element" long-term goals. But where do such goals come from?

Apparently, they somehow pop into existence. They magically appear *before* any analysis has taken place. If you haven't analyzed your business, its competitors, the dynamics of competition, and more, claiming that you want to "be the technology leader" is just vague bloviation. It certainly does not help your organization understand how to move forward. (See Chapter 14, "Don't Start with Goals," for more on this point.)

THE IDEA THAT a person or organization has one or two primary driving goals is simply not true. It is a fantasy invented by economists and certain management thinkers. The reality is that most people and organizations have "a bundle of ambitions." That is, they have multiple intentions, visions of the future, and things they would like to see or achieve. Some things in this "bundle" conflict with one another—not all can be achieved together.

When I was twenty-five, I wanted to be a top researcher, advise senior executives on strategy, have summers off to make ascents in the high mountains of the world, learn to fly, backcountry ski in the winter, master the mathematics of statistical decision theory, be a teacher who could inspire my students, run 10Ks, drive a Morgan Plus 4 Drophead, easily move from the wilderness to the boardroom, marry a woman in a prestigious profession, have happy and talented children, have time to spend with my family, and make enough money to retire early and buy a town house on the Île Saint-Louis. During my life I got to make progress on a few of these. As opportunities and challenges arose, new ambitions grew and old ones were moved to the back shelf. Along the way, as I decided what to do next, I had to pick and choose among the items in my bundle of ambitions.

If I were Reed Hastings in early 2018, my ambitions would, likewise, be many:

- I would want the company to survive and prosper.
- I would be worried about the too-high stock price.
- I would want to preserve the wealth, most in paper, that I have accumulated.
- I don't want to lose the position of being the leading streaming service in the United States.
- I would also dream about becoming a real intellectual property factory, like Disney, making my own movies and finding ways to reuse the content and characters like Disney and Viacom do (toys, books, theme parks, and so on).
- I would like to be different from that "old guard" and find a new and fresher way to work with talent and production people. I would want to keep growing my international footprint, especially in larger countries that can also create content (United Kingdom, Germany, Italy, Brazil, Mexico, South Korea, Japan).
- The European Union (EU) Parliament is considering a streaming-service requirement that at least 30 percent of

content be local—I want to push that and exploit the rule against Disney in the future.

- India is a huge market, and I would want to find a way to stream there at low subscriber rates.
- I also have dreams of being more like a TV station, with daily news streaming and covering sports events.
- Could I take a cue from YouTube and have a separate streaming "channel" for contributed content? From time to time I sometimes wish I could somehow sell out my holdings and start something new again, with a small team and not have to manage thousands of employees.
- Or I want to take a year off to be with my family.

Reed Hastings is a talented entrepreneur and, in reality, probably had some of these ambitions, perhaps even more. These kinds of intents and dreams are precursors to strategy, but they cannot all be accomplished, or at least not all at once. Effective strategy emerges out of an exploration of challenges, ambitions, resources, and competition. By confronting the situation actually being faced, a talented leader creates a strategy to *further some elements out of the whole bundle of ambitions.* Importantly, your ambitions are not a fixed and given starting point. In crafting a way forward, strategists will often have to choose among their values and ambitions. The ambitions made salient in a particular situation are as much outcomes as givens. In 2015 General Electric had an ambition to be a "top-10 software company by 2020." Today, it can't cut GE Digital fast enough. Cruise-ship lines that strove to be the most "fun" in 2020, now, after COVID-19, strive to be the "cleanest." For the Gap, being the leader in trendy denim has been replaced with simple survival.

Diagnosing the Challenges

Diagnosis is the starting point in creating a strategy. At Netflix there are a lot of opportunities for analysis—prices, costs, competitors, buyer behavior, changing tastes, and so on. There is a meaty role for consultants here in analyzing the company and comparing it to competitors. The behavior of buyers (subscribers) is central, and there is much to learn about how different people and different cultures respond to variety, novelty, story lines, change, and pricing. And, importantly, we should look at how others have dealt with similar situations.

Still, after going over the typical two-hundred-page report on costs, prices, markets, buyers, and competition produced by your consultants, how do you then *create* a strategy to face a future where leadership in streaming is being contested?

One frequently hears that managers are decision makers. The theory of decision is highly developed. In one sentence, it says that you should choose the action that provides the highest expected payoff (utility). If you conceive of strategy as decision making, then your job would be to examine each alternative and select the best. You don't have to be an experienced executive to see that this is nonsense. Where do these "alternatives" come from?

The reality is that creating a strategy is not simply pure goal seeking or decision making, unless there are fairly well-structured causal connections between actions and results. If we knew how each possible chess move changed the probability of winning, it would be easy to step through a game. But we don't have that kind of mapping. Instead, to play chess we memorize patterns of clever moves and search for the crux—the place where the patterns of forces may allow us to take advantage of an opponent's (apparent) weaknesses.

Gnarly Challenges

Strategy creation is a special form of problem solving. By a *form* of problem solving, I mean that it treats much less structured and much more complex problems than you found in the traditional homework problems of your school days. When talking and writing about strategy, it seems better to say "challenges." People associate "problems" with math puzzles, "problems at home," and other unpleasant situations. I also want to emphasize that a strategic challenge may be triggered by a large opportunity—the challenge being how best to grasp it.

I think of strategic challenges as arising in three basic forms: choice, engineering design, and gnarly. Most that I see are gnarly, perhaps because companies don't ask for help with easier ones.

A *choice challenge* occurs when we know the alternatives, but there are uncertainties and nonquantifiable aspects that make choosing among them difficult. Situations of strategic choice usually arise when there are large long-term commitments of capital or contract at stake. If you own coal in Australia, and China is buying more each year, should you invest in a railroad to the sea and a harbor? How big a harbor? What kinds of supply contracts?

An *engineering-design challenge* arises when one has to create something new, but you have methods for evaluating your creation before implementing it. If you go to engineering school, you may learn how to analyze the stress on the steel members and cables of a bridge. Later, asked to design a new bridge, you probably copy a previous design. But when Norway asks for a design-build offer on the world's longest *floating* bridge, over the 550-meter-deep Bjørna fjord, you have to create the design—you have to imagine a way of shaping steel and concrete into a floating bridge. Unlike the choice challenge, there are no predefined alternatives. Still, the wonderful thing about modern engineering is that we have good models of structures and water and loads and winds. You can test your imagined designs mathematically and by simulation before making a choice.

A more difficult situation is the *gnarly-design challenge*. Here there are no given alternatives, and there are no good engineering-type models to test your designs against. There is no guarantee of a solution of any kind. There are not clear causal connections between actions and outcomes.

You solve a gnarly challenge by beginning to dig into the *nature of the challenge*—in figuring out "what is going on here." What is the paradox or central knot of the thing? What constraints might be relaxed?

A Diagnosis of Netflix

Putting myself in CEO Reed Hastings's shoes, the overall challenge seems to have these elements:

The central tension facing the company was that it had grown by renting other people's material. But that may not really work in the future. The vast libraries of Disney (including ESPN, Pixar, Lucasfilm, Fox), WarnerMedia, MGM, NBCUniversal, and more will be withdrawn from Netflix and Amazon. There will be a growing war for content.

With new streaming services arriving, each with a monthly charge, and each trying to pin subscribers with "original" content, when will the market saturate from subscriber financial limits and content fatigue? Then what?

Most of Netflix's so-called original content is produced under contract by the same list of studios that have dominated the industry for a century: Warner Bros., Lionsgate, Paramount TC, Sony, and so on. How long can this supply arrangement last?

If Netflix tries to make high-quality movies, ones that would normally go first to theaters, it would be in direct competition with its suppliers. Does that mean it is trapped into making B-grade movies?

International margins, especially outside Europe, remain low.

Some of the series offerings have been A-grade, but as Amazon, Disney, Apple, Hulu, and more begin to compete for them, won't the price to license or hire talent drive out profits?

Netflix's cost of gaining each new subscriber is rising, from about $300 in 2012 to about $500 in 2017.

Cash flow is strongly negative—Netflix has been continually adding new debt to finance its growth.

It can only grow its way to cash profit if its costs of production and content can be spread over a larger subscriber base that has broad common tastes in content. Can international expansion provide this base?

In order to show the value of the crux, of getting to the heart of the matter of the strategic challenge, let me quickly describe some of the alternative policies and actions Netflix could take that easily come to mind. With regard to defending domestically, it could go right up against Disney with a $4 per month limited subscription. This version of Netflix could provide a secondary lower-priced plan aimed at phones and pads, with cartoons and other kids' entertainment. For another $10 per month, the full subscription would also be available for adults.

It could strive to build the "new" Hollywood, breaking from the financial and cultural burdens of the old Hollywood's politics, power plays, and focus on "stars." One of the important lessons of series like *The OA* and *Orange Is the New Black* is that one doesn't need existing stars to make popular content. Going down this expensive and risky road would require a very large subscriber base and continued support from the capital markets—no major mistakes allowed.

With a market value close to $90 billion in early 2018, Netflix could buy a studio, like MGM, and get access to its library and production capabilities. This would, of course, be inconsistent with the idea of being a "new" Hollywood.

Netflix could aim at creating a few huge blockbusters, like HBO's *Game of Thrones*. Content like this can pull in millions of subscribers just to view this one show. There is no formula for doing this.

Netflix could offer more than one streaming service, tailoring each to a different group of subscribers. There is a lot of room here for exploring ways of subsetting the audience and arranging prices.

With regard to expanding internationally, Netflix could focus on the developed world outside the United States, particularly the Anglosphere (Canada, Australia, New Zealand, and the United Kingdom). These and a few similar areas have tastes broadly in common and income levels sufficient to pay for a good streaming service. Along this line, with its current presence in these regions, it could have a new-content advantage in drawing on expertise outside the United States in making video entertainment. In contrast to focusing on the Anglosphere, Netflix could be the worldwide streaming-content distributor. It could tone down its spending on creating content and focus on being a worldwide distributor for international content. By early 2018, Netflix had already done well with *Dark* (Germany), *Money Heist* (Spain), *Sacred Games* (India), *3%* (Brazil), and others.

THE CRUX OF THE CHALLENGE

Think of a set of gnarly challenges as a large tangle of sticks and wire. It blocks your way forward. You could hack at it for days. But find the right spot and cut one thick wire, and the tangle may break into smaller chunks that are manageable. That wire is the crux of the tangle.

Netflix's overall challenge is that it can no longer count on contracting for existing good TV and studio films at reasonable prices. When it comes to streaming, both access to material and subscriber scale are important. With more subscribers, one can pay more for material, and the ratio of needed shows to subscribers falls—you don't need twice as many different shows for twice as many subscribers. So, subscriber scale seems key. But, of course, subscribers will gravitate to good material unless one is playing a pure cost game for an audience with little taste for variety, such as children.

In competition it is useful to look for asymmetries—ways in which competitors differ. Going back to Fontainebleau's Le Toit du Cul de Chien, the crux of a boulder for a short muscular climber may be easy for a taller climber. Or one army may be larger, the other more experienced. One business may have better technology but poorer distribution, and so on. In the case of Netflix, my attention is drawn to its stronger position in the international arena, an interesting imbalance. Netflix had an early start there with good subscriber growth in the English-speaking world as well as parts of Europe and Turkey. Disney and others will try to take their services abroad but will predictably try to use production bases in the United States. Can Netflix gain advantage by leveraging foreign production to a global audience?

In my view, the *crux of Netflix's situation* is the opportunity to use its current international advantage to create sufficient material to feed both its domestic and its growing international markets.

THE MOVE FROM diagnosis to alternatives requires audacity, especially in a gnarly situation such as that which Netflix is facing. Alternative actions are not given but must be imagined or constructed. Then you do your very best to choose among the alternatives you have created. Finally, you need to translate the idea into specific and coherent actions. In shaping and evaluating an alternative course of action, we have to make judgments. And to invent a solution, we have to judge, or assume, or believe, certain things to be true.

For Netflix, the crux analysis leads one to seek a mechanism for stimulating the international creation of good content while, at the same time, making Netflix the favored distribution channel. Scale will help it pay well, but there is more. Creating content that slides across borders is not easy. Can Netflix create and share knowledge about how to do this? Can that be tied to financing? Could it even set up an international academy, teaching skill in scripting, acting, and production? Will developments in artificial intelligence make language translation easier and cheaper? I could lay out other designs for alternatives, but I am not going to take this simulation of strategy making any further. I hope you can see the value of a careful diagnosis and the identification of a crux.

THIS PROCESS OF diagnosing the challenge and then creating a response is the best theory we have for strategy creation. You analyze the challenge and your resources, and you try to think of ways to surmount the challenge and realize some of your ambitions. A myriad of tools exist to help you analyze the challenge. And there are ways of stimulating and helping you think of a response—analogies to other situations, altering the point of view, doing again what worked last time, and so on. But these are only stimuli. You don't "pick" a strategy; you create it. Then you do your very best to choose among the alternatives you have created. Finally, you need to translate the idea into specific and coherent actions.

2

Untangling the Challenge

Finding and Using the Crux

Very early in my career I thought of strategy work as analysis. I would gather data, impose frameworks borrowed from consultants and academics, and look in detail at products and prices and regions and competitive behavior over time. I worked to quantify competitive advantage. If it was an airline, I would disentangle the drivers for one airline's profit advantage over another. For a magazine, I created slides detailing the cost per story, photograph, and so on. But, over time, I came to realize that all of this analysis, while useful, did not really produce a strategy—a way forward that would improve things.

Trying to learn from corporate leaders, I observed many who saw their jobs as pushing people to "make their numbers." Others were well spoken, but really had little idea about the guts of the business they had somehow come to lead. There were some who saw strategy as planning or financial engineering or as long lists of "things to do." Some were insightful but lacked the courage to act.

Luckily, I was able to watch and learn something from leaders who were skilled strategists:

- like Pierre Wack, the legendary head of strategy at Shell, who taught me to see the correlations among the elements of a situation and to be alert for whipsaws as trends overshoot and rebound

- like Steve Jobs of Apple, whose brutal honesty let him cut through layers of baloney and grab the crux of a situation (and annoy many people around him)
- like Andy Marshall (Office of Net Assessment/Department of Defense) who had a fine instinct for defining the competition at just the right level to change the conversation for the better (his paper on redefining the Cold War situation as a long-term competition between the United States and the Soviet Union was pivotal in moving US policy makers away from an armaments view to one that encompassed economic and social dimensions)
- like Andy Bryant, the board chair of Intel who understood how size and complexity can compete with having the technological edge
- like Simon Galbraith of Redgate Software, whose natural talent for diagnosis led him to a canvas larger than a single business

These general managers, and others, did things differently, and, over time, I began to get a feel for the broad outlines of that difference.

Skilled strategists are happy to look at analysis and data, but they are also able to identify and focus on a critical challenge or opportunity and then create a way to address it. They had a "nose" for what was vital and an ability to concentrate energy on such issues. They cared about performance but didn't confuse results with actions. They did not pick a strategy from some popular list or consultants' matrix or from the three choices on a PowerPoint prepared by staff. Perhaps most important, they did not see strategy as a fixed description of "where we want to be" in the future. Of course, they had obvious ambitions of winning, and profit, and success, but they saw strategy as dealing with on-the-ground challenges and with important new opportunities that arose.

The truth is that gnarly challenges are not "solved" with just analysis or by applying preset frameworks. Rather, a coherent strategic response arises through a process of diagnosing the structure of challenges, framing, reframing, chunking down the scope of attention, reference to analogies, and insight. The result is a design rather than a choice. It is a *creation* embodying purpose. I call it a "creation" because it is nonobvious to most others, the product of insight and judgment rather than an algorithm. It is not a deduction, but a design. Implicit in the concept of insightful design is that knowledge, though required, is not, by itself, sufficient.

Writing about how hard design problems are solved, industrial design specialist Kees Dorst nicely described zeroing in on the crux of a problem:

> Experienced designers can be seen to engage with a novel problem situation by searching for the central paradox, asking themselves what it is that makes the problem so hard to solve. They only start working toward a solution once the nature of the core paradox has been established to their satisfaction.[1]

The skilled designer-strategist recognizes the crux of a challenge as something evoking a sense of blockage or constraint. It is a thing blocking easy solution. A strategist-designer's attention is drawn to it because it hints at leverage—that if we could only just move the keystone, the whole wall can be breached. Attention is particularly drawn to a crux that seems similar to those in other situations or where there is a hint as to how to solve it.

THE TRAP OF TRYING TO DEDUCE A STRATEGY

You cannot deduce a strategy from some set of always relevant preset principles. An example of a group of executives making this mistake was 'Paradigm Corp.'[2] The CEO, 'Carl Lang,' of this medium-size manufacturer of specialty paper products asked me to appraise his strategy. "The board," he explained, "wants an independent check on what we have developed." Most of my work would be to interview a few managers and look at various documents they had generated.

Lang's first step had been to clarify the company's purpose. He told me, "Our aim is to produce measurable tangible results. In particular, we want to achieve a return on total assets of at least 9 percent, a market share of at least 25 percent, and reliable sales growth of 10 percent per year."

The top management team had turned to Michael Porter's book *Competitive Advantage*. Their primary tool was his breakdown of strategy into four types, as shown in Figure 5.

FIGURE 5. Porter Generic Strategies

	Price competition	**Attribute competition**
Broad-market scope	Cost leadership	Broad differentiation
Narrow-market scope	Cost focus	Differentiation focus

Carl Lang's strategy team had chosen the broad-differentiation strategy for Paradigm because the company had a history of competing based on having the broadest variety of specialized shapes and sizes.[3]

An article in a business journal was then cited as the source of these (so-called) "operational strategies":

- continuous improvement
- capacity utilization
- just-in-time
- outsourcing
- new-product time to market

Carl's team had chosen "new-product time to market" because the other operational "strategies" seemed impractical to them. Their production facilities were old, in another state, and unionized, and they had little control over the details of production.

Carl wanted to have a strategy created by a logical process that could be defended to the board or even in a court of law. And he wanted me to testify to the board that having "broad differentiation" and "new-product time to market" strategies were reasonable and had a good chance of producing a return on assets of at least 9 percent and sales growth of at least 10 percent per year. Of course, I couldn't do that because Carl's strategy had nothing to do with the challenges Paradigm faced.

Paradigm's basic problems were that it had no effective control over manufacturing and that its largest customers were slowly growing firms. Once we had identified and focused on these issues, the group began to gradually generate ideas about how to deal with them. Over several months, Carl Lang developed a reasonable strategy for shifting marketing and sales efforts to smaller firms that were growing and splitting the manufacturing activities into standard and special items. My contribution was getting them to look at actual challenges instead of financial goals and generic strategies.

DEDUCTION VERSUS DESIGN

Carl Lang was attempting to deduce a strategy from strategy "frameworks" such as Porter's "Five Forces" or Kim and Mauborgne's "Blue Ocean Strategy Canvas." But such frameworks are designed to call attention to what might be important in a situation. They do not, indeed cannot, guide one to specific actions.

Others try to deduce strategies from desired performance goals, such as "grow profitably by 20 percent each year for the next five years." It doesn't work that way because the goal, by itself, has no action implications. If you begin to add nuance, like "focus on the largest potential accounts," that proposed action has a complex set of challenge-based implications hidden within it. Why haven't we been going after larger accounts? What makes that harder? What changes have to be made to be able to sell to larger accounts?

To see the issues more clearly, it is helpful to dig into the difference between deduction and design.

We are all familiar with *deduction*, first formalized by Euclid in his book *The Elements* (300 BC). In high school, we study his presentation of the axioms of geometry (things equal to the same thing are equal to each other, all right angles are equal, and so on) and learn how to deduce geometric relationships from these axioms. The idea of deduction is close to that of logic itself. Given certain assumptions, certain other relationships, or facts, follow.

Given Newton's law of gravity, and knowing the positions and orbit of Mars and Earth, one can *deduce* the velocity needed for a spacecraft to leave Earth and impact Mars. Given your history of music listening, a Web service can make a good guess as to what you might like to hear next. Deduction is one of the most powerful reasoning tools our civilization has created, especially its huge successes in mathematics and physics.

After the atomic bomb showed that physicists scribbling on blackboards could blow up cities, economists and some other social scientists shifted their attention away from looking at actual behavior toward creating a deductive system like the physicists had. One result was a modern economics that had little to do with actual behavior. In it people and firms all act to maximize their expected value, called "utility" because it is not necessarily measured in monetary terms.

Herbert Simon received the 1978 Nobel Prize in Economics for observing that, contrary to this modern economic theory, people don't actually maximize when they make choices. They are not the perfectly rational creatures imagined in economics. Rather, their rationality is *bounded*. This, of course, was obvious to all but academics.

People make local judgments about what action will make them a bit better off at the moment. Better chess players, he found, were able to recognize more chessboard patterns than weaker players. They had access to a wider range of challenging situations and possible responses. Having chess experts verbalize their thinking, it was found that they could not really explain their thought patterns. "My attention is drawn to square QB5 . . . ," one would say, unable to explain how he identified the crux of the situation.

In general, economists were annoyed that Simon's award was in "economics." Most had abandoned the study of actual economic behavior in favor of deducing actions from their complex mathematical system.

Importantly for us, Herbert Simon was fascinated by the difference between deduction and design. He explained that normal science is about understanding the natural world. "Design," he argued, "on the other hand, is concerned with how things ought to be" in order to carry out human purposes. His insights into my own career in professional education struck me with special force. He observed that it was "ironic that in this century," natural sciences drove design considerations from the curricula of professional schools. He noted, "Engineering schools gradually became schools of physics and mathematics; medical schools became schools of biological science; business schools became schools of finite mathematics."[4]

My own life experience supports Simon's comment about the replacement of design with deduction in professional schools. For the academics who currently populate top professional schools, design is a bit like shop class, akin to automobile repair or welding, and residing at a far remove from respectable activities like the mathematical modeling of stochastic processes and the statistical analysis of selection bias.

Study marketing in most masters in business administration (MBA) programs and you will be exposed to theory about consumer behavior and the concept of market segments, but will have little insight into the wide variety of actual company marketing programs. The students will find that they cannot deduce a real-world marketing program from the theory of consumer behavior.

Study finance and you will learn a great deal of theory about security prices, but if you want to be an investment banker you will have to go elsewhere to learn about the fascinating complexity of real-world deal structures. You cannot deduce a deal structure from finance theory.

Take an MBA course on strategy, and you will be exposed to a few case studies of classic business-strategy success stories. But, increasingly, your instructor will use these cases as "examples" of his or her favorite concepts from industrial organization economics.

Again, you cannot deduce a good strategy from theory. Much of design is a combination of imagination and knowing about many other designs, copying some elements of each. The problem for modern professional schools of engineering and business is that you cannot know about the vast variety of designs if all you have learned is deductive logic.

My interest when I was a senior at the University of California at Berkeley, studying electrical engineering, was in large power systems—the big turbine generators that supplied everyone's electricity. I took the only course on generators and motors available. The professor had us study tensor analysis.[5] We never even saw a picture of a generator. The idea was that with tensor math, you could model some of the electrical output performance of generators. But this kind of analysis gave no clue as to what a generator actually was or how to design or build one. It was all math, not engineering. I switched to computer design and then to feedback-control systems design because those subjects actually included a smattering of design.

A few years later, I was a systems design engineer at the Jet Propulsion Labs. My work was the initial design of future spacecraft. On visiting my alma mater, I told my former adviser that one big problem we had was that many spacecraft components failed over time. There were no interplanetary repair people for spacecraft, so we were constantly trying to figure out how to compensate for sensors gone bad and radios that wouldn't start up. Yes, we could calculate reliability numbers, but we didn't really understand why these things failed in the first place. He shook his head and said, "Unless you can find a way to mathematicize it, we cannot research it in the engineering department."

GNARLY SITUATIONS

I introduced the idea of gnarly challenges when discussing Netflix in the previous chapter. Drilling down further to be a bit more precise, gnarly problems have these characteristics:[6]

- There may be no clear definition of the problem itself. Studying various concepts of "the problem" and working to identify or choose a crux issue can be a large part of the work of creating a strategy. In many gnarly situations, there is not really a given "problem." Rather, there is simply a sense of things going wrong or of opportunities just around the corner.
- Most of the time you do not have a single goal but a *bundle of ambitions*, such as those I had when I was twenty-five or those I ascribed to Reed Hastings—that is, a group of desires, goals, intents, values, fears, and ambitions that may conflict with one another and that cannot normally be all satisfied at once. Forging a sense of purpose out of this bundle is part of the gnarly problem.
- Alternatives may not be given but must be searched for or imagined. Much of the time the apparent alternatives—invade or blockade, acquire "BuyCo" or not—have been made artificially sharp by shortsighted staff or parties with vested interests. There are almost always other ways to proceed.
- The connections between potential actions and actual outcomes are unclear. Opinions will differ sharply, even among experts, about the efficacy of various proposed actions. In gnarly situations, there are multiple interpretations of the facts and only weak connections between desired results and specific actions to be taken.

How, then, does one deal with gnarly challenges and develop a solution when unsure about what the challenge really is? Neither individuals nor organizations can attend to everything at once. So, we work to isolate the crux of the overall mix of challenges and opportunities. The crux is an important part of the mixture of problem and opportunity that can (almost) surely be surmounted if we focus resources and efforts on it.

We follow effective strategic leaders because they have done this work—they have replaced the buzzing confusion of reality with a call to attack and conquer a part of it where we can actually win.

Faced with a gnarly challenge, the strategist recognizes or forges an embedded solvable problem—not the whole gnarly challenge, but one with kinship to its key elements. And it is a problem that we are capable of addressing.

For example, in 1999 Marvel had just come out of bankruptcy with a comic-book and toy business and with a huge debt burden. The company had an avid following among comic-book readers, but no general audience. Much of the debt was paid off by licensing out characters just for toys and games. The next opportunity lay in making Marvel characters into feature films. One problem was classic chicken-and-egg: Studio licensing offers were low because there had not yet been a successful major film based on Marvel characters. And because there had been no major feature film, the characters were essentially unknown outside the comic-book crowd. Another difficulty was that although Marvel had forty-seven hundred comic-book characters, Hollywood was chiefly interested in Spider-Man and the X-Men.

After licensing Spider-Man to Sony Pictures and the X-Men to Fox for very low fees, Marvel president Kevin Feige identified the crux of the problem as making the rest of the Marvel characters worth something. To attack that crux, he devised a plan to create value for a large group of Marvel characters by having them all inhabit the same fictional "universe." Marvel raised money from Wall Street to pay for an independent studio. Its first successful film, *Iron Man*, was followed by twenty-eight more feature films. Many of the same characters appeared in these films and in eleven television series: Iron Man, Thor, Captain America, the Winter Soldier, the Black Widow, Hawkeye, Vision, Black Panther, and many more. Marvel was acquired in 2009 by Disney, which continues to develop the Marvel Cinematic Universe.

Mastery over a gnarly challenge arises only after the crux has been exposed when you see or recognize the locus of tension in the web of conflicting desires, needs, and resources. We may want to expand capacity but have no space to do so. The suggested new product may work well for customers but be rejected by distributors because it cannibalizes other streams of profit. Resolution of the crux will usually help resolve major parts of the larger issue. As a number of problem-solving researchers have found, "At the least, problems must be deeply analyzed before an insight solution can be achieved."[7]

Locating the crux is the *first maneuver* in dealing with gnarly challenges. Discovering, or articulating, that solvable problem within the complexity of a gnarly challenge is not easy. Many gnarly challenges seem to pose a bewildering farrago of problems and issues. It seems like there are a multitude of interconnected problems. Some are blessed with an innate talent for teasing out the crux. Andy Marshall, for example, saw that the crux of the Cold War was having a strategy for competing with the USSR, by using US social and economic strengths to greater effect, not with simply piling up weapons. Others simply pretended confidence in the face of complexity. Over several decades, I have seen strategists such as Andy Marshall and Dawn Farrell of TransAlta use the practical tools of *collecting*, *clustering*, and *filtering* to help untangle gnarly situations.

Collecting—making a list of problems, issues, and opportunities—ensures that you are looking at all the issues, not just the first to come to mind. It will grow longer than you anticipate, just like what you need to take on vacation grows from your initial planning. Your initial sense of problems was not complete. Your initial sense of alternative actions was also constrained. You, or other members of your team, know more than you can immediately say. Collecting is aided by reference to outsiders and competitors. (More on this in Chapter 19.)

Clustering places problems and opportunities into groups. When I work with a team in a Strategy Foundry (see Chapter 20), each participant works on identifying a challenge. We write them on the board or on cards and collect them all—usually about twelve or so. Often, these "challenges" are each really more than one challenge, so we break them apart. As things get broken down, we normally wind up with about twenty challenges and opportunities. We then try to cluster them into somehow related groups. If you are working alone, it is a bit harder, but you can do much the same thing as a group if you try to take different points of view and imagine the voices and opinions of others.

The groups produced by this clustering have fuzzy boundaries. The purpose is not to establish scientifically solid sets but to explore the ways in which challenges differ. Some are harder than others, some are about competition, some are about internal issues, and so on. Some will be more critical than others. Some will be easier to resolve. Some can be deferred to the future.

Following collecting and clustering, you realize that there are too many issues, too many problems, and too many different interests at work. They need to be *filtered*. The first step is sequencing: bringing to the forefront those that seem to be immediate, while deferring attention on many where action can be deferred. As Desmond Tutu is credited with saying, "There is only one way to eat an elephant: a bite at a time."

Once these challenges have been winnowed down, the next step in filtering is rating their importance and addressability. Importance is the degree to which the challenge either threatens the core values or existence of the enterprise or represents a major opportunity. Addressability is the degree to which the challenge appears to be solvable. (Chapter 4 covers this in detail.)

The judgment about addressability is the more contentious. Some challenges are clearly addressable. Some are very important yet fairly hard to address—that is where the crux will usually lie.

A critical challenge that does not seem easily addressable deserves great attention. Can it be divided into subproblems? Is it like any similar problem others have faced? Is there anyone who might be an expert on such situations? What is changing that might alter its addressability? What is the single keystone constraint, which if broken, would make it addressable (the crux of the crux!)? Or, more drastically, one can break this critical yet hard challenge into pieces and start the process of collection, clustering, and filtering over again, all focused on just this topic.

The crux of a challenge is a point of tension where a constraint or conflict between resources and issues, or among policies, seems to chafe. When Amazon first opened its Marketplace service, it allowed outside firms to sell their products through the Amazon website. The conundrum was that some of these firms might gain scale and scope to challenge Amazon, even taking their suppliers and products to their own websites in the future. Yet denying these sellers would limit the scope of a company that aimed at being the world's biggest store. Like so many insights, the solution seems simple in retrospect. Amazon began to greatly improve its logistics system and offered the Marketplace sellers use of its warehouse and shipping services. It was an offer of marriage most could not refuse. And its continued expansion into more and more products countered threats from almost all suppliers.

Another case of seeing the crux was Apple management realizing that Steve Jobs's devotion to doing everything in-house was in stark conflict with the concept of an app store. They began to realize that opening up the iPhone's app store to outside programmers would produce enormous competition among app makers, driving down their prices, increasing their quality through comparison, and thereby increasing the value of each iPhone.

You will have a much harder time dealing with a gnarly challenge if you have not distilled it down to a crux. No one solves a problem they cannot comprehend and hold in their mind.

DESIGNING ALTERNATIVES

Formulating a hypothesis about what will work follows from filtering the set of issues and breaking gnarly challenges into components. The design of action alternatives is the *second maneuver* in dealing with gnarly challenges. You can check the proposed actions against existing knowledge to see if any elements of the idea are ruled out by very strongly supported evidence. For example, a proposal to build more low-income housing should be confronted by the fact that people in such developments have, in the past, been the frequent victims of crime.[8] Without a law-enforcement or crime-control substrategy, simply building the project may do more harm than good. Given this history, a new solution to low-income housing requires an audacious leap to a novel mixture of policy, architecture, planning, and action.

Elon Musk, as we noted earlier, saw the crux of the challenge of cheaper cost to orbit as reusability. His audacious leap occurred when he realized that fuel is cheaper than hardware. His new rocket would include extra fuel so it could return to Earth without burning up. Here are some more examples of audacious leaps to action based on a recognition of a crux:

- Like Russia, China had traditionally collected tax and operating revenues centrally and then allocated funds based on various plans. Deng Xiaoping saw that China's crux economic problem was dulled incentives to be efficient (or profitable, in Western terms). "Being rich is glorious," he said, a truly revolutionary statement in a country that held up the equality of poverty as a virtue. Deng's most important new bold action was to allow local communist collectives selling products and services to keep most of their profit. This policy became a coherent strategy for development when it was connected to export-based activity and the careful importing of outside skills.
- In Singapore the 1960 gnarly challenge was horrendous unemployment, with the majority of the population of the small island living as homeless squatters. One approach might have been searching the world for charity. However, Lee Kuan Yew believed that the crux of the challenge was that Singapore was a terrible place to do business. He determined that it could become rich by becoming one of the most attractive places in the world for business. His actions were intensely coherent and, by developed Western standards, draconian. There would be no homeless squatters, no labor unions, no unrest. There would be strong private property law and a stable economic climate. Drug peddlers were executed. Dissenters and union organizers were jailed. Foreign money began to pour in, and employment

boomed, creating a trained labor force. Today, more than three thousand multinational firms operate there, unemployment is very low, the gross domestic product (GDP) per capita is $58,000, and life expectancy is eighty-four years.

- In 2003 Jason Fried was struggling to use email to handle the growing collection of contractors, consultants, and designers connected to his Web-design company's expanding client base. The crux of the problem was having to use email, Excel, memos, telephone calls, and various other management tools that did not talk to one another well. There had been a similar challenge in the early days of spreadsheets when one had to use different tools for calculating, graphing, importing, and exporting data. Fried's team boldly decided to invest in creating their own tool, now called Basecamp. This software handled to-do lists, message boards, schedules, real-time group chat, questions and answers, and more in a single application. The Basecamp client base grew from forty-five in 2004 to three million in 2019.
- During the 1980s, the Walt Disney Company's performance began to sag. Both feature films and cable TV operations were bringing in little profit. Corporate raiders began to circle, seeing an opportunity to split the company into its theme-park and movie components and make a quick gain. Michael Eisner was named chairman and CEO in 1984, backed by the oil-rich Bass group. He began to see the crux of the challenge at Disney in its much-admired classic animated films such as *Cinderella*. These almost defined Disney to each generation when they were rereleased, but they could not be replicated. The costs of the hand painting of each frame, originally borne during the Depression, could not be justified in the 1980s. The solution Eisner and Disney president Frank Wells designed was remarkable. One key was breaking Disney's culture of handcrafting its films by investing in computer-based animation. The other was expanding the company's profit and growth beyond animated films to also center on creating new

animated characters. Whether it was *The Lion King*, *Beauty & the Beast*, or *Pocahontas*, each new character, or property, generated profits far beyond the film. Toys, games, TV specials, Disneyland rides, and other synergies were carefully exploited. It was a wholly new strategy in entertainment.

THE MECHANICS OF INSIGHT

The creation of strategies like these fascinates because they are the connection between intellect and grand outcomes. With insight, you see what others have not or what they have ignored. Yet how one designs a creative response lies at the very edge of our understanding, something only glimpsed out of the corner of the mind.

How does insight happen? It springs upon us, taking us by surprise. Or it arises unasked, catching us in the middle of some unconnected activity. An insight "feels right," its truth self-evident. And we are unaware of how insight is attained. Introspection fails to reveal the underlying process.

Cognitive neuroscientists have uncovered some of the brain activity associated with insight. One especially interesting finding has been a preinsight (one-second) burst of activity in the right-side (rear) visual cortex. This low-frequency (6–10 Hz) "alpha" pulse appears to block external senses for a moment. This jolt to the visual cortex means that the phrase "flash of insight" is not just a figure of speech.[9]

The flash of insight is the experience of creation, and we share it when we recognize a good strategy. It is Gordon Moore, the cofounder of Intel, realizing that photolithographic scaling would let him cram ever more transistors onto a square millimeter of silicon, now known as "Moore's Law." It is Jeff Bezos seeing, in 1994, that the Internet was the perfect medium for selling paper-and-ink books. It is Marc Benioff "dreaming" the design for a cloud-based customer-relationship management (CRM) system. It is Sam Walton seeing his discount stores as nodes in a logistics system rather than individual stores. When the flash of insight remakes a part of our world, we see in new ways. Rivals who fail to achieve the new insight are put off balance, striking at the edges rather than the center of our strength.

People who study or write about insight usually imply that it is instantly gratifying—the falling of an impasse between a problem and its solution. After his voyage on *The Beagle*, Charles Darwin was struggling with the problem of how different species arose over time. The idea of natural selection, of differential survival among existing variety, occurred to him instantly: "I happened to read for amusement Malthus *On Population*, and being well prepared to appreciate the struggle for existence which everywhere goes on . . . it at once struck me that under these circumstances favourable variations would tend to be preserved and unfavourable ones to be destroyed."[10]

Such moments of insight can indeed be sublime. However, the predisposition to see insight as pleasant arises from a biased attention to the emotions of the successful. Insight is not always "aha"; it may instead be "uh-oh." When Kmart's senior management first understood that Walmart was not simply a rural specialist but a competitor that had undermined their whole approach to business, they did not feel Darwin's joy at discovery.

Insight does not automatically awaken at our call. It cannot be guaranteed, but it can be aided. If you have not grasped the thorns of the problem, you cannot expect insight into a solution. Insight is helped by practice at the feel of sliding and shifting points of view. Insight into strategy is much aided by understanding the power of focusing coherent action upon a point of leverage. Insight into strategy is also greatly aided by having examined a broad repertory of past strategies. And insight is helped by looking in the right places. I start my own search for insight in the yet-to-be-questioned assumptions about how things work, in the asymmetries among interests and resources, and in the habits and inertia of others.

There is a large literature on how to generate new ideas—brainstorming, meditation, visualization, collect many before evaluation, hypnagogia, adopting another's point of view, "what if . . ?", imaginary mentor, and others. Yet John Dewey's original argument remains sound. He wrote that the most reliable source of new design ideas is "reflection" on a "felt difficulty."[11] The key source of design insight is a clearheaded diagnosis of the structure of the challenge, especially its crux, by employing a tool kit of persistence, analogy, point of view, making explicit assumptions, asking why, and recognizing your unconscious constraints.

In chasing insight, you need persistence. In facing difficult problems, persistence means being willing to endure the anxiety and frustration of "being lost" and work on a way out of difficulty. And when the first idea appears, to test it and critique it and then be willing and able to work on still another way to deal with the challenge.

I have been lost a few times: in the wrong ice gully as the sun set on a snowy evening high on Mount Washington in New Hampshire; at eighteen thousand feet, thinking muddled by altitude, descending the wrong side of snowcapped Mount Damavand in Iran; and in the forests of Maine, where the land was flat and each tree looked like another, on and on for miles.

When you get lost, there are rising feelings of helplessness and anxiety. It is frustrating not knowing which way to go, with the temptation to grasp onto the first hint of a way.[12] Those two rocks piled on one another—don't they mark a path out of the forest?

This, to some extent, is the same feeling one has when facing a gnarly strategic challenge. At first glance, there is no obvious solution. It may be embarrassing to not have a ready answer. The strong temptation is to adopt the first solution offered. To hold that proposed solution in mind but continue to look for another is very hard. It is accepting anxiety and frustration all over again. The discipline of persistence—of thinking again about the situation from a different angle—is vital.

There is a theory that people have difficulty seeing a subtle yet superior solution to a complex problem when there is an attractive, seemingly simpler alternative—a distraction. (This is the basis of the "think again" advice discussed in Chapter 20.) In a fascinating experiment, researchers gave experienced chess players problems where there was a classic "smothered mate" set of moves available.[13] But there was also a less obvious but quicker way to win. The players were told to seek a win in the fewest possible moves. They could take all the time they needed. The researchers found good players were indeed "distracted" by the familiar five-move smothered-mate attack. But master players were not distracted. The masters quickly saw both solutions and chose the quicker three-move solution.

One conclusion is that it pays to be a master. More interesting, though, is the conclusion that it should pay to increase your awareness of "bright, shiny objects" responses to problems. When the problems are strategic, by searching more widely, you may dramatically improve your ability to see better solutions.

The most direct source of insights are analogies, the examples and lessons of others. Direct examples from direct competitors are the clearest, but also risk a head-on competitive shoot-out. In competition, the strategist normally seeks to come at the situation in a way that is different from that taken by competitors. Interviewing Toyota engine designers in Japan, I asked them a hard question: "Why not use Honda's methods? They are the best at engine design." The answer was that the Toyota team did not aim to be just as good as Honda; they wanted to be better. In the same vein, many of the most useful analogies are taken from other industries, other countries, or other times. Or they can come from other situations entirely. There is no avoiding the fact that wide knowledge and experience are very helpful in tapping into appropriate analogies.

Marc Benioff started Salesforce.com as a direct analogy to Amazon. Howard Schultz started Starbucks after observing a coffee shop in Milan, Italy. Bill Gross started GoTo as an analogy to the yellow pages. Ryanair used Southwest Airlines as one of its models to design its strategy (see Chapter 3). Facebook started as an online analogy to a college yearbook.

We may also seek analogies that are closer to metaphor. If I draw a picture of this challenge, is it a spiral or a box? As Pepsi are we a grazing animal or a predator or a scavenger? In the United States, are we Rome in 50 BC, rising to world dominance, or Rome in AD 400, with barbarians using the empire's own roads to invade?

Or are we Athens, and is China the new Rome? As Microsoft do we protect our territory by building castles, by patrolling the borders, by punishing neighbors, or with alliances? What are other points of view? How does this situation look to a competitor? To a customer? To a high school kid? How will we look at this in a few years? How will lawyers and politicians view the situation? How do these issues look to the database manager? To the loading dock?

Focusing in on the problem—looking only at a part, but in more explicit detail—can make parts of it clearer and easier to deal with. If you have a problem with the "customer experience," looking just at the returns process, for example, may stimulate insights that can be used more broadly.

Focusing out is the converse, where one sees the challenge as part of a larger landscape. In my home state of Oregon, wildfires are a problem. Most summers the sky is smoky in August as fires burn in the nearby Cascade forests. Most of the people looking at this issue argue about prevention versus containment or about thinning and controlled burns versus fire being natural. However, a broader view of the situation shows that most of the large fires occur in National Wilderness Areas. These areas are protected from development, but they also lack any kind of fire roads, firebreaks, or other development. So the larger problem is the definition and management of wilderness—do we really mean for it to support large fires every year only a mile from towns or cities?

Making assumptions explicit can sometimes indicate how a point of view can be usefully changed. For example, a large US automaker assumed that, by standardizing its parts-shipping containers, it achieved economies of scale and reduced the costs of their acquisition. This was true, but the additional, unstated, assumption that no other costs were imposed by this policy turned out to be false. Moving many parts in too large containers made for more damaged parts and costly rework.

Asking "why" about the assumptions or about the way things are done is a way to break the existing frame. Why don't movie theaters adjust prices to demand rather than have long lines for the openings of popular films? Why do home remodels always take two to three times longer than estimated? Why does it take two months to bring our software up and running for a large client? Why does a discount store have to be so large?

A MAJOR IMPEDIMENT to insight is unconscious constraint, an unrecognized assumption or belief about the world, or about the problem situation. What keeps us from seeing in new ways may be the burden of the old, softly holding one's mind in a rut. The impediment may not simply be a lack of vision; it may also be the unconscious fear of casting aside whole doctrines, beliefs, or operating principles.

Consider animation. In 1833 the oddly named phenakistoscope was invented. It was a toy—a cardboard disc with a series of slits around the perimeter. Below the slits, a sequence of images was printed. Turn the disc to face a mirror, peer through a slit at the reflected image in the mirror, and spin the disc about its axis. As each slit passes your eye, you see one of the images; the sequence creates the illusion of motion. With a phenakistoscope, one could, for the first time in history, see an image move, see the image of a horse appear to gallop.

The animation insight was not technologically difficult. When I was a boy in fifth grade, I used to amuse the girl sitting next to me with short animated stories about boxes, arrows, and circles. Drawn in the margins of our books, the stories came to life when I flipped the pages: boxes advanced on and consumed fleeing circles, only to be hit by flying arrows. Once you understand how an animation is made, it is obvious how to make another.

The unconscious constraint was the overwhelmingly powerful universal belief that perception maps reality. If you believe that you perceive continuous motion because motion is continuous, you know that a sequence of still images cannot possibly look like motion—it can only look like what it is, a jerky sequence of still images. To understand animation, one must entertain the disturbing idea that perceived reality is constructed by the mind—that our perceptual system fills in the blanks, performing massive acts of interpolation. Constructing early animations required shifting or removing an unconscious constraint.

SOLUTIONS

I. M. Pei's design for a new entrance to the Louvre is a wonderful example of someone finding the crux of a problem and then having insight into a solution.

In 1984 French officials decided that the world-famous Louvre needed renewal. Built as a castle in about 1200, it became a palace for French kings when François I rebuilt it in 1546. Becoming a museum in 1793, by the twentieth century it was literally a maze of rooms and connections, with too little office space and no decent public entrance. President François Mitterrand hired Chinese American architect I. M. Pei to consult on a solution. Walking and studying the grounds, Pei quickly concluded that the great empty courtyard had to be the center of the renewal. At that time, it was a dusty parking lot. The courtyard would be dug up, and new offices and storerooms would be built under it. But what about an entrance? Pei didn't like the idea of an empty courtyard but, at the same time, didn't want to erect a structure that would block views of the classic buildings surrounding it.

The crux of the problem: create an entrance and transform the empty courtyard while not blocking views of the classic palace. Pei's design insight was a transparent glass structure in the center of the courtyard. The glass concept meant that a flat roof was out of the question since it would kill part of the view and collect debris. A slanted roof would pose the same problem. Pei settled on a transparent pyramid. It would be the entrance from which one could see the surrounding buildings and not block views from outside. (I would have chosen a transparent fluted dome, but they didn't consult me.)

Once I. M. Pei had decided on the pyramid design, the problem became solvable. There were hundreds of engineering, aesthetic, and political issues to address, but they were all solvable, given the overall concept of a transparent pyramid.

There was great furor over this design when it was announced, and there are people today who still hate it. But the transparent glass-pyramid entrance to the Louvre is widely admired and has become one of the top three tourist attractions in Paris.

A SECOND FASCINATING example of identifying a crux and then a solution are the stories of GoTo and AdWords.

In early 1999 I was visiting Bill Gross's Idealab, a Web incubator, in Pasadena. He suggested that I try his newest search engine, GoTo.com. I typed in "best new cars," and I immediately saw entries for Ford, Toyota, and so on. This was interesting, because in 1998 Web search was a mess. Look for "best dog food for Labradors," and you were just as likely to get porn as anything about dogs or food. One part of the challenge was that the Web was basically free, and anyone with some skill could put up a site. Search engines would be triggered by their titles and hidden keywords.

Gross's insight into the crux came from looking at the telephone yellow pages. Almost every company had a listing, with those paying more having larger ads. Could he build a search engine where companies paid for their positions in the results?

Gross's idea was to make search more effective and to also solve the other part of the challenge plaguing the industry—how to make any money. He explained that search engines like Yahoo, AltaVista, and Lycos take some keywords and try to find websites that the words describe. "At GoTo we let people bid on the keywords—the site bidding the most gets its search result placed first, the second-highest bidder places second, and so on." Then GoTo listed all the sites that didn't bid at all. He explained that "when someone clicks on the search result, we collect the fee. And the site can monitor its position in real time, adjusting its bid to achieve its goals."

Gross's insight was novel and clever—the bids generated considerable income for the search engine, and the procedure automatically eliminated the thousands of "spam" sites trying to lure unwary searchers. Yet GoTo worked well only as a form of advertising. If you were looking for information on how to fix a car, you would have to wade through pages of sponsored links. GoTo went public later that year, changing its name to Overture Services in 2001. In 2003 it was acquired by Yahoo! for $1.6 billion. A financial win for Bill Gross, GoTo held the seeds of the core problem of how to make money with search. But there was further innovation on the way.

When I had been talking with Bill Gross in Pasadena, Google founders Larry Page and Sergey Brin were receiving their first round of $25 million in venture capital. They were also trying to fix search and had invented a clever algorithm (PageRank) that became best in the industry. They had solved the search problem, but they also struggled with the how-to-make-money problem. They saw Gross's GoTo but were dead set against ruining their PageRank search results with paid-for links. Their challenge was to provide accurate search results but also, somehow, to make money. Sometime in early 1999, Sal Kamangar, Google's ninth employee, managed a team that defined and built Google's AdWords system.

The AdWords design idea was to put text advertisements *on the side* of the search-results page. Instead of contaminating the search-results list, this design kept results and paid ads separate. It seems so simple in retrospect, but they broke the industry-wide unconscious constraint about search results being a single list. They had advertisers pay per thousand times their ad was displayed. Later, the company would switch to the pay-per-click system.[14]

The AdWords insight launched Google, now Alphabet, into being one of the most valuable companies in the world.[15]

3

Strategy Is a Journey

There was a time when I was a mountain climber, spending all my summers in the Tetons or the Wind River Mountains or the Alps. When you try a new route on a mountain, you do not have a clear map of exactly how you will get to the top. Your plan is normally more like "Let's go up that gully and exit on the ledge to the left. Then we will see if that crack above goes." On the ledge above, you may see that the crack doesn't go and search for a different way forward, perhaps a traverse to the right and then up rough rock to another ledge. And so on.

Real-life business strategy is a bit like that route up a mountain. You may have an ambition to get to the top of a particular peak, but the route requires overcoming a series of difficulties. Climbers call them "problems." And, as each difficulty is overcome, there are new views of the problems and opportunities that lie ahead. And, if you make it, your ambition evolves. Next time, you will try the northern face or a bigger peak.

Real-life strategy, whether your own or a company's, is an ongoing process of dealing with critical challenges and deciding what consequential actions to take. Some challenges are long-term and broad in scope. Others are more immediate blockages, or sudden opportunities, encountered on the way forward. In all cases, strategy is the process of confronting and solving critical challenges.

I emphasize this because there is a widespread misconception that a business strategy is some sort of long-range sketch of a desired destination. I encourage you to think of strategy as a journey through, over, and around a sequence of challenges. If you were the CEO of Intel in 2014, you might have said, "Intel executes Moore's Law to make the world's best semiconductors." But in 2017, you would be asked about Intel's strategy for dealing with the slowing of Moore's Law. And in 2019, you would be asked about Intel's strategy for dealing with the rise of special-purpose processors, as developed by Google and Microsoft. And in 2021, you would be asked about the company's seeming loss of process leadership to the Taiwan Semiconductor Manufacturing Company (TSMC). The idea that Intel has a single unchanging "strategy" that spans these challenges reduces the concept to a slogan or motto, like "Be the best." Strategy is problem solving, and it is best expressed relative to a particular challenge.

Strategy should be an ongoing process. This concept of strategy allows a company to have a strategy process that is not a constant restatement of some vague overall purpose and intent. The strategy process becomes the much more entrepreneurial task of solving challenges and grabbing opportunities, as they appear, along the way. An organization doesn't face a single "battle" or even a single "war." If it is to persist over time, it will face an ongoing series of challenges, each of which should be dealt with. Existence is an ongoing quest, and making strategy is ongoing work. There can be no one approach, or "strategy," for dealing with them all, as we will see from the challenges that Salesforce.com and Ryanair have faced.

SALESFORCE.COM

The development of Salesforce.com nicely illustrates the sequence of challenge and strategic response that shapes a company over time. To say that Salesforce.com had a "strategy" during its development so simplifies the concept as to make it almost meaningless.

Marc Benioff was the kind of kid who wrote adventure games for his Atari. In college he was able to get a summer job writing code at Apple for the forthcoming Macintosh. After college he took a job at Oracle in customer service and was later promoted to vice president of the client/server division. While at Oracle, Benioff became familiar with Oracle's OASIS system for customer-relationship management.

Customer-relationship management systems started as index cards and evolved into computer databases in the 1970s. Such databases listed customers, contacts, order histories, evaluations, identification of leads, and other information useful in managing sales activities. Later, the databases began to include accounting, shipping, and other operations information. In the late 1990s, the term *CRM* began to be used to describe this kind of software, and it began to become even more complex, absorbing much more than customer data—product planning, supply chain, payment systems: all began to be integrated into CRM software.

CRM software traditionally ran on a company's computers, managed by the internal IT (information technology) department. In the late 1990s the leading suppliers were Oracle (OASIS system), Siebel, and SAP. Total cost to a company for a standard CRM system for two hundred users was estimated by the Yankee Group (2001), a technology research firm, to be $2.8 million, with $1.9 million being license fees for the software, plus support fees and customization fees.[1] The systems were complex and somewhat difficult to both install and maintain.

Marc Benioff recalled how in 1996 he *dreamed* how to build a cloud-based CRM: "I came up with the idea about how to build Salesforce.com in my sleep. Literally. I had a weird dream in which I envisioned Amazon.com, but instead of the tabs with Books, CDs, or DVDs, they said Accounts, Contacts, Opportunities, Forecasts, and Reports."[2]

Of course, Benioff didn't dream up the idea out of nowhere. He had been thinking about CRM systems for years and was deeply involved in looking for ways to reduce the large start-up costs customers had to bear. The crux of the difficulty was the software.

Installation had to be tailored to the client's internal systems, and there were constant updates and bug fixes to manage.

What Benioff envisioned was the simplification gained by putting all of the software in the "cloud," so that anyone with a Web browser could use it. With a cloud-based CRM, the user could simply sign on via the Web and have a CRM for a monthly fee. There would be no local servers, no charges for installation or maintenance, and no IT department.

Benioff left Oracle in 1999 with the blessing of CEO Larry Ellison plus some $2 million in seed capital; other chunks of venture capital were fairly easily attracted. It was the boom years for dot-com, and the endorsement from Ellison was significant.

The initial critical challenge he faced was attracting very good developers and more capital to feed them. How would you choose to attract the best developers? Benioff's approach was to build publicity. He courted reporters and writers, held extravagant Silicon Valley parties, and did everything he could to spread the word. He described Salesforce.com as a radical disruptor, aiming to obliterate the standard software industry. Benioff adopted a symbol showing the word *software* with a red slash through it and coupled it with the slogan "No software." A video promotion showed the Salesforce.com jet fighter shooting down the old "software" biplane.[3] The buzz and sense of creating the future did attract a group of talented developers.

The first important product was SFA (Sales Force Automation). The next big challenge, not surprisingly, was getting companies to actually buy the product. The crux of this challenge was that such decisions were largely made by the IT department. Salesforce.com was relatively unknown, and signing up might well make the CRM people in the IT department redundant. The initial attack was to bypass corporate purchasing and have individual users directly purchase access for a low charge. That did not go well. So Benioff changed the policy to allow up to five users at a company to sign up for free. There would be a $50 per month fee for each user over five. Over time, the company began to use telemarketing and direct sales to reach larger customers. With a better product and a lot of positive word of mouth, sales began to grow.

The initial hypothesis was that the free sign-ups would generate inside influencers who would lead large companies to sign up. But sales analysis showed that smaller firms were actually the fastest-growing source of new customers. The company changed its policy to target small businesses, especially the many being suddenly created by the Internet boom.

With the Internet crash in 2000, Salesforce.com faced financial difficulties. Many of its small business customers disappeared. An internal debate arose about billing—could the company remain true to its no-contract, no-discount claims? Or should it change its position and allow annual or multiyear contracts? It was a strategic issue given the firm's positioning as the "No software" company. In the end, Benioff chose to raise the rate for monthly customers and press his best customers for longer-term deals, with salespeople getting good commissions for signing annual contracts. The original "vision" of a simple monthly plan faded away.

As the technology began to mature, Benioff sought to add new solutions, some broad and some industry specific. This was a new competitive idea—taking advantage of the installed base to offer "apps" and, eventually, bundles of apps. This idea then morphed into one of letting customers adapt the product to their own circumstances. Salesforce.com took the original tabs (Accounts, Leads, and so forth) and added "blank tabs" that the user could customize.

The key to making this work was AppExchange, which was essentially an app store for business software. When it was introduced in 2005, several reviewers called it an "iTunes for business." Then in 2006 came tools for writing code to actually run on Salesforce's servers (Apex) along with tools for building custom visual interfaces. With these steps, Salesforce.com was moving away from simply being a cloud-based CRM to being a cloud platform for a wide range of business applications.

In 2010 the company added Chatter, which Benioff called "a Facebook for the Enterprise."[4] The idea was to differentiate from competitors by social networking, but also by being able to offer this ability to clients for their own social networking programs.

Clearly, Benioff began with some underlying set of ambitions for Salesforce.com. Yet there were numerous strategic challenges that had to be met during his ongoing quest. And, obviously, as each challenge was met, the ambition shifted and escalated. At each step, the response was a *design* for dealing with the challenge. It is common to say that strategy is about choice. The word *choice* implies a set of given alternatives from among which to choose. But you will look in vain for a handbook for CEOs on the "best ways to attract developers." There is no solid rule from economics or marketing about whether to initially target small, medium, or large accounts. The approaches Benioff took were designs, not choices. And the power was in these designs coupled with a willingness to shift and adapt as well as in forceful implementation.

Salesforce.com was the first dot-com listed on the New York Stock Exchange. In early 2021, it had sixty thousand employees, was valued at $243 billion, and was ranked number two in the *Fortune* list of "best companies to work for." The free sign-up has evolved into free trials. Point your browser to www.salesforce.com to get one. Benioff's design has become known as software-as-a-service (SaaS) and is the model for a host of other ventures.

RYANAIR

In 1984 Irish businessman Tony Ryan and two fellow investors formed Ryanair. Tony Ryan had worked for the Irish airline Aer Lingus and afterward built one of the largest airplane leasing companies in Europe. The Thatcher government had loosened the rules about who could run an airline, and Ryan's intent was to compete with Aer Lingus on the London–Dublin route. He knew that Aer Lingus costs were bloated, as were sole competitor British Airways', on that route. Ryan calculated that Ryanair could emulate the cost structure of American Airlines, offer good service and lower prices than did the government-owned carriers, and take share on the London–Dublin route.

The company's original strategy didn't work out. Good service and low prices were themselves inconsistent. And aiming at the London–Dublin route against two state-subsidized carriers was inconsistent with being a small start-up. British Airways could afford to lose money on one of its routes. That is exactly what happened. Its lower prices on London–Dublin kept upstart Ryanair from making a profit. Over the period 1984–1992, Ryanair fought for share on the London–Dublin route, gaining passenger traffic, but it went bankrupt in 1992. The crux of the challenge was the staying power of the established players on the major routes.

During the company's restructuring, CEO Michael O'Leary visited the United States to look closely at low-cost carrier Southwest Airlines. There he saw a cost structure much lower than American Airlines and a clever strategy of not competing head-on but, instead, serving nonmajor airports on at least one side of a trip (for example, Chicago to Baltimore rather than to Washington, DC). Recalling that visit, O'Leary said:

> We went to look at Southwest Airlines in the US. It was like the road to Damascus. This was the way to make Ryanair work. I met with Herb Kelleher. I passed out about midnight, and when I woke up again at about 3am Kelleher was still there, the *******, pouring himself another bourbon. I thought I'd pick his brains and come away with the Holy Grail. The next day I couldn't remember a thing.[5]

With new capital, Ryanair resumed business with a bare-bones cost structure, flying Dublin to Luton rather than London's Gatwick Airport. It went farther than Southwest in trimming costs, and it unbundled parts of its service to keep its basic price very low. That is, at Ryan, the paid ticket was for air travel for the person only. Baggage was extra, having your boarding pass reprinted was extra, food was extra, there were no refunds, and the inside of the aircraft was covered with advertisements. Ryanair began to add routes to smaller European towns and grew rapidly and profitably.

CEO Michael O'Leary liked to emphasize the bare-bones nature of Ryanair service and the fact that everything was extra. His foul-mouthed pronouncements included "I'd love to operate aircraft where we take out the back ten rows and put in hand rails. We'd say 'if you want to stand, it's five euros.' People say 'Oh but the people standing may get killed if there's a crash.' Well, with respect, the people sitting down might get killed as well." And "You're not getting a refund so f**k off. We don't want to hear your sob stories. What part of 'no refund' don't you understand?"[6]

Ryanair's cost of carrying most passengers was about equal to its fares. Its profit came from its fees—the charges for baggage, for priority boarding, for fast-tracking through security, for choosing your seat, for chips and drinks aboard.

As it gained confidence, Ryanair began to expand to the European continent, again aiming its routes away from the major airports and carriers. A few years back, for example, I wanted to fly from the London area to a music festival in a small medieval town in France. Ryanair was the only carrier serving the area, and the fare was about $75.

Ryanair grew rapidly over the ensuing twenty-five years, becoming the largest budget carrier in Europe and carrying more international passengers than any other airline in the world. From the United Kingdom, it served forty countries. In 2019 revenues were €7.7 billion, and profit after tax was €885 million. The readers of *Which?* surveys voted it the least-liked short-haul airline six years running. Nevertheless, low prices and flights to many otherwise hard-to-reach destinations kept boardings growing at 10 percent per year.

Today, Ryanair faces a new gnarly challenge brought on by COVID-19 and the delays in Boeing's production schedule. The pandemic has forced a drastic reduction in air travel, and, in April 2020, O'Leary had to dismiss three thousand employees, including many pilots. The number of flights by all European carriers collapsed. The United Kingdom began requiring COVID tests of passengers that made scheduling flights even harder.

O'Leary also took particular exception to the way several European governments were subsidizing the major carriers and ignoring the low-cost start-ups. He said that the carriers "who went in weakest, which is the legacy airlines, Air France, Alitalia, Lufthansa, have either been nationalized or are receiving extraordinary volumes of state aid. These are going to hugely distort the level playing field for aviation in Europe for three to five years."[7]

This new set of gnarly challenges put the company's low-cost structure at risk, as it had to dismiss employees to keep costs down. Can its leadership find a way to hunker down until the pandemic subsides and still ramp up low-cost operations when that happens? The crux is creating confidence in a successful return to scale sufficient to attract the required financial support.

4

Where You Can Win

The ASC

There is an old aphorism that the key to strategy is playing the games you can win. Of course, life is not a game, nor is corporate management or statecraft. But the essential idea of focusing where you can "win" is neither trivial nor always followed. People can concentrate on meeting social expectations, or looking good, or local political infighting, or avoiding embarrassment, or becoming addicted to superficial pleasures. People and organizations can spend enormous resources and effort on what, based on history, they think they "are good at," or what others say they are good at, or doubling down on a losing position, instead of on what promises the greatest gain. Such concentrations become habit. And having a habit makes it harder to break away and do something more rewarding.

Designing or choosing often means leaving aside multiple issues and desires and focusing, instead, on what will make the most difference. Musa Majid, who runs a small bodega, a corner grocery and convenience store, in the Bronx, New York, did just that.

Musa was an immigrant from Yemen, arriving in the 1970s and going to school in New York. At first, he had a series of part-time jobs helping grocers unpack crates. Then he married and wanted a more reliable income. He was able to set up the bodega business in the mid-1990s with help from connections in the Yemeni community. These connections were crucial resources that allowed him to find a landlord, suppliers, and employees at favorable rates. They also helped him obtain bank loans and the necessary permits. The licenses for beer and cigarettes they helped him obtain were, he said, very important for the business. Musa's margins on goods were low, and he had to work at least twelve hours a day, seven days a week. A key part of keeping the business alive was to know the repeat customers and greet them cheerily by name. He didn't trust other ten-dollar-an-hour employees at the register and had his nephew fill in when he could not be there.

Musa Majid's bodega business had a guiding policy—an underlying logic. Getting from place to place was neither easy nor simple for people living in some sections of New York. So, local neighborhood people shop at a nearby bodega, despite its tiny stock compared with suburban grocery stores. Musa's connections within the Yemeni community were a substantial resource, as were his energy, basic good humor, and willingness to work long, hard hours. He made enough money to support his daughter's education and took pride in being in business rather than having a menial job working for someone else.

Given his resources, running the Bronx bodega was, for Musa, an *addressable* strategic challenge. It was a space within which Musa could "win." It was not the win a person with much greater initial resources might seek, but for Musa it was a win.

PLAN DOG

Diagnosis will always reveal multiple challenges. To focus, some challenges must be put aside or deferred. One must choose which challenges to confront. In this sense, the crux itself may be a choice. Choose the crux that strikes at critical issues and can be surmounted, a logic exemplified in Plan Dog.

Germany had conquered France in June 1940. That summer the Battle of Britain, the air war between the United Kingdom and Germany, began. In the Pacific, Japan had signed an alliance with Nazi Germany and, three years earlier, invaded China. To US military planners, it looked like the nation might soon be involved in war in both Asia and Europe. In this context, Admiral Harold Stark, chief of naval operations, wrote a memo outlining the challenge: "If Britain wins decisively against Germany we could win everywhere; but if she loses the problem confronting us would be very great; and, while we might not lose everywhere, we might, possibly, not win anywhere."[1]

As a naval officer, he thought in terms of the two different hemispheres, or oceans. For him, the crux was that the United States could not really fight two world wars at once. With that frame, he listed four strategic options, lettered A through D, summarized below:

A. hemisphere defense against forces in both oceans
B. full war with Japan; defend in the Atlantic
C. strong assistance to the British for their war in Europe and to the British, Dutch, and China in Asia
D. strong offensive in Europe as an ally of Britain; defend in the Pacific

President Roosevelt chose Admiral Stark's option D, which became known by its letter as "Plan Dog." General George Marshall, army chief of staff, supported this choice, and, following talks with the British, a March 1941 agreement codified the "Germany First" choice. After the attack on Pearl Harbor, the United States entered the war against both Germany and Japan, with the majority of its war effort focused on Germany. None of this was made public.

The two critical judgments behind Plan Dog were that the United States could not decisively prevail in both Europe and Asia at the same time and that defending Britain was *more important* than defending territories in the Pacific. Facing challenges in both Europe and Asia, US leaders chose to make the European challenge the first priority. Not everyone agreed. Many, like General Douglas MacArthur, saw America's future with Asia, with Europe being the tired past. Nevertheless, most of the US war effort went to arming the

USSR and building up for a cross-Channel invasion. Seven thousand tanks (40 percent of US production), more than eleven thousand aircraft, and much more went to the USSR and Britain via the "Lend-Lease" program.

XRSystems

'XRSystems,' or XRS, provides an interesting example of how a leadership group worked to identify where they could win. XRS was a maker of measuring instruments for acidic, cold, and high-temperature environments. In late 2012 I was asked to help the company with strategy. 'Stacy Diaz' had been working for XRS for ten years and had been CEO for three. The headquarters was a two-story building off the interstate in the suburbs of a major city in Ohio. We met in Stacy's understated office. There, Stacy explained that she was facing a number of complex issues. Here are my interview notes (converted into complete sentences):

> XRS is privately owned by the 'Borault' family, and the family has been thinking about a public offering in the next year or two. We are organized as an LLC [limited liability company]. If we are going down that path, we need to get our ducks in a row. But, right now, there are a bundle of unresolved issues.
>
> XRS was formed twenty years ago to commercialize temperature, pressure, and shock sensors for very difficult environments. Today, the product line also includes vibration and change-of-position sensing. These devices are used in nuclear power plants, jet engines, rockets, industrial furnaces, certain science laboratories, and in some chemical industry applications.
>
> One problem we face is new competition from an Israeli company with a sensor that combines pressure, vibration, and temperature readings, cutting the costs of having both. We aren't sure how to respond to this. For now, we think our reputation and customer relationships will carry us, but in the longer term . . . ?

Our development efforts are currently concentrated in Ohio, where we have seventy-five people working on three different efforts. One is drone-based sensors. A second is working on sensors to be integrated into undersea cables, and the third is looking at integrating our sensors into Wi-Fi and Internet environments. Right now, they are wired rather than wireless.

The owners brought new blood into the board last year, and . . . I would like to say it was a breath of fresh air. One of the new board members, 'John Cherold,' is from a finance background, and he says XRS is underperforming. He wants to outsource our development work to contractors and brings this up at every meeting.

Much of our product line requires encapsulation in quartz bulbs. We were experiencing quality and cost issues at our Ohio manufacturing facility, so three years ago the board decided to buy a small facility near Beijing and move quartz-bulb production there. It is a small facility with under one hundred employees. After we bought the facility, the Chinese government decided that it was adding to air pollution and made us move to the suburbs. After the move to a new building, production rates fell dramatically. I and some other senior leaders traveled to the plant to try to understand what was going on. We met with the former owner/manager, Mr. 'Chi.' We explained the problem. Mr. Chi told us that "if you are having problems with the workers, I can have my former works manager come in and break a few fingers." Well, that's not how we do things. We have hired a new works manager and are hoping that will do the trick.

Sales growth has been slow. The sales force are ex-engineers, and they try to visit each customer twice a year. Most of our sales come from customer orders from companies who know about our products and how to use them. We have exceptional skills at sensors for very difficult environments, but there is only so much demand for that. We have good customer relationships, but there is nothing new happening in nuclear power, jet engines, industrial furnaces, the chemical industry, or supercold environments.

'Kurt Kamper' was the person who originally figured out how to put these sensors in tough packages. He was a genius. He has passed away, and the original engineering team that worked with him on most of our products have left or retired by now. We have brought in good engineers, . . . but, I have to say, they have a hard time modifying or improving the original designs.

In confidential interviews with the senior management team, more information was forthcoming. One executive told me that the company "has been a bit sleepy, coasting on the achievements of a decade past." Another wondered why quartz production had been moved to China: "They could have fixed the issues here in Ohio. There was an issue with OSHA [Occupational Safety and Health Administration], and the board wanted nothing to do with safety complaints. They treated the complainers like subversives." A third commented, "There really is no marketing team. The sales team doesn't have the skill set required to push market boundaries." A fourth told me, "There are no metrics to gauge our progress."

Stacy Diaz assembled a small team of herself and four other senior executives. This group worked to flesh out a diagnosis and examine alternative actions. Their summary diagnosis was that there was a saturated low-growth market for their sensor products; the company had a complacent internal culture, with marketing and sales adapted to the low-growth markets; and there was a lack of new technical ideas. They were attracted to working on sales and marketing, as that challenge seemed to be the familiar. Yet, at the same time, the group recognized that market saturation was a more critical challenge.

On the morning of the second meeting, I conducted an exercise I call "Instant Strategy" (see Chapter 20). I asked each group member to write down one sentence describing their guiding policy solution to the most important challenge. They had two minutes to write it down. Then we shared the results on a white board. Their five Instant Strategies were:

R&D refocus only on wireless
Phantom stock plan for most managers (LLC specific)
Reorganize sales for more expeditionary work
More sales visits to nonclients
Automotive sensors

CEO Stacy Diaz said that she could, in a short time, redirect R&D to just wireless. There would be grumbling, but it could be done. The financial officer said that phantom stock was not hard but would take board approval.

The group then quizzed the manager who had written "automotive sensors." He explained that he had been off-roading with his Jeep and would have appreciated some shock and tilt sensors. Such sensors would have to stand up to rocks and water and hard hits—and be wireless. And he would need a display of some kind. The others began to chime in on the topic. Did the army need sensors for its vehicles? What about big rigs?

They decided on a small task force to look into the vehicle sensor issue. Who else was in that market? The group put the sales and marketing issue on hold.

In a month the vehicle task force came back with an opportunity. A small privately held company, 'Autosense,' was working on wireless automotive sensors for shock absorbers and tires. They were interested in measuring inclination. Their engineering group was small but imaginative. It took three months for the board of directors to arrange an acquisition deal.

XRS embraced the new opportunity and began to grow. It found ways to make its sensors rock proof and, eventually, bulletproof. It moved its manufacturing to North Carolina, closing the China plant.

My view was that XRS's basic strategy had been so successful in the past that the company went to sleep. The management had nestled comfortably down into its high-profit niche. When looking at challenges, the issue of sales and marketing seemed to them both important and addressable. Yet they knew the challenge of market saturation was the crux. It was *important*, but defining it that way made it seem unsolvable. The critical comment, one that pointed at the crux, was by the engineer who defended his idea about vehicle sensors by saying, "If our market is saturated, we have to find a market that isn't."

Many times, in retrospect, good strategy seems to be just good management. Yet its actual creation is a set of tough insights and choices about how critical issues can actually be addressed.

THE CLASH OF AMBITION

Values and desires are usually seen as guiding and motivating action to their accomplishment. As described in Chapter 1, individuals and organizations have a bundle of ambitions, all of which clamor for attention. All too often the crux of the challenge is not an external threat but a clash among our own ambitions.

If we desire peace, it limits our warlike responses. If we want a sustainable production system, it may limit our ability to generate high shareholder returns. Seeking a successful career may limit the time we can spend with our children. When there are multiple values and desires, they together act to reduce the space of possible action as each creates new limits on action. When these limits overlap, there may be no feasible action satisfying our multiple values and desires.

Especially in personal or political situations, the conflicting ambitions may be irreconcilable. A woman may wish to stay married but detest her husband. A university faculty may be committed to the principle of free speech but, at the same time, have a majority that wants to limit "hate speech." In such cases, there does not seem to be a feasible policy satisfying these conflicting desires.

Strategies are usually what I call "corner solutions." The phrase comes from linear programming, where the solution to a problem is normally a set of actions defined by the intersection of various constraints—geometrically, a corner of intersecting lines or planes. When the constraints are so strong that no solution is possible, I call the strategy a "null set." There is no solution without relaxing at least one of the constraints.

The standard human response to a null set is to behave myopically, giving obeisance to whichever value is most salient at the moment. One can see this clash at work in the US escalating involvement in the Vietnam War. President Lyndon Johnson did not want to be blamed with losing Vietnam as President Truman had been blamed for "losing China." At the same time, he did not want to distract Congress from legislation and spending on his Great Society programs. The cadre of decision makers he assembled wanted to maintain the reputation of the United States as a reliable ally and treaty partner, yet at the same time did not want to engage in a major war. They wanted victory in Vietnam but did not want to unleash the full fury of the military. They conducted extensive bombing of the North, stirring protests around the world, but, at the same time, ruled out striking most key economic and logistical targets. Secretary of Defense Robert McNamara designed what was essentially a war of attrition, seeing all the while that the North was more willing to keep losing lives than was the United States. North Vietnam meant to stay the course no matter how costly or how long it took.

If you have ever faced difficult competing values, you know what it means to "be of two minds." By 1966 McNamara wanted compromise, but he knew it would mean defeat. At the same time, he knew that victory was unattainable within existing political constraints. Yet he argued that eventual victory was possible if the United States could convince North Vietnam that US determination had no limit. At the same time, he knew that there was a real limit to the cost the United States was willing to bear. He faced a null set.

President Johnson turned from one adviser to another, from hawk to dove, asking over and over again for someone to solve the problem. The United States escalated in response to setbacks and then halted bombing and other operations to convince the North that the

United States really sought peace. Then, when the North did not reciprocate, more troops were sent and more bombs dropped.

Near the end of McNamara's stint as secretary of defense, in 1968, there was a meeting of top advisers to the president to consider the request by General Earle Wheeler, the chairman of the Joint Chiefs of Staff, for an additional 205,000 soldiers on the ground in Vietnam. McNamara exploded: "I have repeatedly honored requests from the Wheelers of the world, but we have no assurance that an additional 205,000 men will make any difference in the conduct of the war. . . . Nobody knows whether it will make any difference. It still may not be enough to win the war. There is no plan to win the war."[2]

When there are many conflicting desires, and conflicting theories about how they can be met, the consequences are indecision and myopic vacillation among various half measures. Creating effective strategy in such situations is extremely difficult or impossible. The central challenge is not the outside world but the conflicting mix of values and purposes within the organization or society.

The crux in such cases is the strongest conflicting policies or values. To move out of the null, some constraints must be relaxed or removed. Some values held dear must be foregone. That probably entails a change in leadership. We expect our leaders to have firm resolve, but that very firmness becomes a liability when it impedes a change in priorities. In the case of Vietnam, the new secretary of defense, Clark Clifford, had been a hawk but quickly changed his mind about the utility of escalation and began a concerted campaign aimed at reducing the US commitment. The new president, following the election of 1968, Richard Nixon, then made commitments to a reduction in force to match his slogan of "Peace with honor." Of course, after the United States completely withdrew combat forces, the war ended with the North victorious and US honor lost.

The US strategy in Vietnam was a null set defined by the political constraints. To get a better outcome, some of the constraints on doctrine and action had to be relaxed. But leadership never saw the dilemma as their own conflicting desires and policies. At no time could any envision using enough force to destroy the North's ability to fight. Nor could anyone envision a way to simply help the two parts of Vietnam to peacefully reunite.

Competing ambitions and political constraints were also the issue at Microsoft in the years right after Apple's iPhone appeared. At that moment, Microsoft's top management needed to modernize its Windows-based mobile phone software. And, also facing the search-engine challenge from Google, it needed to break into the exploding Web-search marketplace. Instead of directly meeting these challenges, it put its best engineers on a complete redesign of Windows, trying to realize chairman Bill Gates's dream of having a database-oriented file system and advanced "universal canvas" display. The tragic result of that project was the widely disliked Windows Vista that delivered none of the promised advances. The company never mastered the mobile phone issue, purchasing the failing Nokia, and then exiting the whole phone business. After fumbling the acquisition of Yahoo!, its Bing search engine did not become profitable until 2016.

It is tempting to say that Microsoft would have done better had it concentrated on just one of these challenges. Then CEO Steve Ballmer recalled that "I put the A-team resources on Longhorn [Vista], not on phones or browsers. All of our resources were tied up on the wrong thing."[3] But, as many Microsoft employees have reported, there was a deeper challenge: a politicized internal culture combined with low skill at integrating newly acquired talent. Key creative talent abandoned the company. It is clear, in retrospect, that neither Bill Gates nor Steve Ballmer was capable of honestly diagnosing or dealing with this crux challenge.

THE ASC

I call what passes the joint filters of critical importance and addressability an ASC (addressable strategic challenge). The number of ASCs that can be simultaneously worked depends on the size and resource depth of the organization and the graveness of the most serious. "Plan Dog" was selected because it responded to critically *important* issues and because it was *addressable*—concentrating on Europe was judged to be achievable rather than simply a wished-for outcome.

The idea that some issues are more important than others is almost self-evident. In one of the earliest (1924) articles to use the term *business strategy*, John Crowell noted, "He who cannot draw a clear line of cleavage between the essential and incidental in a situation has no business in the field of strategic planning."[4] But what is really meant by "important," and how can one assess "importance"? A teacher once told me that "good judgment is knowing what is important in a situation." But this simply shifts attention from the word *important* to the equally mysterious role of *judgment*.

What is "important" depends on the situation and the interests of those asking the question. For example, surveys showed that the issue of systemic racism became the leading issue for millennials during the summer of 2020, surpassing earlier concerns of climate change, war, and income inequality. In the context of business or organization strategy, an issue is important when it strikes at a vital interest. Put differently, a challenge's importance is measured by the degree to which it threatens the basis of a group's or company's strategy or even its existence. An opportunity is important because it is large and risky and because it requires an adjustment in the company's strategy.

Given that, with good judgment, one has determined which challenges are truly important, the second test is *addressability*—the degree to which the challenge can be surmounted. Addressability depends on the skills and resources of the organization and the time span being considered. The United States could almost surely send a crew to Mars within a decade if the resources were committed to the project. We almost surely cannot make Afghanistan into a functioning liberal democracy within a lifetime. Warlord societies, like Japan, Scotland, and fifteenth-century France, did evolve into democracies. It took one warlord or power conquering the rest and then a few centuries of evolution to get there. Plus, there is no evidence that the United States has any skill at doing this sort of thing.

Working on corporate strategy with Mark Kott, vice president of strategy at O-I, the leading glass-bottle manufacturer, we were preparing for a strategy workshop when I described the idea of using addressability and importance to jointly winnow issues. Mark remarked that "these are difficult judgments on two dimensions: there will be big differences in opinion. Whose should prevail?" His was a deep question about how people should pool their opinions and information. The simple answer is that one purpose of hierarchy is to resolve such disagreements. The more complex answer is that intense discussion over why such judgments differ can lead to valuable insights.

CHUNKING THE CHALLENGE

'Paul Dekalb,' the chief executive of a German apparel company, took issue with making "addressability" a key constraint on strategy. "If we only look at what is addressable right now, we will forgo the long term. Out strategy is to create real differentiation—truly distinct positions in the market. And, we have to have the patience to invest in true transformation—developing new capabilities."

I asked Paul to stop thinking of "creating real differentiation" and "developing new capabilities" as being strategies. "They are," I said, "more accurately described as being ambitions, intentions, or aspirations. However wise they may be, there is no bite to them. You need to take each and break off a smaller 'chunk' that can be tackled and overcome, now."

"But isn't that just tactics?" Paul complained.

"No," I said. "The distinction between strategy and tactics arises in the military and denotes the difference between the general's action plan and the top sergeant's action plan. It is not about long-term versus short-term."

Paul was a very smart person. Yet, like many executives and political leaders, he had adopted the modern notion that "strategy" should describe a broad long-term path into the future. This certainly makes the job of writing down your strategy easier, but it dances around the hard part—distilling broad intent into actions that can be taken now.

On the campus of INSEAD (Fontainebleau, France) there is a statue of Georges F. Doriot, one of the school's founders. Doriot was an educator, military leader, and entrepreneur. Behind the statue is a plaque showing one of his most famous sayings: "Without action the world would still be an idea."

The discipline of addressability does not pass over complex long-term challenges. It encourages breaking such challenges into smaller chunks, one of which can be tackled today. As a Chinese proverb reminds us, "A journey of a thousand miles begins with a single step."

THE INTEL EXERCISE

How to winnow challenges and get to an addressable strategic challenge was part of a "master class" on strategy I conducted in early 2020. I worked with a group of five executives from different companies. Each read selected articles and a short summary on issues facing Intel, the leading microprocessor company. The purpose was to help develop skills at identifying challenges and evaluating their importance and addressability.[5]

In the semiconductor industry, the drumbeat was Moore's Law, a principle that promised faster and cheaper transistors as size was shrunk, a process called scaling. Intel had gained dominance in microprocessors through its skill at leading the industry in scaling down, node after node, from 1000nm feature sizes in 1984, down six scaling steps to 130nm in 2001, then six more scaling steps to 14nm in 2014. (A nanometer is one billionth of a meter. The COVID-19 virus is about 100nm in diameter.) And, by having its x86 processors become part of the Windows-Intel standard for personal computers (PCs) and most laptops, its margins were higher than any other semiconductor maker.

After reading the materials, some in the group voiced the view that the company seemed to face an almost bewildering range of challenges. Others countered that most large companies face this range of issues but rarely recognize them all. A spirited discussion produced a list of eleven key challenges facing Intel. Here is a summary of their list:

- *The End of Moore's Law.* The industry's continued ability to make smaller, faster semiconductor chips was rooted in continually reducing the scale of transistors, a pathway called Moore's Law. But, by 2018, it appeared that Moore's Law scaling was coming to an end. Even if transistors could be made smaller, the cost seemed to be ballooning. This posed a large challenge to Intel's strategy of constantly being at the performance edge in microprocessors.
- *AMD.* When IBM chose the x86 as the processor for its PC in 1981, it insisted that Intel license competitor Advanced Micro Devices be a second source for these and future related processors. Recently, AMD's share of the market increased because its new Ryzen chips outperformed Intel's current offerings.[6]
- *Manufacturing.* Intel was having major problems moving from its 14nm node to the 10nm node. Intel's delays not only were embarrassing to the company, but put other tech companies plans at risk.[7] Contract chip foundry TSMC did not seem to have experienced these problems at this node, allowing Intel's chief chip rival, AMD, to jump ahead in its processor performance.
- *Missing Mobile.* Intel's strategy in mobile had been to develop the Atom, a small x86 processor optimized for mobile devices. The offering did not win many mobile phone placements. In early 2014, CEO Brian Krzanich had announced a new program aimed at placing Intel "Atom" systems in forty million tablets. To do this, Intel prepaid customers the costs of switching from Arm to Intel. It is estimated that Krzanich spent about $10 billion in the failed attempt to get manufacturers to adopt Intel's Atom. The line was discontinued in 2016. Would Intel forever miss the huge mobile phone market?

- *Arm Holdings.* The processor winner in mobile was UK-based Arm Holdings. It held patents on a simple processor architecture quite different from Intel's x86. Its business model was to license its proven designs and let foundries in Asia fabricate the chips. Key licensees were Apple, Qualcomm, and Samsung. The Arm threat to Intel was ramped up in 2019 when Amazon announced it would produce Arm-based Graviton2 processors for its cloud servers. Qualcomm launched an Arm SOC (system on a chip) aimed at laptops.
- *Modems.* A "modem" is the "radio" part of a mobile phone. Intel struggled for years to make and market a modem for phones,[8] but the only significant buyer was Apple, which was in a legal wrangle with top modem maker Qualcomm. With the Apple-Qualcomm lawsuits settled in 2019, Intel closed down its modem development activity, and Apple purchased Intel's modem business for $1 billion. Again, was Intel never to have a successful entry into the mobile market?
- *IoT.* In 2016 Intel announced a major commitment to the Internet-of-Things (IoT). This was the market for wireless computing devices. Much lower power than phones, these chips would connect home appliances, smartwatches, drones, dog collars, automobiles, and hitherto unthought-of applications to Wi-Fi systems and the cloud. By mid-2017 Intel halted development of its low-end IoT chips and cut 140 employees in the area, refocusing on industrial applications. There had been uptake there, with increasing revenues. Some analysts were excited about the prospects for Intel's growth in the IoT market. The market remained fragmented with no obvious major leader. Companies like Texas Instruments and Silicon Labs were also hoping to ride an IoT growth wave.
- *AI.* Although sales of x86 processors for desktop and laptop computers had leveled off, there was great demand for huge processing power in the burgeoning artificial intelligence sector. The AI training market was dominated by Nvidia, which had morphed its game-based graphics processor into

a powerful machine-learning engine. In 2016 Intel acquired Nervana, which used x86 processors to power a complex inference engine. Then, in a surprise move, Intel spent $2 billion to acquire Israel-based Habana in December 2019 and, soon after, halted the development of the Nervana products. Management indicated that it intended to keep Habana operating as a separate company.

- *Cloud.* Intel dominated the data-center processor market with its x86-based Xeon product line. Its share of the server processor business was thought to be in excess of 90 percent. With the recent decline of the PC market in conjunction with the rise of big data and cloud computing, Intel's data-center business has become one of its primary growth drivers. The challenge here was that several tech giants were putting custom chips to work in the cloud. Amazon had designed an Arm-based processor for use in its Web-services cloud servers. Microsoft was sampling an eighty-core Arm chip for its cloud data centers.
- *China.* In 2019 China was Intel's largest market, accounting for 28 percent of its revenue. In addition, almost one-tenth of its fabrication facilities are located in China. In late 2019, China created a $29 billion state-backed fund to advance its chip industry and reduce reliance on US technology. The 2020 coronavirus outbreak also generated uncertainty about this deep relationship. Would demand in China diminish? Would world demand for Chinese products containing Intel chips diminish? Would new trade disputes break out between China and the United States?
- *Culture.* Robert Swan became Intel CEO in early 2019. Unusual for Intel, Swan had a background in finance rather than engineering. Soon after taking charge, he identified Intel's culture as a major challenge. The evidence of many years was that Intel had difficulty developing devices other than x86 processors and that it was not very good at integrating new acquisitions. Swan adopted the motto "One Intel," echoing the "One IBM" motto adopted by Lou Gerstner, the CEO

of IBM from 1993 to 2002, who was then resisting demands that he break up the company and sell off different parts. The *New York Times* reported that Swan believed Intel had deep problems stemming from its years of dominance. "Managers, complacent about competition, battled internally over budgets. Some of them hoarded information."[9] An important pivot point seemed to be Intel's failure to deliver the 10nm chips on the promised schedule. Swan believed that these problems showed employees that things needed to change.

Study-Group Analysis

The study group agreed that the set of issues facing Intel were gnarly. They differed in their opinions about importance. Ashok, one of the participants, said, "They have to solve the manufacturing issues. If they don't, they will lose the cloud and all their revenue. If Intel cannot make the next 7nm node, it might as well just become another customer for TSMC."

Differing sharply, Abigail felt that culture was issue number one. She offered that "the whole race to smaller and smaller is coming to an end. The cloud is turning into a cost game, and Intel is not ready for that. It has coasted on the Wintel standard for years and is not prepared for cost competition."

They argued over the addressability of the IoT, AI, and cloud challenges. One basic issue was that to vigorously meet these three challenges, Intel would have to really commit to high-volume, lower-margin production. Could the company do this? These technologies represented engineering problems of mixing hardware and software, closeness to customers, and lower margins that were not in synch with the bulk of the company's x86 high-margin, down-the-nodes business. A majority felt that the AI challenge was both important and addressable. The group judged that if Habana were kept separate, it had a chance to carve out a good position in the deep-learning market. But how big would this specialized market be?

The culture issue was intertwined with each upside challenge. The group believed that internal beliefs, habits, and processes had been ingrained over many years by market dominance, high margins, and clockwork scaling down through the steps of the Moore's Law nodes. If the company was to be successful at making money with high-volume, lower-margin products, it would need to change how engineers and marketers worked and its whole expense regime.

One vocal participant, Patrick, was more concerned about opportunities. "The real challenge is grabbing the moment. Opportunities like AI and, maybe, IoT only come along once in a while. Intel has to grab these and not get wrung out over saving its traditional business."

The group was not so sure about the end of Moore's Law. Intel was claiming it could forge ahead. Most felt that the slowing could not be avoided. Other modes of competition and growth had to be sought.

After several hours of discussion, each of the five participants was asked to score the challenges on importance and their addressability. That is, how strategically critical was each challenge for Intel, and how likely was it that Intel could successfully address that challenge over the next three to four years? Each challenge was scored on a 1–10 scale, and the scores were averaged over the group members. For example, the AI challenge had an average importance score of 8.1 and an average addressability score of 7.6. As each challenge had two different scores, it was helpful to plot the challenges as points on an XY graph. In Figure 6, the X axis is importance and the Y axis is addressability.

As is usual in such an exercise, no challenges were rated below 4 on either scale. If they were not important, they wouldn't have been discussed as "strategic" in the first place. One interesting result, common in such exercises, was that a few challenges were deemed fairly easy to address. In this case, the AMD challenge was seen as "business as usual" for Intel.

The graph clearly showed the group's view that the two addressable critical challenges were manufacturing (10nm) and culture. Not

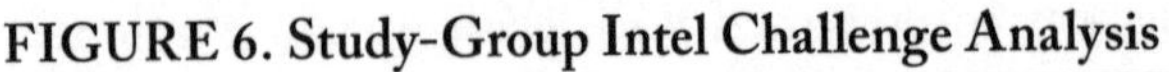

FIGURE 6. Study-Group Intel Challenge Analysis

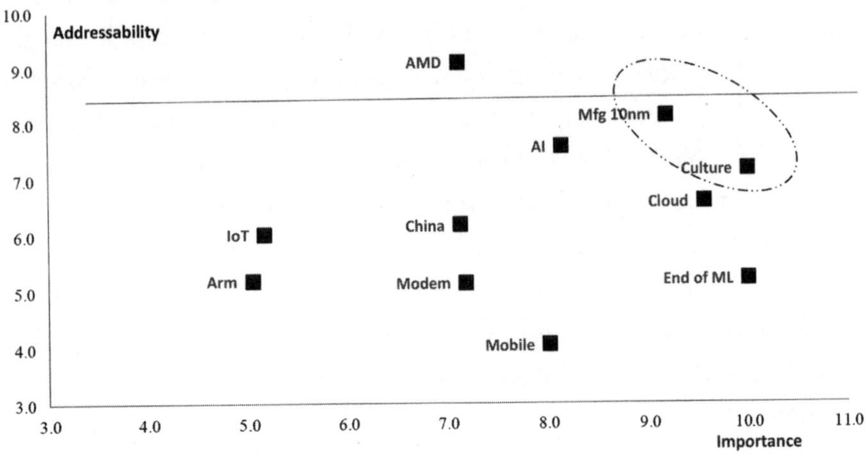

shown in the chart are the ranges of scores. The most significant spread was around the AI challenge. Some thought it subsidiary, and others thought it was the wave of the future, an opportunity outweighing the other troubles clamoring for attention.

This analysis suggests that the crux of the challenge for Intel lay somewhere within the manufacturing and culture challenges. They were interconnected. The profits from the Wintel standard had kept the company pecking at this succulent target year after year, unable to fully attend to other lower-margin businesses and, perhaps, narrowing the range of skills of its manufacturing engineers.

To truly identify the crux at Intel, we would have to know more about its internal culture and about the sources of its recent difficulties in manufacturing. The crux will most probably be a place where one can conjoin a significant opportunity to a program of organization change. Its core engineering culture must change if it is to compete with other firms on both design and cost rather than collect profits from being part of a de facto standard.

It would be wrong to suggest that this study group had the answers to Intel's strategic issues. The purpose of the exercise was to demonstrate the process of winnowing challenges to find ASCs, which, in turn, give a region to search for a crux. This process of narrowing choice is essential to focusing attention on solving complex problems.

Postscript

In May 2020, TSMC announced it would build a $12 billion fabrication plant in Arizona, aimed at the next 5nm node. In July Intel announced that its 7nm chips would be at least six months late. CEO Bob Swan raised the possibility that Intel might move away from manufacturing its own chips.

In January 2021, the Intel board announced that Pat Gelsinger would replace Swan as CEO on February 15. Gelsinger had begun his career at Intel and had, most recently, been CEO of VMware, an important actor in cloud infrastructure. In March 2021, Intel announced new "Rocket Lake" chips that used the designs it had intended for the 10nm node but were being "backported" to be produced on its older reliable 14nm process. This was a disappointing development to those looking for a quick fix to its 10nm node problems.

In July 2021, Gelsinger laid out a plan to regain chip leadership. The plan included a new transistor design, a new way of delivering power to the chip, and a commitment to extreme ultraviolet lithography. Tech observers were impressed but wondered if Intel could really make these new ideas work.

5

The Challenge of Growth

"Our main challenge is growth," the CEO said. "Our growth rate has been slowing, and it has hurt our stock price and our image. We must increase our penetration of existing markets, relentlessly seek out new opportunities, and create new growth options."

This CEO's short meditation on growth was hardly unique. Growth being "too slow" or "slowing down" is the diagnosis I hear most frequently when I ask company leaders for their challenges. More often than not, slowing growth is a natural outcome of a maturing product offering or a whole market. For example, total global mobile phone subscriptions grew from 2007 to 2012 at a rate of 13 percent per year. However, from 2013 to 2020, the rate slowed to 3.4 percent per year. The slowing was due to saturation. By 2020 there were 5 percent more mobile phone subscriptions than there were people in the world. Subscription provider Verizon was forecasting a slow 2 percent growth for 2021.

Diagnosis of the challenge of growth begins with history and expectations. Management's desire to "grow" must be balanced against size. For example, Walmart had revenue of $560 billion in 2020. To double its size, it would have to "acquire" Amazon plus AT&T. For such large companies, the wise strategist must look for the relative growth of specific new lines of business and new ventures rather than of the whole.

For most firms, the growth challenge is a mixture of competitive pressures and the limitations of both organizational agility and entrepreneurial insight. Finding the crux in a particular situation means assessing all three factors, plus having access to the logic and mechanisms for value-creating growth.

True value-creating growth is the secret sauce of firms that have become the household names of corporate success. The ingredients to that secret sauce cannot, by themselves, magically ignite growth, for true profitable growth is an entrepreneurial feat, not a series of steps that can be followed mechanically. But they can help one look in the right directions and keep one from making serious mistakes.

THE MEANING AND MECHANICS OF GROWTH

The word *growth* has ancient roots in the concepts of "increase" and "health." In early America, "Increase" was the name of prominent members of the Puritan community, such as clergyman Increase Mather, the president of Harvard College from 1681 to 1701. In biology the word means an increase in the size of an organism or in the number of cells in an organism or culture. In business, it means almost any improvement in a measure of success, but especially an increase in revenue and profit. In macroeconomics it normally means an *increase* in GDP or some other overall measure of economic activity.

Whenever I look at growth-rate data across numerous firms, I am always impressed at how truly *random* it is. I vividly recall one client early in my consulting career wanting to examine what he called "growth persistence." He believed that each firm had a characteristic rate of expansion—say, 9 percent per year—and that it would more or less grow at that rate, though with a slow decay. He asked me to prepare some analyses and charts to illustrate his ideas.

When I first looked at a plot of corporate sales growth rates over two or three years versus the same company's growth during the following two or three years, I was flabbergasted. It looked like a poorly choked shotgun blast had been aimed at the printout. The plot of points looked random. There was no persistence. Given a company's three-year rate of growth, you could predict virtually nothing about its expected rate of growth during the next three years.

There is an important distinction between growth in the size of a company, measured by sales, profit, assets, or other accounting terms, and the growth rate of its share price—or, more precisely, its total shareholder return (TSR), which is the annual growth rate of its share price plus its dividend yield.

As much as CEOs may desire growth in their companies' share prices, the connection between corporate growth and share-price growth is neither simple nor direct. In my MBA classes I used to introduce this subject by calling attention to prospective grades in my course. "I normally grade you," I would say, "on how well you do on written papers and tests." But then I would suggest a different scheme for the current course. "This term I will forecast your performance in this course based on your past grades in other courses. Then, I will grade you on the degree to which you beat, or fall below, those forecasts." That plan would elicit groans of displeasure and complaints. "That process is arbitrary and unfair," I would hear. "Well," I would explain, "that is how the stock market appraises CEOs: not on how well they perform but on how well they beat expectations of how well they will do."

The stock market is a noisy mechanism for summing up and discounting the value of expected future corporate payouts and buyouts. A stock price will, more or less, follow earnings, or free cash flow, as long as the growth rate is slow compared with the overall equity market return. If a slow growth rate were to unexpectedly increase to, say, 20 percent per year for two years, the stock price would jump up at each increase. That would happen because the earnings jumps were *surprises*. A soon as it became evident that the fast growth was over, the stock price would drop sharply. The collapse would occur because hopes of continued growth had been quashed.

That is the fascination with fast growth. With rapid growth we *know* it must eventually slow. If a company grows at 20 percent per year for fifty years, it turns $100 million into $1 trillion. Fifty more years and it would be worth $10 quadrillion—much bigger than the global economy. So, we know that very rapid growth will not go on forever. The drama is in guessing when it will slow and stop or even reverse. This uncertainty about the life span of rapid growth is what actually keeps a stock price appreciating fast. At each period, price is balanced between the hope of continued growth and the possibility that this is the end. When it is discovered that growth has continued, the market price lifts. It lifts because we have found that *the end is not nigh*. However, hang on long enough to stock in a rapidly growing company, and you will live through the inevitable painful readjustment of expectations to slower growth.

If you are a very long-term investor and reinvest all your gains in a diversified portfolio, all you should expect is about a gain of 7 percent per year. If you are a speculator, you can ride a growth wave, and your job is to get out before it stops. This is not always easy, as hope springs eternal. For a growing business, the market is always discounting the chance that the end of the good times is nigh. Management's job in a growth firm is to surprise them with evidence that the good times are still there. Management's job in a slow-growing firm is to surprise the market with an uptick in performance.

INGREDIENT 1: DELIVER EXCEPTIONAL VALUE TO AN EXPANDING MARKET

"Unremarkable," you might say, yet delivering exceptional value to an expanding market is the basic formula for business success in the vast majority of cases. It is a useful counter to what companies try to do to satisfy growth-ravenous equity speculators.

Invited to help with strategy for 'Varnico' in the spring of 2016, I attended the company's "Strategy Day" meeting in which past and ongoing work was discussed. Varnico was a worldwide company providing services to the food-processing industry. It had been public for about twelve years. CEO 'Bob Haller' provided a presentation of the company's recent performance. After the financial crisis of 2008–2009, it had been growing at a fairly steady 6–7 percent a year. Haller, however, was under pressure from the board to "get the share price moving." Over lunch he told me he was looking at ways to grow revenue by acquisition and by adding product features that could boost prices.

The following week I had a morning with Bob Haller to discuss the direction of my work with the company. Responding to his ideas for growing revenue, I had come prepared with a chart showing the association between revenue growth and annual TSR for the S&P 1500 over the three years 2013–2015.[1] As can be seen in Figure 7, there is no clear association. I told Bob, "If there is a lesson here, it is don't let your sales growth slip below 2 percent."

Bob Haller was a bit surprised by the chart. Like many executives, he tended to believe that there was a strong association between revenue growth and stock-price appreciation. "Back in the 1960s," I told him, "I was originally trained as an engineer and initially had all these engineering ideas about business performance—that one could figure out the secret of performance from data like this. But it doesn't work that way. In a competitive economy, real performance data almost always looks random.

"If the market expected your earnings to grow at 12 percent a year for the next decade," I told him, "the stock price would *already* be quite high." The trick to increasing a company's value is

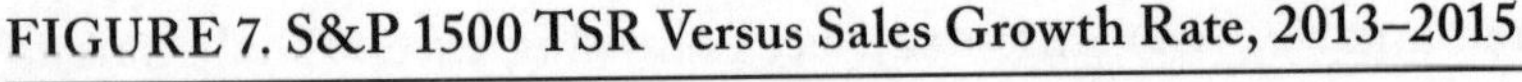

FIGURE 7. S&P 1500 TSR Versus Sales Growth Rate, 2013–2015

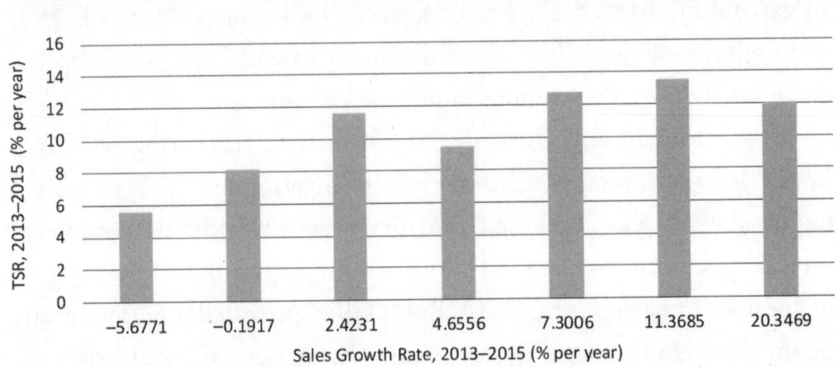

unexpected growth that hasn't been bought and paid for through acquisitions or other tricks for raising accounting results. I told Haller, "Your stock price is moving with the market averages, because Wall Street doesn't expect you to do anything new and value creating. *You are going to have to surprise them.*"

Two key elements in stock-market value creation for an existing company are strategy effectiveness and extension. Effectiveness comes first because extending an ineffective system builds an even larger future problem. And both must be better than expected to have an equity-market payoff.

Strategic effectiveness in a business is the combination of the *unique value* you are able to create and how strongly that position resists competitive erosion and imitation. Creating value means being able to provide products and services that buyers value more highly than it costs to make them. A good measure of value is the *value gap*—the difference between what a buyer is willing to pay and your cost of provision. The measure of *unique value* is the amount by which your value gap exceeds those of your competitors. A company increases its unique value whenever it can either reduce its costs of provision or increase the value to buyers of its services or products.

Strategic extension is the act of taking your unique value system and extending it to cover more buyers or similar products, or both. This is mostly what Google's growth has been. Their uniquely powerful search engine has continually brought in more and more advertising buyers each year. Extension may also mean new territories. After that, extension comes from stretching the unique value logic to cover adjacent markets—to somewhat different products or buyers or both.

Finally, a more entrepreneurial form of extension is entering wholly new product markets with a novel unique value proposition.

At Varnico the first step was to improve the company's *effectiveness*. The delivery of services was reasonably well managed, but there was little learning across regions and customers. In best-of-class companies, sales and service managers meet (nowadays virtually) monthly to share insights into customer problems and how they were solved. And these details are incorporated into training programs.

As part of the new set of initiatives, Bob Haller assigned one person from each region to meet biweekly with other regional representatives and to share issues and problem-solving approaches.

A second issue seemed to be some difficulty in bringing second-level service personnel up to the level of the first tier. The judgment was that top performers were not bringing subordinates along. Human resources (HR) was then given the task of developing a tracking and reward system for top service performers that included their contributions to on-the-job training and development.

The third effectiveness issue was the IT support—it tracked company expenses but did nothing to help understand customer problems. Fixing that took a year.

With these changes underway, the next challenge was the nature of Varnico's customers. They were typically smaller food processors who did not have a large technical staff. They relied on Varnico to set up the equipment for new inputs or new mixture densities and for anything more than routine maintenance. The strategic question was whether it could penetrate the market for the larger processors.

Varnico analyzed the nature of the challenge and decided that the blockage was the larger firms' internal service staffs—they felt Varnico was a threat to their own jobs. The executive team and IT came up with the idea of polishing the newly developed customer-oriented data system and selling it as a service to the larger customers: a strategic *extension*. That way, the Varnico product would help the internal staff do their jobs better with no threat of being replaced or looking bad.

After several new contracts of this type were signed, Varnico acquired a small software-as-a-service specialty firm and had it improve and maintain the customer-oriented data system.

As Bob Haller implemented these steps over three years, the company's stock price increased nicely. During this three-year period of strategic renewal, Varnico's share price increased by 55 percent, helped along by the general tailwind of the market (about 31 percent) during this period.

Varnico was a solid company serving a fairly mature market. It was able to increase its return to shareholders by renewed attention to effectiveness in ongoing activities followed by an extension from smaller to larger customers. Much of that return arose because these moves were unexpected. The challenge for Bob Haller going forward was to surprise the market once again.

INGREDIENT 2: SIMPLIFY TO GROW

In high school I had to study William Strunk's classic *The Elements of Style*. Strunk's most incisive command was "Omit needless words." In business, and other organizations, the parallel is "Omit needless activities."

Activities, or whole chunks of business, are needless when they don't generate a surplus. The resources they consume may or may not show up on financial statements. The resources may be money, public controversy, or management attention. In any of these cases, "weeding the garden" is necessary because of the tendency, like "the stuff" in your garage, for such activities to accumulate. Sometimes they are the favorites of a powerful executive or of a past CEO. Other times, they are parts of a larger unit, kept alive by its ability to subsidize them. In any case, when they are not needed for a vigorous program of growth, they sap time and energy from more important things.

To grow a company, it is very helpful to get it trimmed and focused on the business areas that will grow. "Weed the garden" of stale activities and business units. This idea of concentrating to grow or to create value works because value creation may not even be noticed on too large a base. If you add $100 million in value to a $100 million company, you will be applauded as a managerial genius. If you add the same $100 million in value to ExxonMobil, no one will notice.

The idea of concentrating to grow also reflects the very different managerial systems, compensation systems, and levels of agility needed for growing versus stable businesses. Mixing them together may dilute the effectiveness of either. In addition, we are all bounded in the number of issues and challenges we can simultaneously address. Concentrating and simplifying the managerial task at the top yields the advantages of focus.

S&P Global

The McGraw-Hill publishing organization has a history dating back to 1888, but its position as a major publishing house started in 1917, with an important position in educational publishing. It started the successful *Business Week* magazine in 1929. In addition, it published a number of trade magazines such as *American Machinist* and *Coal Age*. In 1966 it acquired the Standard & Poor's credit rating agency. On the road to becoming a publishing conglomerate, it became the biggest education publisher with the acquisition of the Economy Company in 1986.

With the 2008–2009 financial crisis, CEO Harold W. McGraw III asked new chief financial officer (CFO) Jack Callahan to help streamline the company. The next few years were a model of weeding and concentration. They set the stage for strong future growth.

At McGraw-Hill, there were a lot of committees and interconnections among the publishing, education, and financial-information businesses. These added costs created complexity by mixing executives with very different experience bases. No one wanted to be left out, even when they had little to add. In addition, the company was in trouble about its S&P subsidiary's credit ratings on subprime mortgage bundles. These were among the securities that turned out to be much more susceptible to risk than claimed, one of the causes of the 2008–2009 world financial crisis. There was the obvious temptation to ditch that business. But, after thinking it through, leadership went in the opposite direction. They decided to center the company on actual financial data rather than paper publishing.

To start its program of simplifying to grow, McGraw-Hill sold *Business Week* to Bloomberg and then sold off its broadcasting business in 2011. The next big move was the sale of the entire education business. Its education publishing revenues had fallen each quarter for two years, as state and city governments cut back. Investors increasingly saw the firm as a conglomerate and had no confidence that top management could redirect the century-old textbook business around digital publishing. To make the education business more attractive to potential buyers, the company first broke out and outsourced the overbuilt finance, IT, and HR functions. It then cut back on the size of the division's management overhead. McGraw-Hill Education was sold to Apollo Global Management in late 2012 for about $2.5 billion.

The following year the company was renamed McGraw-Hill Financial. It then sold off its construction publications. Finally, in 2016, it changed its name again to S&P Global and then sold off its J. D. Power division (consumer surveys). All these steps left the firm totally concentrated on financial-information services.

Early on, the concentration, or weeding out of businesses, dropped its revenues from $6.2 billion to $4.2 billion by 2012. With the company refocused on financial information, it began to develop new products and skills in that area. Its business mix became ratings, Dow Jones Indices, and specialized financial data (Capital IQ). In these areas, margins were high and increasing: up to 40 percent in 2015 and up to 50 percent by 2019. From the 2012 low to 2019, revenue grew a compound growth rate of 7 percent per year. Earnings before interest, taxes, depreciation, and amortization (EBITDA) grew at a compound 19 percent per year. Over the same period, the company's stock price grew by a handsome 24 percent per year. By concentrating its resources on financial data before it started to grow, the company magnified the rate of shareholder return. Had it been somehow able to achieve the same growth in its financial data business without concentrating, its shareholder return would have been diluted by its previous stable of slow-growing businesses.

S&P Global is a prime example of ingredient 2: "simplify to grow." It worked here, in part, because it is very hard to grow a conglomerate. Even if you grow a part, that performance can be lost in the mix. Second, developing the elements of growth is made easier by focus. Of course, if you focus on the wrong thing, not much will happen. But if you can focus on a business that has growth potential, and has or can have a competitive edge, then you are closing in on the secret sauce of profitable growth.

INGREDIENT 3: BE QUICK

Reaction time is critical in competitive situations. When a new opportunity or challenge arrives on the scene, the first capable response often wins: not necessarily the first mover, but the first one to provide a competent reaction.

John Boyd flew F-86 Sabres during the Korean War and went on to run the academic program for US Air Force training. His insights gained from studying air combat became known as the Boyd Loop. In Korea he saw USAF pilots down Mig-15 jets flown for North Korea by Russian pilots, despite the Migs being faster and climbing better.

Boyd diagnosed two reasons for this anomaly. First, the F-86 had a canopy that permitted better visibility so that the pilot could see his opponents' position more clearly and stay better oriented. Second, and more important, the Russian pilots were trained to execute precise maneuvers, like the compulsory figures in Olympic ice skating. By contrast, the American pilots were trained to be quick, flexible, and very aggressive.

In Boyd's language, the pilot who won in air combat was the one who was able to "go around the loop" faster. The "loop" was a sequence—observation, orientation, decision, and action. Boyd taught that if you could go around this loop faster than an opponent, the opponent would become disoriented and confused and you would win. He became known as "forty-second Boyd" because he would bet other fighter pilots that, in training, he could get on their tail in forty seconds. The legend is that he never lost.

You can see the Boyd Loop in action in a tennis match. The better player places the ball so as to catch her opponent a bit off balance, so he makes a hurried return from the right edge. With a quick and accurate rereturn to the left edge, she puts her opponent even farther off balance. Once he is rushing from side to side, he has almost surely lost that point.

In business, competition quickness is normally most important in customer responsiveness and in the cycle of new product development and introduction. Nvidia, as recounted in detail in my previous book *Good Strategy/Bad Strategy*, pushed aside its competition by shortening its product introduction cycle from the normal eighteen months for semiconductors to six months. Nvidia did this by creating three development teams, each taking eighteen months to deliver a design but each on a schedule offset by six months. With a new design hitting the market every six months, competitors could not keep up.

With a faster release cycle, Nvidia not only beat its graphics-card competitors, but also kept semiconductor giant Intel's i740 graphics chip from gaining any traction in the market. According to industry analyst Jon Peddie, this was exactly the Boyd Loop at work: "Intel developed the i740 with the same processes and same approach that it used to develop its CPUs [central processing units]. This didn't work in the extremely competitive 3-D graphics industry. Intel's development cycle was 18–24 months, not 6–12 months. It didn't adapt to this quick development cycle. It wasn't about to redesign its whole development and fabrication process just for a sideline business."[2]

In the intense competition over smartphones, Nokia and Microsoft were slow to go around the Boyd Loop. Currently, there is intense competition between the United States and China in AI technology. Boyd theorized that when one competitor thinks they are being lapped, they become disoriented. Frederick Kempe, CEO of the Atlantic Council, described a whiff of this mental state after attending the Davos Forum in 2019:

> Most troubling for the American business leaders in Davos, who had grown accustomed to being atop the global technological heap, was that they heard time and again how quickly they were falling behind their Chinese peers. Though it is a technology race most Western executives feel is only on its first laps, they heard how President Xi had declared a sort of space race or Manhattan Project around AI that is already delivering measurable results.[3]

Of course, it is also important to have a competent development effort for AI. But since no one today knows how this technology will evolve over several years, it is also important, at the level of the nation-state, to have multiple initiatives. Boyd's insight was that being in the lead may be less important than having your opponent believe you are in the lead. Thinking you are behind can induce mistakes. Be oriented to the combat, and be fast to observe, decide, and act.

Can a bureaucracy be quick? Most of the time, large complex organizations cannot move quickly around the Boyd Loop unless there is strategy, unity, and trust among the major actors. Digital "transformation" plans at GE and Ford failed expensively because, in part, these efforts were set up as separate business units that were supposed to, somehow, create new digital worlds for each company as a whole. But the leaders of the main business units were not really interested in this program. Lacking broadly based initiatives, hundreds of billions were wasted.

As I write this paragraph, I am homebound by the COVID-19 virus. Unlike South Korea, the US government was unable to quickly respond to the new virus. The media wanted to blame President Trump, but, for all his failings, the main problem was systemic. The US Department of Health & Human Services is a giant bureaucracy that manages both the Food and Drug Administration (FDA) and the Centers for Disease Control (CDC). As the COVID-19 pandemic hit the United States, there was mistrust, infighting, politics, and incompetence throughout the whole system. Despite years of warnings and studies about possible pandemics just like COVID-19, no one had an action plan. There was no road map about how to test, whom to quarantine, and how to manage this on a state or federal level.

In discussing the issue with people in other nations, I have had to constantly explain that the United States is a federal system with four layers of government. There are legislators, courts, and police at the federal, state, county, and city levels. Authority over various elements of public health is divided among these levels. As the crisis unfolded, many were surprised to find that authority over lockdowns and social distancing were local rather than federal. In these areas, the president can suggest but cannot command. Similarly, most emergency stockpiles and health care capacity are local responsibilities. Despite years of warnings about pandemics, none of these four levels of government had any detailed prepared plans on how to react, the importance of testing, or whom to isolate and where to house them, nor did they have the necessary stores of medical materials.

The South Koreans are just as bureaucratic, but their bureaucrats did have prepared plans and did quickly create a test for the virus. The difference is the degree of skill, trust, and executive power at the top.

In a pandemic, in a fight, in a world of technological competition, in grasping new emerging opportunities, quickness is critical.

INGREDIENT 4: USE MERGERS AND ACQUISITIONS TO SPEED AND COMPLEMENT A STRATEGY

There have been literally hundreds of studies on the impact of mergers and acquisitions on corporate performance and value. The results of these studies are mixed. Looking at total dollar value gives a negative result because the very largest deals are the worst. For example, looking at the huge merger wave from 1998 to 2001 (the dot-com and telecommunications wave), researchers found that shareholders lost 12 percent in value for every dollar spent on acquisitions, for a total loss of $240 billion. Nevertheless, they found that during this period, the *average* acquisition had a small positive return to the acquirer's stock price. The reason was that the huge losses on the largest deals overwhelmed the gains on smaller deals.

Studies like this almost always measure the gain to shareholders by looking at a short window around the announcement of the deal, usually three days before and after. This research design basically assumes that the stock market is perfectly efficient. The problem is that mergers and acquisitions tend to come in waves, and research on them measures upticks in value on deals during the hopeful upswing of the wave. Then, after the wave crests and recedes, and problems set in, there are massive restructurings as the acquirers try to digest what they have bought. These negative processes don't show up as "events" in the researchers' methods. Thus, studies like the one cited previously see only the upticks on the deals and not the shrinkage of value at a later date. The net result is an upward bias in these kinds of research results.

So, is there any hope to add value by acquisitions? Yes, of course. The fundamental ingredient of the secret sauce of adding acquisitions to growth is to keep it focused—only use acquisitions to speed and deepen your basic competitive strategy. Don't use acquisitions to simply bulk up revenues or earnings. And, above all else, don't buy complex, multiproduct, heavily staffed companies that will take years to untangle. And, even above that, don't ever engage in a "merger of equals." If you do, the infighting over who is in charge of what will go on for years.

The basis of profitable growth is to deliver exceptional value in a growing market. Acquisitions that deepen value or speed its expansion across buyers are very worthwhile (at the right price!).

If you look at who does the biggest deals, it is usually the older mature companies. For example, in 2016 the biggest deals were AT&T and Time Warner ($85 billion) and Bayer and Monsanto ($66 billion). On the announcement, AT&T stock value fell by $18 billion. Bayer's market value also fell by $18 billion after its deal, and it suffered stockholder lawsuits.

I call these Niagara deals because they are huge and because they seem to be mostly done by older companies looking to restore some excitement to life (*Niagara* rhymes with *Viagra*). Having worked with such firms, I can attest that watching the monthly and quarterly results roll in for a very large complex business can become pretty boring. All the business and product entrepreneurship, if any, is down three levels and done by younger executives who work closer to the coal face. So, at the top, the only real excitement, apart from a crisis, is a deal. With a big deal there are high-powered lawyers and investment bankers appearing on the scene, there are trips on private jets to special secret meetings, and very large amounts of money are offhandedly discussed. There are side payments to all and sundry, payoffs to the acquired CEO, and bragging rights about size to the acquirer.

Some CEOs do these money-losing deals because of bad incentives. For example, at Men's Wearhouse, in 2014 CEO Doug Ewert did a deal to buy Jos. A. Bank for $1.8 billion. His company's stock fell 70 percent. But because the merged company was bigger, Ewert's compensation rose by more than 150 percent to $9.7 million. As *Forbes* contributor David Trainer observed: "Executives seek and execute acquisitions that have little to do with shareholder value because they help boost metrics such as sales, EPS [earnings per share], or EBITDA that determine their bonuses. In addition, a big acquisition will put the company in a peer group with larger competitors, which also tends to boost executive pay."[4]

Another trigger to overpayments is a surplus of internal resources. I recall, many years ago, in 1997, talking to Charles Ferguson about how Microsoft had acquired his private Web-page maker called Vermeer. Microsoft initially offered $20 million, which was a bit more than Ferguson had thought it was worth. A good negotiator, Ferguson said he would think about it. The Microsoft negotiator came back after the weekend and said, "How about $130 million?"

Ferguson took it. Later, talking with the Microsoft executive who had been involved, I asked how Microsoft justified such a large overpayment. He explained that Bill Gates had ordered the company to catch up with the exploding Internet. He explained, "It was 'Internet money.' The price didn't matter."

Microsoft was a very rich company with a huge competitive advantage in its key products, and it has continually tended to overpay. In 2007 Microsoft bought online advertising company aQuantive for $6.2 billion, writing it completely off in 2012. In 2012 it bought Nokia for $7.5 billion and wrote it off completely three years later.

If you look at who does the most acquisitions in a year, it is usually the big stars of the day! In 2016 Microsoft led with nineteen deals. Alphabet (Google) did eleven deals. Apple did nine. Look at Alphabet's acquisitions in Figure 8. These are all smaller firms with intellectual property or small systems that Alphabet can use to deepen its existing businesses. Most of these were private transactions conducted without the complexities and expense of buying public companies. None were complex organizations with large managerial structures. Alphabet's growth has been powered by such acquisitions, with Android (2005), YouTube (2006), and DoubleClick (2007) being among the most important. It tends to buy companies to fill in where it has already been conducting research. Thus, it was trying to make its Google Video platform work when it turned to buy eighteen-month-old YouTube in 2006.

There can be many motivations for acquisitions. Companies try to pick early winners. They try to exploit economies of scale. They try to change their own culture with the injection of a new culture. They believe they can fix a broken target company. They try to consolidate an industry. My strong advice for a company seeking profitable growth is to restrict your purposes to two: to acquire skills and technologies (including growing platforms) that are complementary to the existing strategy and that would be hard to create internally and to provide broader and stronger market access for the target's products.

FIGURE 8. Alphabet Acquisitions in 2016

Company	Business	Complement to
BandPage	Platform for musicians	YouTube
Pie	Business communications	Spaces
Synergyse	Interactive tutorials	Google Docs
Webpass	Internet service provider	Google Fiber
Moodstocks	Image recognition	Google Photos
Anvato	Cloud-based video services	Google Cloud Platform
Kifi	Link management	Spaces
LaunchKit	Mobile tool maker	Firebase
Orbitera	Cloud software	Google Cloud Platform
Apigee	API mgmt and predictive analytics	Google Cloud Platform
Urban Engines	Location-based analytics	Google Maps
API.AI	Natural language processing	Google Assistant
FameBit	Branded content	YouTube
Eyefluence	Eye tracking, virtual reality	Google VR
LeapDroid	Android emulator	Android
Qwiklabs	Cloud-based training platform	Google Cloud Platform
Cronologics	Smartwatches	Android Wear

Source: https://en.wikipedia.org/wiki/List_of_mergers_and_acquisitions_by_Alphabet reproduced via Creative Commons license https://creativecommons.org/licenses/by-sa/3.0

INGREDIENT 5: DON'T OVERPAY

One reason so many research studies keep showing negative returns to acquiring firms is that acquirers are overpaying for what they get. Particularly when buying a public company, there is a premium for control of about 30–40 percent over its inherent value. If it is a buoyant moment, there is a premium on the premium. It is even worse if the company is contested. Getting into a bidding war with another firm is a sure way to grossly overpay. And the more paid, the larger are the fees taken by investment bankers and other advisers.

I well recall a February 1998 gathering of telecommunications company leaders in Scottsdale, Arizona, led by Salomon Smith Barney analyst Jack Grubman. There were ten or fifteen shaded tables with a CEO and their helpers at each. The industry was recently deregulated, and with the new Internet booming, valuations were skyrocketing. Grubman was urging larger companies to bulk up quickly before it was too late. I was able to overhear the conversation at the table next to me where the CEO of a fairly large company was being advised to grab Winstar Communications. Winstar was putting small broadband antennas on rooftops all across the country, promising to bypass the copper wires of the telephone companies. The CEO looked at the paperwork and said, "This is very pricey. Yes, Winstar's sales are up this year, but losses are growing and equity is negative. At $45 a share, that's well over $1 billion for the company." The Salomon Smith Barney banker pushing Winstar nodded and then said, "Yes, but your paper is also sky high." The argument being made was that Winstar's stock was well overpriced but that the potential buyer's stock was also way overpriced, so why worry? The CEO didn't bite, and he was right. Winstar had grown fast using debt. But its revenues couldn't cover its expenses, especially interest, and it went bankrupt in 2001.

To avoid those premiums, try to buy private, nonpublic companies. The premium will be less, and there is less chance of a bidding war.

Another premium is paid by using stock. Try to pay cash. Paying with stock is equivalent to issuing stock, and there will be a hit on your stock price. Equity issues by established public firms tend to cause a stock-price dip of 2–3 percent. This, in fact, may be one reason for some of the statistically negative results from large deals.

It seems reasonable that the greatest benefits, the largest synergy, would come from an acquisition that is closely related to the business of the acquirer. Unfortunately, this does not seem to be the case. In a thorough meta-analysis of sixty-seven studies of acquisitions and relatedness researchers concluded, "The overall effect of relatedness on [stock-price] performance is negligible. It is also possible that synergies exist but that their effect is too small to pay-off a (high) acquisition premium."[5]

The largest premium is due to hubris—overconfidence. This is not the problem of hidden faults, as in the used-car market. It is, rather, the problem of grossly overestimating "synergies," of overoptimism in growth prospects, and overweening pride in one's ability to fix persistent managerial problems in the target company. Within the behavioral economics tradition, this overconfidence is often attributed to *reference-group neglect*.[6] This occurs when a person focuses on their own history and apparent skills and does not consider the skills and outright trickery of adversaries. As a professor in a graduate school, I would sometimes ask students to privately estimate their rank in my class, based on their test performances to date. No one put themselves in the bottom quarter. More than half put themselves in the top quarter. That's reference-group neglect.

In spite of all these reasons to avoid paying a premium, there are cases where you simply must pay more than the going value for a company. This occurs when the firm holds unique intellectual property, or a special market position, that you absolutely do not want a competitor, or potential competitor, to acquire. In such cases, you are not simply buying the company; you are paying to prevent the competitive hit that will occur if you do not.

Nvidia, for example, passed on acquiring ArtX, a small cadre of talented former Silicon Graphics engineers. It was the last such cadre from the failed Silicon Graphics. Competitor ATI snapped up ArtX, moved to copy Nvidia's six-month release cycle, and began to introduce graphics boards that matched Nvidia's. Then, in 2006, CPU maker AMD, Intel's major rival, merged with ATI. Passing on ArtX was a strategic blunder by Nvidia. Although Nvidia did not need its resources or talent, acquiring it would deny these scarce resources to others.

The same sort of logic can also apply in a rapidly consolidating industry. During most of the 1900s, for example, the major accounting companies were called the "Big 8." Today, mergers, and the failure of Arthur Andersen, have brought the number down to the "Big 4": KPMG, PricewaterhouseCoopers, Deloitte, and Ernst & Young. Each of the original firms had to do some kind of deal to maintain a prominent world presence in the consolidating industry.

INGREDIENT 6: DON'T GROW THE BLOB

The "blob" is the complex interconnected structure at the heart of so many older organizations. It is fairly bureaucratic and has numerous policies and norms that have evolved over many years. I have worked with some companies in this category who would like to accelerate their growth. Much of my advice is to simplify, weed the garden, and focus. When they won't go down that path, my advice becomes, "Don't grow the blob."

There are two reasons for this admonition. First, you don't want that bureaucratic structure trying to manage a growth business. It would be like the US Department of Homeland Security trying to write a new video game. It might even get done, eventually, but it would take years, cost a fortune, and be out of date when it arrived. Second, you don't want the blob restricting choices made by a new growth business because of conflicts of interest and various other power games.

A larger company can find growth opportunities within itself or via acquisitions. I call such growth opportunities "seedlings," and they need to be cultivated and shielded from the blob. Starting within, the C-suite must maintain close and direct connections with no more than six to eight seedlings. Not all will succeed. But those still within the blob need extra protection. The trick is to nurture them until they can exist as a separate division outside the older mainline. Acquisitions are easier to shield by keeping them separate. This, however, poses the intricate problem of leveraging the parent company's skills and market position. If it doesn't use this leverage, it is just trying to be a venture capitalist or private equity fund.

In today's fast-moving tech world, it is probably not a good idea for a large company to nurture seedlings that better belong with a venture-capital firm. The large company simply cannot offer the same "make you a billionaire" incentives that the VC can. The kinds of ventures a large company should seek are those that require more than just a small cadre of engineers or programmers. What the larger company is trying to achieve is a greater level of risk-taking along with some leverage from the parent's reputation, skills, and market position. To make this work, the company has to go easy on, or eliminate, the standard hit-your-numbers reviews and, instead, conduct monthly help sessions on the seedling's challenges and action policies. If the seedling fails, the managers in charge should not be punished or let go. Such actions spray herbicide on your garden.

INGREDIENT 7: DON'T FAKE IT

Wall Street analysts love a company that generates predictable increases in earnings—not just increases but predictable increases. The only problem is that the economy, technology, and competition are obviously not really predictable. So to generate predictable earnings, a company must engage in smoothing, manipulating accounting elements, normally accruals, to compensate for fluctuations in earnings. General Electric's amazing 1985–1999 streak of hitting its earnings targets was widely known to be largely due to smoothing via its GE Capital subsidiary. Financial assets were quickly bought and sold to generate end-of-quarter gains and losses that compensated for gains or losses in manufacturing. As a *Forbes* article put it: "Like a professional baseball player revealed to have been dabbling in steroids, GE prolonged a nearly decade-long record of meeting or exceeding analyst expectations by resorting to tricks including 'selling' locomotives to financial institutions in transactions that looked a lot like loans, and fiddling with the accounting for interest-rate hedges."[7]

A survey found that 97 percent of the senior executives preferred smooth earnings.[8] A study of four hundred chief financial officers found that these financial executives believe that 20 percent of public companies misrepresent their earnings in order to achieve predictability. Their estimate was that "10 cents on every dollar of earnings is typically misrepresented for those companies."[9]

Back in the 1990s, one of the companies that managed earnings best was Microsoft. As Justin Fox described it:

> Starting around the unveiling of Windows 95 in August 1995, Microsoft has followed a uniquely conservative method of accounting for the software it ships—deferring recognition of large chunks of revenue from a product until long after the product is sold. The reasoning is that when somebody buys software in 1996, they're also buying the right to upgrades and customer support in 1997 and 1998. If it hadn't been for the new accounting technique, the company would have had to report a sharp rise in profits in the latter half of 1995, then a sharp drop in the first half of 1996—a turn of events that might have sent its stock price reeling—instead of the smoothly rising earnings that it did post.[10]

Do these earnings smoothing efforts pay off? The bulk of research on this topic says no. An intriguing study found that companies that smoothed earnings had a much greater incidence of subsequent stock-price crashes.[11] Another careful study found "no relation between earnings smoothness and average stock returns over the last 30 years."[12]

The evidence is that managers and analysts prefer smoother earnings. But the stock market doesn't really care. Manipulating earnings to be smoother messes up accounting results and wastes time and energy. Spend your IQ on something else.

NO EARNINGS AT ALL

The rise of the Web economy and, especially, the "sharing" economy has created a number of growing firms with no earnings at all. The premise is that they are playing the Amazon game of "get big fast" and will then, at some future time, make a profit. I cannot honestly say "Don't do this" because you might fool people long enough to become a billionaire. Back in 1999 we discovered that the market tolerated losses at the newly minted dot-com companies as long as revenue grew smartly. But when profits of just $10,000 finally appeared, there were agonized cries as scales fell from eyes.

Right now, the poster child for this effect seems to be Uber. It appears that the company's price for a ride does not cover its variable costs, but it is able to subsidize both the rides and the rapid expansion with investors' capital. Despite creating the largest loss on initial public offering (IPO) in history, Uber continues to expand. The payoff to the original investors has been huge. For example, First Round Capital's $510,000 seed investment was worth $2.5 billion by mid-2019. The original founder cashed out and left the board in 2018. Still, CEO Dara Khosrowshahi claimed that Uber would become profitable by the end of 2020. By early 2021, that hasn't happened. It would seem that the only way to get to profits is to either raise prices or cut drivers' pay, and management does not want to do either.

More evidence that whole classes of speculators have a "bright, shiny object" reaction to any evidence of growth is WeWork. This company was created to sublease office space to people who wanted a small workplace apart from their home. No one would ordinarily think this would be a very profitable business. After all, there are already plenty of small firms that lease office space, a business that has been around for thirty years. But WeWork wanted to lease a lot of space in a lot of cities and then make that space available on a Web app, sort of like Airbnb. And it was signing new leases fast, showing rapid growth in the space available. Despite the fact that this business plan wouldn't pass muster in an undergraduate make-up-a-plan competition, it got funded by Japanese investment house SoftBank. The initial investment in WeWork was $4.4 billion, implying a valuation of $18–$20 billion. Despite claims by CEO Adam Neumann that the company was profitable, it was not—it made huge losses. By 2018 the company had burned through its cash and needed more, so an IPO was planned. The deal, arranged by Neumann and SoftBank CEO Masayoshi Son, valued WeWork at $47 billion. As part of the deal, $1 billion would go to buying shares from existing investors, including the board of directors. When the IPO prospectus became public, reactions to the history of losses, the increasingly erratic behavior of Neumann, and the company's fluffy mission concept were negative. SoftBank backed away from the IPO. The board wanted Neumann out, giving him a payoff of $185 million to just step aside. SoftBank reentered the deal with $5 billion, valuing the company at $8 billion, a long way down from $47 billion.

The gloss on WeWork was that it was a "tech" company building the sharing economy. It actually seems more like an office-space lessor in a competitive world with excess office space. Yet billions were thrown around. Supposedly sober Goldman Sachs investment bankers claimed that it might have a path to a $1 trillion valuation. Their fees on a successful IPO would have bought many new homes in the Hamptons.

There is an old aphorism in the poker world that Warren Buffett made more widely famous: "If you sit in on a poker game and don't see a patsy, get up. You're the patsy." In the world of fast-growth, no-earnings companies, you'd better know who is the patsy.

WITH ALL THE business media attention to growing companies, it is hard to remember that profitable value-creating rapid growth is not the norm. It is fairly rare, and, when it occurs, it lasts for only a while.

6

The Challenge of Power

Attacking the crux of a problem or challenge requires action. And that means making some activities, people, and departments more important than others. These shifts in roles, influence, and resources are the concomitant of focus, making some objectively more important than others. There is no escaping that strategy is an exercise in power.

The issue of power often makes people uncomfortable, especially in an era when so much thinking about management and strategy boils down to the quasi-religious notion that intense drive and belief will be rewarded, that fervent resolve, clarity of purpose, and visionary leadership will all, somehow, get things done. Shouldn't a leader be able to ask everyone to devote their full measure to the company's mission? If everyone is fully informed, shouldn't they move to do the right thing, the effective thing, without being ordered around?

SONS AND DAUGHTERS OF VIKINGS

In 2013 I was invited to give a talk on strategy to a group of businesspeople in Stockholm, Sweden. As part of the visit, I met with a group of eight strategy academics in the afternoon following the talk. I didn't know them, but it is always interesting to meet new people who share an interest in your specialty.

After some get-to-know-you preliminaries, the group asked me to briefly explain my views on strategy. I provided my basic definition that a *strategy is a mixture of policy and action designed to surmount a crucial challenge*. Before I could elaborate, the senior person held out his hand, palm first. "We are looking at things a bit differently," he explained.

"We see businesses as part of a complex social fabric," he continued. "The reality is that business, government, and nonprofit organizations form an interconnected network, one that extends globally, a web of relationships, where each organization responds to signals from the others. It is this network, which evolves over time, adapting to changes in tastes and technology. We were wondering how you would see strategy in this context."

I had heard all this before. His "reality" was not reality; it was a model, actually a metaphor. "In your model," I responded, "there isn't any room for strategy. A strategy is a design and direction imposed by leadership on an organization. Strategy began when people realized that telling warriors to 'go out and fight the invaders' didn't work. Leaders had to impose a structure, a design, on how the group would fight. In a modern business, a strategy is the exercise of power to make parts of the system do things they would not do, if left to themselves."

When I said the phrase "exercise of power," there was an audible gasp from some in the room. Had they been practicing Catholics, they would have crossed themselves. They were very uncomfortable, both intellectually and emotionally, with the idea of power. How had the sons and daughters of the Vikings and of Gustavus Adolphus come to this pass?

These Swedish academics were not alone in looking at the world as a natural system, absent human agency. The root has been intellectuals' fascination with evolutionary theory since the latter part of the nineteenth century. If God didn't make the world, then it is the outcome of natural evolutionary processes. Similarly, intellectuals have reasoned, business organizations have "evolved" under the force of natural selection. And, as Herbert Spencer argued, isn't society itself really an organism? According to this way of thinking, cities grow like forests (no architects?), bridges appear across rivers near population centers, and a business firm's success or failure stems from its being fit, or unfit, to its environment. This natural-system metaphor allows the intellectual, having erased the deity, to also erase human design, human purpose, and human choice from society and organization. (No one has, as yet, offered a natural-systems theory of how academic books get written.)

In 1976 I moved from the Harvard Business School in Boston to UCLA. The move was much more than the difference between the East and West Coasts. At HBS I had been immersed in the study of how leaders created and modified corporate strategy and structure. At UCLA I was part of the broader academic world in which business issues were subordinate to the intellectual supremacy of economics and sociology. That was when I first discovered the sociological penchant for viewing organizations, and strategy, as "natural" systems.

Despite the view that things "just evolve," strategy *is* an exercise in power. In a typical organization, if senior executives don't pay attention to anything strategic, most things will go on pretty much as before, at least for a while. People will continue to sell, factories will produce, software engineers will continue to improve code, and so on. Department heads will sign contracts, and accounting reports will be generated and audited. What will almost never happen is something important that is nonroutine, something new and different. It won't happen because important changes always mean shifts in power and resources. Strategy means asking, or making, people do things that break with routine and focus collective effort and resources on new, or nonroutine, purposes.

SHARON THOMPSON

This discomfort with the exercise of power is not just a Swedish or an academic condition. It is reflected in the popularity of work on "vision" coupled with seeing strategy as inspirational and motivational messaging.

In 2014 I was asked to consult with 'WebCo,' a smaller supplier of website commerce software. 'Sharon Thompson,' the CEO, explained to me that the management team had spent weeks on developing the vision, mission, and strategy statements for the company. She showed me her draft statement. It said:

> *Our Vision*: Constant progress in connecting people and commerce
> *Our Mission*: To help our customers seamlessly conduct business through the Web
> *Our Strategy: To provide products and support to individuals and Website developers in building commerce into their Websites. Our advantages are the breadth of our scope, having applications for PHP-, HTML5-, and JavaScript-based websites, and the speed and clarity of our developer support.*

"What do you hope to accomplish with this?" I asked her.

"What I want," she replied, "is to provide everyone with a set of principles and objectives about how we conduct our business. When this is communicated and accepted, it will ensure that everyone understands what we are trying to accomplish. Then everyone will know what to do.

"My concern," she continued, "is that this document is neither very inspirational nor very specific. I have been reading about strategy, and it should be a call to arms that embodies our dreams and aspirations. And it should also, at the same time, offer financial and nonfinancial goals that are precise and measurable. Can you help me get there?"

Sharon's strategy statement embodied a great amount of the popular advice about strategy. Try Googling "strategy statement," and see the hundreds of chunks of popular advice on the subject. As she notes, the doctrine is that your "strategy statement" should inspire, define the product and the customer, define the source of competitive advantage, and set specific financial and other goals. It should be both precise and flexible, short-run and long-term.

One of Sharon's difficulties was that such "strategy statements" aren't really strategies. Rather, they are a pop-culture literary form, like the "business plans" business students are asked to invent, which are designed to garner approval from colleagues and friends and, in the rarest of instances, help entice someone with money to invest in the company. The truth is that venture capital is invested not in plans but in the individuals who have proposed the venture and have committed themselves to running it.

I asked Sharon about how she hoped to displace the dominant player, WooCommerce, which offered a free plug-in for the WordPress site builder, which was also free. She explained that neither WordPress nor WooCommerce really worked to full potential without additional themes and plug-ins that were not free. Such chunks of software were offered by many players, and some worked well with WooCommerce and WordPress, while some caused difficulties that appeared only down the road. And when WordPress offered a major free security update, it could break some of the existing themes and plug-ins. She said that "the whole thing is a bit of a mess and a lure for the unwary." Someone might want to set up a simple e-commerce website and sell some items. But, she explained, "as their business grows, or as the underlying patchwork quilt of software updates evolves, things go wrong." The customer would then have to go to a professional Web designer and "pay the big bucks for a full redesign and then monthly maintenance."

There were other players than WooCommerce, and there were other site builders than WordPress. But, she emphasized, it was hard to avoid the pattern of free software followed by expensive fixes. Sharon said, "It is really an entire ecosystem delivering a bait-and-switch experience."

"I see the challenge," I noted, "but your strategy statement doesn't really explain or confront it. The statement says you provide plug-ins for PHP-, HTML5-, and JavaScript-coded websites and that you have speedy response to developers. None of that solves the beginners' problems you just highlighted to me."

Sharon went on to explain that beginners weren't willing to pay much for the software and had a lot of support questions, which were expensive to service. WebCo had better acceptance among Web developers who knew how to code. In a real sense, her competition was full-feature software that offered the whole package of website design and e-commerce support, which was increasingly being supplied as a cloud-based service.

Sharon's explanation covered some of the major features of the challenges she faced. Yet it lacked an appreciation for the problems of creating solutions for all these different issues with a small team of engineers. Her explanation also highlighted the fact that WebCo lacked a focus on solving a particular customer's problem. It was trying to sell to beginners, small businesses, developers, and so on. And the software engineers worked in three different languages, further diffusing effort. Perhaps a big company could do that, but WebCo was burning capital and needed much more focus. It would have to show much better market success to attract another round of funding.

Most critically, however, was that Sharon did not have a taste for the exercise of executive power. In her heart, she disliked telling anyone what to do. She wanted a strategy statement so that "everyone will know what to do."

The typical advice executives like Sharon receive is a description of a total solution to the problem she faced, along with a definition of the target market and the product and service features recommended to give it an advantage over rivals. But Sharon wasn't really interested in a strategy makeover—she basically wanted a better "strategy statement." She shied away from directing any significant changes in the company's business pattern. Perhaps I am not the salesperson I should be, but we parted ways without devising a strategy for WebCo to become the Salesforce.com of the Web-commerce world. WebCo never developed a strategy that would enable it to "grow up." Today the company remains small, has a different name, and sells graphics elements for Web designers.

METALCO

Some years ago, I worked with 'Stan Hastings,' a CEO who had been recently hired to turn around a company with three divisions.

From him I learned a lesson in how someone, even a CEO, builds a power base.

Stan had previously been a senior staff person at a larger company. The board brought Hastings into 'MetalCo' as CEO in order to solve the problems of the Electrometals Division and make investments in new growth markets. At MetalCo, the central Metal Division was the source of cash and earnings, while the Electrometals Division's products had been battered by competitors.

When Stan Hastings called on the division heads to meet with him for the first time, the head of Metals refused. "You come to my office," he demanded.

Hastings told me that the Metals Division needed major changes, but that the board wasn't ready to support him in such a step. So he decided to act where he did have the leeway. He fired the head of the weak Electrometals Division and took over its direct management. He spent seven months working to improve its profit. He then sold the whole Electrometals Division, using the cash to acquire some new businesses, still connected to the firm's metals base, which looked to have brighter futures. With the board's now strong backing, he fired the head of Metal and began work on improving its operations.

Stan Hastings's actions are a vivid real-world example of how a person gained executive power in a new situation. The board had hired him to turn the company around, but would not, initially, support him in a conflict with the head of the strong cash-earning division. In this case, he acted with indirection. First, he demonstrated hands-on management ability at Electrometals and then in developing new growth opportunities, all without initially touching the Metals Division. Only then had he developed the executive power to lead the whole company.

THE DC AGENCY

There are times when the job simply doesn't grant enough power to deal with real challenges. In 2005 I was invited to attend a large gathering of academics, lawyers, judges, politicians, and government agency managers. After giving a talk on strategy to a group of about a hundred, I was taking questions from the listeners. A woman identified herself as the head of a fairly important government agency, not a top-level agency like Homeland Security, but two levels down. Still, she had the responsibility for the direction of her agency's priorities and its two thousand employees. Her question was that at her agency she had the responsibility for operations and setting priorities within the basic charter. "I have two thousand people reporting to me," she said. "But I don't see how I can really set any strategy, at least not as you describe it." She argued that the people working for her knew that she was appointed for a short term and would be replaced in a few years by someone else. "They are polite and helpful," she explained, "but I can tell that although my ideas are given attention, they will never be acted on." She argued that the agency was really run by the permanent civil-service cadre. "People like me have little impact. There is actually resentment that the very best civil-service types will never be promoted to my job."

My response to her wasn't that helpful. I sympathized and recognized that hers was a common problem. Still, it was a year before I was able to formulate the problem in a simple and direct way: she simply did not have enough executive power to create and implement a strategy. She was hired to administer the agency, like someone who manages an apartment complex. Without sufficient executive power, she could not direct its purpose or even intervene much in how it carried out its functions.

GRANDCO

'GrandCo,' a producer of geolocation products for nautical markets, also designed and manufactured a line of surveying instruments for agricultural and land surveying. In late 2009 I was asked to help 'Nora Frank,' the head of R&D for nautical products, with strategy work. From her I got a dramatic lesson in how one might build a power base inside a large company.

After only an hour of talking with Nora on the telephone, I realized that she was caught within a dysfunctional organizational structure. Her direct responsibility was R&D for nautical products, with manufacturing under another manager. Sales and marketing were split between an Americas division, one for Australia, and a third for the "rest of the world." The land-survey products divisions were not quite as fragmented but were also broken down functionally. In other words, no one in the company had any profit-and-loss responsibility for any business except the CEO.

I told Nora that my expertise was business strategy, not R&D management. Nora was not put off. She explained that nautical-products revenues were in slow decline due to new competition, but she felt it could be turned around. The trick would be to concentrate R&D on products for whole-fleet management, from oil tankers to fishing boats. But corporate wanted her to keep doing R&D on products for the yachting market. Corporate wouldn't approve a budget for other purposes. Nora argued that the yachting market was vulnerable. The new smartphones with Google Maps showed everyone that you didn't need a piece of $40,000 equipment to find out where you were at sea.

I liked Nora's spirit and agreed to help her flesh out an approach to the fleet-location business. After a few days of work on the project, I became convinced that the idea had merit but that Nora's real challenge was that there was no business unit to present to. After intense conversation, Nora became convinced that she had to create a "virtual" division within GrandCo—a group of individuals in R&D, manufacturing, sales, and marketing who would meet regularly to discuss the issues in nautical products. The virtual division would assemble a virtual profit-and-loss statement for the business and begin a coordinated effort to plan product policy. Nora had a good relationship with someone in marketing as a start, and he, in turn, had fairly good relationships with individuals in Americas and rest-of-world sales.

Over the next two years, the virtual division planned and gained grudging approvals for product-line extensions in nautical from yachts to smaller commercial vessels like fishing boats and long-distance ferries. By year three, Nora had gained budget approval for work in the fleet products. In year four, a new CEO, impressed with her entrepreneurial zeal, made the virtual division real and put Nora in charge.

Nora Frank's journey from head of R&D to head of a business division was one of gathering executive power. At the start, she had a vision for a business strategy but could not implement it. Her real personal strategy had to encompass the path toward having enough executive power to actually enact the business strategy she envisioned.

SCICO

'Fletcher Black' called me in the fall of 2015. Fletcher's business was named 'SciCo' and was a division of a larger corporation. He said that he needed help with competitive strategy. After some discussion, I agreed to a preliminary visit and discussions with him and two other senior leaders in his business.

After arriving at Fletcher's offices, we began to talk specifics. The company sold a variety of scientific equipment to a range of universities and private research laboratories. Their products ranged from analytical balances to centrifuges to new gene-editing tools. The company's origins lay in balances and had expanded it by adding product lines, both internally developed and acquired, over the previous twenty years.

That morning, Fletcher explained his challenges in some detail. He told me (I turned my notes into complete sentences):

> The business has good potential to improve the bottom line. To do this we need to drive sales efficiency while navigating quality concerns. We expect to close the year with about $1 billion in revenue, up 2 percent. But no real increase in profit.
>
> One key problem is in SciCo-branded centrifuges. These have been a mainstay of the company's volume and profit for many

years, especially because the tubes it uses have to be replaced frequently. Recently, however, we have had strong competition from a new French firm. Its products are less expensive and, frankly, just as good. Even more troublesome, it is beginning to offer a line of wireless measuring instruments. These wireless instruments feed results directly to the screens of researchers, often displaying multiple measurements on the same html page.

I am concerned that the sales force has been cobbled together from various product acquisitions. As a whole, they do not have a common sense of what SciCo is and why it exists. In particular, the sales team is poor at driving consumables utilization—they tend to be wannabe researchers and engineers.

Costs are rising, and we are constantly under pressure to move our price up to keep margins healthy. We have had, unfortunately, any number of recalls in various lines, which have hurt our reputation.

I was interested in SciCo's new French competitor and its new wireless products. I asked Fletcher about his company's own plans for lower-cost designs and for wireless-measuring instruments. He said, "Oh, there is nothing on the new product road map for the next three years."

It took me a few minutes to realize that SciCo had no control whatsoever over product development or manufacturing. Development was handled by a "global" division based in Italy. Manufacturing was carried out in a variety of locations, none in the United States. SciCo was not really a company. It was a North America marketing and sales group masquerading as a business.

I asked Fletcher why the corporation let this structure persist, leaving North American marketing and sales powerless to create a competitive strategy. He said that corporate leadership saw the North American market as saturated and wanted to increase its business in the less developed world.

The corporation that owned SciCo had, rightly or wrongly, deemed it to be something like a "cash cow." Without the ability to affect product design or manufacturing costs, the best Fletcher could do was a marketing or sales plan. I told him the story of Nora Frank and how she created a virtual division and, over time, reshaped the larger corporation. Fletcher was impressed but did not believe he would prevail in such an effort within SciCo's parent company.

Fletcher's problem is all too common in large corporations. Businesses are split into parts, and integration is through corporate committee. The parts are placed under action restrictions that limit their ability to compete. Like Fletcher, the leaders of all these damaged businesses lack the executive power to create and execute effective strategy. They can do their best, and that can be quite impressive. What they cannot do is deal successfully with a competent competitor who has power over all the sinews of strength and action.

7

Creating Coherent Action

In my youth I was a rock climber with a few first ascents. When you are high up with just a rope to keep you from falling into what looks like the void, you pay attention to your equipment. In those days, the high-quality names were Edelrid (rope), Chouinard (pitons), and Cassin (carabiners). Today, if you do anything while dangling from a rope, you will have heard of Petzl, a private French company, that designs and makes high-performance climbing, caving, skiing, and industrial safety equipment.

Fernand Petzl (1913–2003) was initially a caver who established a number of firsts in exploring underground labyrinths. Beginning in about 1968, he began to use his workshop to produce pulleys and brakes useful for cavers. His products became known for both high quality and safety, qualities seated by his deep knowledge of caving and the intimacy of the caving community. Incorporated in 1975, the company began to make products for the mountaineering and rock-climbing markets. Fernand's son, Paul, led the company into climbing, eventually organizing a subsidiary in the United States.

Mark Robinson, president of Petzl America, explained that "Petzl is not specialized in rock climbing, work at height, or cavers, but creates tools for anyone who is trying to move up or down under the constraints of gravity."[1] The challenges for a company making climbing equipment are quality and trust. If you are going to trust your life to a small piece of equipment, you have to trust the maker.

There are literally hundreds of firms making outdoor clothing, tents, and backpacks. But which would you trust to make a self-breaking belay device that wouldn't snap in extreme cold or have some hidden flaw? Which craftsperson working alone would you trust? What about a company that also had a huge business selling fashion campus outerwear and casual boots? Only a few firms pass this test of quality and trust. Petzl is possibly the leader, followed by Black Diamond, also led by a real-life climber.

In 2005 the New York City Fire Department (FDNY) reached out to Petzl to create, on a tight schedule, a quick building-escape system for firefighters. Traditional rappel devices wouldn't work on the thin rope firefighters carried. Petzl engineers came back with a design in only a few weeks. Training firefighters followed—they had to learn to place a hook and then exit an opening or window and control their descent with the new device. During training, the descender rope of a firefighter who was bigger than the others began to tear apart. Two days later, the Petzl technicians had a fix, and the system became standard for the FDNY. The quality of Petzl's Exo personal evacuation system and the quickness and surety of their response became a legend in the firefighting and broader work-at-height communities.

The company's product line includes specialty items for climbing, mountain rescue, wind-turbine maintenance, arborists, search and

FIGURE 9. Petzl EXO AP Descender

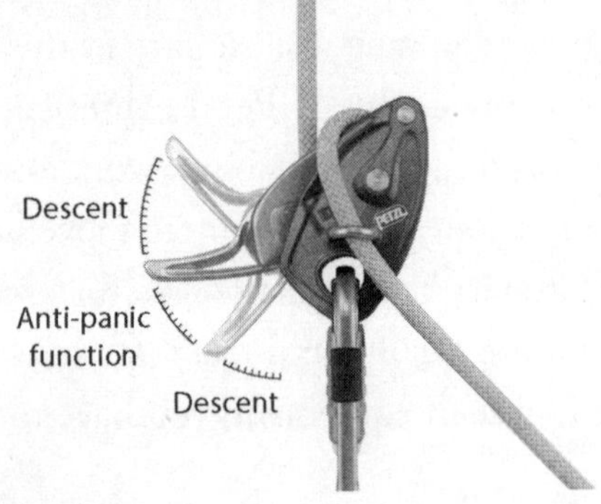

Source: © Petzl Distribution.

rescue, bridge and high-tension power-line maintenance, and more. In 2008 the company opened V.axess, a special facility in Crolles, France, to spur R&D into product performance and stress in vertical environments. V.axess supports research, testing, and rapid product improvement.

The coherence of Petzl's guiding policies and its actions is in their intense product focus, in the deep knowledge of its principals, in the quality of their products, and in the carefully cultivated image of safety in risky situations. In companies like Petzl, coherence is the consequence of a deep narrow focus, assiduously avoiding product proliferations and growth for growth's sake.

COHERENT ACTIONS SUPPORT one another. At the simplest level, coherence means that actions and policies do not contradict each other. In the best of cases, coherence comes from actions working synergistically to create additional power.

- More Americans start their online shopping at Amazon than on a search engine. The company's fantastic growth rate has astounded Wall Street and put down many competitors. The company's strategy is almost totally customer centric and coherently focused on quickness. Its prices are competitive, so there is little incentive to search elsewhere for better prices. Its website works smoothly. You don't have to reidentify yourself each time you pay for what is in your shopping cart. Goods can come the next day, even today. Product reviews are never perfect, but Amazon's are the best available for making a purchase decision. Returns are easy. The wide range of products, like the traditional department store, lets the shopper economize on trips to other vendors. The whole picture, across all of its activities, shows very little compromise with the central idea of offering the customer the quickest, best, easiest online shopping experience for the widest variety of goods.

- Southwest Airlines' original strategy remains a classic example of coherence. It obtained low operating costs by a nonunion, high-hourly workweek policy combined with short turnaround times (fifteen versus sixty minutes). It tried to serve routes where one end could be served by a smaller airport, did not work with online booking services, and provided no reserved seats and minimal in-flight food. All of these policies, combined with an enthusiastic culture, made it very focused and hard to emulate. Today, the challenge is maintaining that cohesion as the company tries to expand to international destinations.
- Redfin is a Web-powered real-estate brokerage business. It is trying to reinvent the real estate market. It charges a small initial listing fee (1 percent) and then provides signage, flyers, photography, and so on to aid in selling the house. It uses salaried agents instead of commissioned brokers and collects a fee (3 percent) from the buyer. It consolidates listing, appraisal, title, inspection, loan origination, and agents. The concept is to use technology, consolidation of operations, and quality human assistance to make more gross profit per customer and then invest that back to provide more value to each customer. The coherence around an integrated real-estate transaction experience can be a substantial advantage, especially as its scale and bargaining power grow. It insists on honest customer reviews, firing agents who violate its customer-first doctrines. Thus far, Redfin is going slow on the iBuying craze, preferring to keep a sober reputation. (iBuyers are middlemen who offer cash to quickly buy a home as is and sight unseen based on statistical estimates of its value, avoiding agent fees and closing costs.)

A. G. Lafley and Roger Martin's *Playing to Win* is an excellent book about strategy at Procter & Gamble, and their story about Olay is a fine example of coherent action.[2] It starts with Oil of Olay being seen as "Oil of Old Lady," no longer relevant to today's consumers.

The challenge was to somehow renew this brand or extend some other brand into the skin-care space it had occupied. Competitive products were fairly high-priced and were sold through department stores and even higher-end channels.

Lafley and Martin say that Procter & Gamble developed a genuinely better skin-care product—let's take that as a necessary claim. P&G's coherent actions were to

1. maintain the Olay name as Olay Total Effects, later extended to several closely related Olay products
2. do consumer research about pricing, research that led to the discovery that pricing at $18.99 garnered more response than pricing at $15.99
3. establish a marketing campaign consonant with the brand's already embedded promise of "Fight the Seven Signs of Aging"
4. work with mass retailers to establish a special display section creating what they call a "masstige" channel—buyers willing to buy higher-end products in a mass channel
5. redesign packaging around this new concept of a prestige product sold in a mass channel

There was nothing magical about these actions. In retrospect, they were just good, insightful management. But look at what might have happened. They might have focused on breaking into prestige channels, places where P&G had little experience. They might have tried to simply rename and reprice the product without putting the effort into a special display area consistent with its higher-quality positioning. They might have priced it too low, signaling another me-too mass-channel skin-care product. When done well, coherence doesn't jump out and smack you on the head. It just looks sensible.

THE SPACE SHUTTLE

The space shuttle was a magnificent achievement of engineering and human courage. In 133 successful missions it put many valuable payloads into orbit. Still, it was intended to make it cheap and easy to put many payloads into orbit each year. It never did that. Two of the five shuttles were destroyed in accidents, killing fourteen astronauts. After the reentry destruction of the shuttle *Columbia* in 2003, the project was slowed, and its last mission flew in 2011.

The two fundamental problems with the space shuttle were fabricated cost estimates and design by committee. The result was an incoherent design.

In 1972 NASA claimed that it could build a reusable space shuttle such that "the cost of placing a pound of payload in orbit can be reduced to less than $100."[3] In actuality, the system as designed and operated had an average cost per pound of about $28,000.

How did that happen? Like the case of Project T (see Chapter 10), the complex projections were cooked. People within NASA and its contractor community desperately wanted to justify a new program.[4] Estimates of cost and risk were *adjusted* to Congress's funding thresholds. In the process they trashed the successful Saturn family of rockets and crippled the US space program for decades. The risk Congress apparently ignored was that the economic analysis was a fabrication. The fancy capital budgeting analysis of the proposed shuttle was a distraction, drawing attention away from the crux issue of reusability.

The design incoherence came out of committee thinking: to get approved, a project or program has to be all things to all people. NASA had wanted to go beyond the moon, build a space station, and explore the asteroids and Mars. Nuclear-powered rockets would explore the solar system. On the other hand, German rocket-scientist Werner von Braun's dream was of a flying space plane that would make orbital access easy, cheap, and safe.

When I was in college studying engineering, my mother, a career civil servant, worked for the air force on project Dyna-Soar. The air force hated space capsules. A space pilot, it felt, should be able to fly missions anywhere in the world, and his vehicle should have wings. The fairly large wings on the shuttle were there to satisfy the air force. Congress wanted a low cost per satellite put in orbit.

The crucial compromise among all these competing interests and ambitions was to tell Congress that the shuttle would perform *all* of these functions and handle *all* anticipated future launches to Earth orbit.

In a discussion with an air force colonel about fighter-jet performance, I once asked what the "perfect" fighter would look like. He said, "The perfect design would have contractors in each state and a part made in each congressional district." In the case of the space shuttle, it wasn't perfect, but by the colonel's standards it was very good. There was virtually no dissent in Congress—the very complex project had something for almost every interest group.

As the project went forward, costs ballooned. Operational costs were many times higher than forecast. To fly the vehicle through the furnace of reentry, the large wings had thirty-five thousand separate thermal tiles. Each had to perform perfectly, and each had to be inspected after each flight and then fitted back into its unique slot. The Office of Management and Budget had overruled NASA on engine design and insisted on "lower cost" solid-fuel rockets that were supposed to be recoverable but, in reality, proved very costly to refurbish. Various interests had driven the rocket-motor business toward Morton-Thiokol (Utah), which had made solid rocket motors for a variety of military missiles. The two deadly failures in 135 launches were partially due to the selection of solid-fuel rockets.[5] (It is worth noting that the 1.5 percent failure rate of the space shuttle was quite a bit lower than the historical 6 percent failure rate of standard launch-to-orbit unmanned rockets. Rocketing into space just isn't that safe.)

The space-shuttle strategy was incoherent. The program was supposed to keep costs down from economies of scale gained by cornering the market for low-Earth-orbit missions. But the shuttles had to have a human crew. You don't have to be a rocket scientist to see that flying a human crew is vastly more expensive than flying an unmanned rocket. The system had to keep humans alive and unharmed on the ascent, in orbit, during the fiery reentry, and on landing. This was a huge premium to pay for routine trips like putting a communications satellite into orbit. Having a human crew made failure catastrophically expensive. National pride was at stake on each mission.

THE UN SUSTAINABLE DEVELOPMENT GOALS

It is all too easy to set goals or objectives that are incoherent. As a simple example, seventeen Sustainable Development Goals (SDGs) were set by the United Nations in 2015. Each goal points to a desirable outcome. The seventeen are shown in Figure 10. They are admirable aspirations, but they are not coherent.

- Goal number 14 asks for healthy and resilient oceans and coasts. But many in the poorer parts of the world make their living by fishing, a negative relationship with number 8 (employment), number 2 (hunger), and number 1 (poverty).
- Goal number 2 (hunger and sustainable agriculture) is inconsistent within itself because withdrawing the use of petroleum-based fertilizers would sharply cut crop yields.
- Goals number 7 (energy for all) and number 13 (climate change) are unfortunately inconsistent within current technological constraints, and without energy, there is little hope of reducing poverty (number 1).
- Increasing food production (number 2) means more land under production, which seems to raise problems for goal number 15, preserving ecosystems. In the past thirty years, China has done much to eliminate poverty (number 1) and hunger (number 2) and improve health (number 2). But in doing so it has become the world's largest emitter of carbon dioxide, mainly from the burning of coal.

Many in the world look with distaste on the ranchers burning tracts in the Amazon to raise cattle. This is a huge negative for goal number 15 (sustainable ecosystems). The meat produced there provides higher incomes for many in Brazil (number 1) and is mainly

FIGURE 10. UN Sustainable Development Goals, 2015

1	End poverty in all its forms everywhere.
2	End hunger, achieve food security and improved nutrition, and promote sustainable agriculture.
3	Ensure healthy lives, and promote well-being for all at all ages.
4	Ensure inclusive and equitable quality education, and promote lifelong learning opportunities for all.
5	Achieve gender equality, and empower all women and girls.
6	Ensure availability and sustainable management of water and sanitation for all.
7	Ensure access to affordable, reliable, sustainable, and modern energy for all.
8	Promote sustained, inclusive, and sustainable economic growth; full and productive employment; and decent work for all.
9	Build resilient infrastructure, promote inclusive and sustainable industrialization, and foster innovation.
10	Reduce inequality within and among countries.
11	Make cities and human settlements inclusive, safe, resilient, and sustainable.
12	Ensure sustainable consumption and production patterns.
13	Take urgent action to combat climate change and its impacts.
14	Conserve and sustainably use the oceans, seas, and marine resources for sustainable development.
15	Protect, restore, and promote sustainable use of terrestrial ecosystems; sustainably manage forests; combat desertification; halt and reverse land degradation; and halt biodiversity loss.
16	Promote peaceful and inclusive societies for sustainable development, provide access to justice for all, and build effective, accountable, and inclusive institutions at all levels.
17	Strengthen the means of implementation, and revitalize the global partnership for sustainable development.

exported to China (38 percent), Egypt (10 percent), and Russia (10 percent), improving diets there. In any event, mandating that everyone stop eating meat would take a level of violence inconsistent with number 16 (peace).

A realistic strategy for pursuing these agenda items would have to set priorities for the goals and for their accomplishment over time. And it would have to make addressability a key element in the calculation. We more or less know how to reduce poverty. But we don't know how to do it without burning oil or gas (absent a resurgence of nuclear power). Would it be better to aim at poverty and let the climate do what it must? Or should the world strictly control the use of fossil fuels and put up with large tracts of poverty for the rest of the century? Finally, it would have to admit that all of these goals would be made much easier with a world of 2.5 billion (when I was born) rather than today's 7.9 billion—and that it all becomes almost impossible in a world of 15 or more billion.

Having seventeen inconsistent goals is the indulgence of politicians. A strategist would face such an exuberance of inconsistent ambition by selecting a consistent subset and pushing the rest aside, at least for a while.

BOLERO

Even before the United States entered World War II, "Plan Dog," as introduced in Chapter 4, was the Roosevelt administration's decision that defeating Nazi Germany was more important than war with Japan (and that a full fight with both at the same time was not winnable). After the United States entered the war, General George C. Marshall, chief of staff for the army, brought Major General Dwight D. Eisenhower into a top position in war planning. On March 25, 1942, Eisenhower presented his strategy, code-named BOLERO.

BOLERO's chief element was an invasion across the English Channel (Operation Roundup). In justifying this difficult challenge as the crux, Eisenhower had to reject proposals to add American troops to the Russian front, to focus on the Mediterranean, to come up through Spain, or to come down through some part of Scandinavia. In BOLERO he insisted on a focus of securing the United Kingdom and keeping Russia in the war. That his priority was focused was evident when he wrote, "Unless this plan [BOLERO] is adopted as the central aim of all our efforts, we must turn our backs upon the Eastern Atlantic and go, full out, as quickly as possible, against Japan."[6] General Marshall and President Roosevelt agreed, and after a briefing in London so did Winston Churchill.

Surprisingly, one month later, President Roosevelt caved into navy and Australian pressure and announced a commitment of one hundred thousand soldiers and one thousand aircraft to Australia. If that was done, coherence would be lost. General Marshall quickly went to the White House and confronted Roosevelt. He told the president that if he wanted to defend Australia, there should be a "complete abandonment" of BOLERO. Historian J. E. Smith wrote: "FDR was sometimes too quick off the mark, and this time he recognized that he had overstepped. As he often did when caught out, he dissembled. 'I did not issue any directive to increase our forces in Australia,' he wrote Marshall. Roosevelt said he merely 'wanted to know if it were possible to do so. I do not want BOLERO slowed down.'"[7]

One sees how coherence is easily lost. The cost of coherence is saying no to many interests with reasonable values and arguments. A strategist tries to not be a politician. The art of compromise and building the big tent that everyone can shelter under is not that of the strategist. Rather, it is coherence aimed at the crux of the problem. The politician arrives after the strategist's victory, sharing the gains among those who have won the day and those who stood aside.

Central to BOLERO was Operation Roundup, the planned cross-Channel invasion of northern France in the spring of 1943. Russia's Stalin pressured Churchill and Roosevelt to quickly open a front in the West against Germany, to take the pressure off the war in Russia, which was killing Russian soldiers and civilians at a high rate (at the war's end, twenty million Russians had lost their lives in the conflict). This pressure led Churchill and Roosevelt to shift the focus to an early fall 1942 invasion of North Africa, called Operation Torch. This was a political decision to shift and spend the men and materials accumulated for BOLERO on a nonstrategic battle in order to assuage Stalin. General Marshall had fought the decision, arguing that it would be better to put the nation's full strength to bear in the Pacific than engage in half measures in the West. Eisenhower, then a lieutenant general, commanded Torch.

In the spring of 1943, when BOLERO was originally supposed to take place, the Allies agreed on a 1944 invasion of France, now code-named operation OVERLORD. Dwight Eisenhower was named supreme allied commander of the Supreme Headquarters Allied Expeditionary Force (SHAEF). On June 6, 1944, about 160,000 troops crossed the English Channel to land in Normandy. Two months later, nearly 2 million Allied soldiers were in France. It would take another year of hard fighting before Germany surrendered unconditionally, on May 7, 1945.

AFGHANISTAN

It is perhaps hard to remember now, but when the Twin Towers fell in 2001, policy makers became convinced that if the al-Qaeda-inspired attackers had possessed nuclear weapons, they would have used them. From that came a resolve to "clean up" the situation in Afghanistan and the Pakistan border, eliminating the al-Qaeda leaders, operatives, and training centers.

Over time, the objective expanded. New values and ambitions were added to the mix. US leaders like to think that the rest of humanity wants to live in a neoliberal democracy. In 2008 President George W. Bush said, "We have a strategic interest and I believe a moral interest in a prosperous and peaceful democratic Afghanistan, and no matter how long it takes, we will help the people of Afghanistan succeed."[8]

The Taliban had grown out of a student movement in the early 1990s, filling in the power vacuum left after the departure of the USSR. The Taliban were supported by the Pakistani intelligence agency, the ISI, in their own move to control Afghanistan. When the

United States invaded in 2001, the Taliban were the de facto government. After the United States quickly defeated them and their allies, a pro-US government was installed, headed by Hamid Karzai. Over time, the Taliban, with secure redoubts in Pakistan's "tribal areas," fought both the US troops and the new Afghan government troops. After twenty years, we now know that President Bush's "peace and democracy" in Afghanistan was not within our grasp.

In December 2019 the *Washington Post*, using the Freedom of Information Act, obtained and published interviews conducted by the special investigator general for Afghanistan reconstruction. The general conclusion the *Post* seemed to draw from these documents was that the US public had not been informed about the difficulties and setbacks occurring in Afghanistan. My own reading was a bit different. I was not surprised or even concerned about public transparency regarding military operations. What I did see, however, was policy incoherence. The most influential single incoherence was the switch, as President Obama came to power, from a counterterrorism strategy to one of counterinsurgency, or, more specifically, from fighting al-Qaeda to fighting the Taliban. Plus, there was Obama's decision to set a short deadline for ending the war, which, in turn, signaled the Taliban that they had to lie low only until the US withdrawal.

In the following quotes from Craig Whitlock's *Washington Post* article, his writing is unquoted, while the snippets from the interviews are in quotation marks:

> Jeffrey Eggers, a retired Navy SEAL and White House official under Bush and Obama, said few people paused to question the very premise for keeping US troops in Afghanistan.
>
> "Why did we make the Taliban the enemy when we were attacked by al-Qaeda? Why did we want to defeat the Taliban?" Eggers said in a Lessons Learned interview. "Collectively the system is incapable of taking a step back to question basic assumptions."
>
> Boucher, a career diplomat who also served as chief State Department spokesman under Bush, said US officials did not know what they were doing.

> "First, we went in to get al-Qaeda, and to get al-Qaeda out of Afghanistan, and even without killing bin Laden we did that," Boucher told government interviewers. "The Taliban was shooting back at us so we started shooting at them and they became the enemy. Ultimately, we kept expanding the mission."[9]

Although the Taliban had been the de facto government before the US intervention, they were deemed "insurgents" and fought with a variety of counterinsurgency methods inherited from the Vietnam War. In addition to that fundamental incoherence, there were many different agencies and objectives being pursued at the same time:

> Fundamental disagreements went unresolved. Some US officials wanted to use the war to turn Afghanistan into a democracy. Others wanted to transform Afghan culture and elevate women's rights. Still others wanted to reshape the regional balance of power among Pakistan, India, Iran, and Russia.
>
> "With the AfPak [Afghanistan-Pakistan] strategy there was a present under the Christmas tree for everyone," an unidentified US official told government interviewers in 2015. "By the time you were finished you had so many priorities and aspirations it was like no strategy at all."

The issue of opium was and is central to politics and economics in Afghanistan. The devastation of the war with the USSR had eliminated agricultural diversity, leaving opium as the country's main product. Seeking international recognition, in 2000 the Taliban government banned opium production, successfully cutting production to very low levels. They framed the edict in religious terms, emphasizing Islamic prohibitions against drugs. But, at the same time, rural incomes plummeted, and the Taliban alienated many warlords and rural farmers. It was a moment when Western powers could have stepped up aid for legitimate farming.

The quick success of the US invasion in 2001–2002 was strongly helped by support from anti-Taliban factions who had previously controlled the opium business—a group of Pashtun drug lords. Gaining control, the United States then began a policy of trying to eradicate the opium trade, incoherently undercutting those who had supported the overthrow of the Taliban.

Opium production employed about four hundred thousand Afghans. The country's drug exports flowed through Turkey and Russia to Europe, providing the majority of the heroin and hashish consumed there. Afghanistan supplied perhaps 90 percent of the world's illegal opiates. But there was no coherent US guiding policy with regard to the drug trade. The United States forced the government to outlaw opium production. The military was charged with various programs to eradicate poppy production. Processing in Helmand was bombed. Fields of poppies were burned. On the other hand, key drug lords were US allies, and their poppy fields were left intact in return for intelligence about the Taliban. The Taliban had been able to quickly stop poppy growing in 2000, but despite the efforts of the United States and the British, opium production flourished. From the *Post*'s "Afghanistan Papers" article: "The main problem is that opium cultivation is a livelihood strategy for a significant part of the population in the poorest country in Asia and one of the poorest in the world. You can't criminalize people's livelihood strategies and expect them to support you."

No single agency or country was in charge of the Afghan drug strategy for the entirety of the war, so the State Department, the Drug Enforcement Agency, the US military, NATO allies, and the Afghan government butted heads constantly. "It was a dog's breakfast with no chance of working," an unnamed former senior British official told government interviewers.

The United States spent about $2 trillion on the Afghan project. When large amounts of money are thrown at a problem, not only is there corruption, but each element of the military and each civilian government agency sees the opportunity to fund its own favorite programs. This, of course, leads to incoherence of action on the ground. What happened in Afghanistan was incoherent strategy on all fronts. The diagnosis was incorrect: the country was suffering, but it wasn't from a lack of democracy. Democracy doesn't really work when the majority want to kill the minority or when an armed minority is capable of killing the majority. The action policy of establishing a democratic central government in a warlord society was not addressable, and the actions taken were incoherent.

THE MINIMUM COHERENCE

Southwest Airlines' original strategy, Petzl, Ryanair, Netflix's original DVD-by-mail business, Enterprise Rent-a-Car, IKEA, and Progressive Insurance are all examples of especially tightly knit coherent strategies that we can learn much from. Much of that tight design comes from having a very narrow product focus.

What about more complex organizations? Larger, more complex organizations cannot have that degree of coherence. They must compensate by bringing more resource depth to the battle. Just as the whole US Navy cannot all be SEAL teams, more complex businesses should probably not attempt to emulate companies with super-strong niche specialization based on highly complementary policies.

Instead, when actions are taken, they should at least meet the test of minimum coherence. That is, simply, actions should not directly conflict with one another. For example:

Don't base your competitive edge on continuing development but then cut R&D to make your numbers.

Don't adopt new trendy marketing presentations for a product that is supposed to be stable and reliable.

Don't base your strategy on your data wizardry and then outsource your software development.

Don't close down one of two warehouses to cut costs while having marketing and sales seek sales based on quick delivery.

Don't claim that your Web platform is about free speech and then shut down sites based on their political positions.

PART II

Diagnosis

Strategy is a form of problem solving, and you cannot solve a problem you have not understood. Deepening your understanding of the challenges being faced is the process of diagnosis. In diagnosis the strategist seeks to understand why certain challenges have become salient, about the forces at work, and why the challenge seems difficult. In this work, we use the tools of analogy, reframing, comparison, and analysis in order to understand what is happening and what is critical.

8

What Is the Problem?

Diagnosing Through Reframing and Analogy

To find the crux of a challenge, you must see the warp and weave of its elements. In arriving at a clearheaded diagnosis, two powerful tools are reframing and analogy, that is, building a mapping between your specific challenge and similar situations faced by others at different times and places.

A properly chosen analogy can open the door to new insight. At the same time, the largest obstacle to creating a *clearheaded* diagnosis of a situation is the tendency to get wrapped in unseen webs of unconscious analogy and bias. Whether in politics or corporate life, we live in echo chambers of self-reinforcing opinion and viewpoint. A clearheaded diagnosis, does not, indeed cannot, mean a perfectly accurate understanding of reality. The real world is far too complex to fully comprehend. In our attempts to structure and understand a situation, we simplify. Most often, we do so by taking certain facts and concepts to be more germane than others. Another way is the power of analogy, either to a known circumstance or to familiar frameworks, theories, and models. To be clearheaded is to be *aware* of the concepts, analogies, frameworks, models, and other assumptions being used to simplify and structure the situation.

A CHANGED POINT OF VIEW

Awareness of an organization's common frameworks and assumptions is easier for an outsider such as myself. When I work with organizations, I have the outsider's advantage and can ask dumb questions without looking too stupid. Diagnosis is basically a process of focusing on challenges and asking "what" and "why" over and over again. If, in interviews with managers, I promise confidentiality on who said what, I hear crisper and more pointed identification and analysis of issues. Being an outsider also aids awareness of the framing power of the stories and analogies insiders use to understand their situation. Diagnosis is quickened by introducing alternative analogies and frames that highlight different issues and different patterns of causation.

The most powerful tool for diagnosis is reframing the situation. At the simplest level, a "frame" is a way of looking at a situation. There are literally hundreds of academic papers on the subject, but a frame is simply a person's point of view on something. Often, individuals have developed frames that work for them and the organization. The frame used by senior leaders focuses their attention on some issues and measurements rather than others. A key step in diagnosis is testing, adjusting, and changing the frame, or point of view.

QuestKo

In 2016 I was meeting the CEO of 'QuestKo' to talk about strategy. After some preliminaries, the CEO showed me the company's strategy, or its "strategic plan." Nowadays, this is normally a PowerPoint presentation with colorful graphics.

In the strategic plan there were numbers about financial results, competition, market segments, buyers, estimates of market sizes and growth rates, and more. Near the end was the section on strategy labeled "Strategy for Growth." It was very positive—really a sales pitch for the company. Over five colorful pages, it promised that the company would "provide more value to the buyer through an improved experience," "continue investing in the growing segments of the market," and deliver substantial growth in revenues and an increase in profitability.

A common obstacle to a clearheaded diagnosis of the situation is that some managers believe that leadership means emphasizing the positive and hiding the negative. The obvious bias this creates is the origin of disasters ranging from the war in Vietnam to Jeff Immelt's debacle at GE. At GE insiders reported that Immelt had an aversion to hearing about problems or negative news. When the once super-stock collapsed in 2018, the *Wall Street Journal* summed it up in one story title: "How Jeffrey Immelt's 'Success Theater' Masked the Rot at GE."[1]

QuestKo's past leaders had assembled the company from five acquisitions, and that era was held up as one of great accomplishment. Portraits of these leaders adorned the boardroom walls. At QuestKo the strategic plan was all positive news and forecasts. There is nothing wrong with trying to please buyers and making continuing investments in the growing segments of the market. But why was the CEO spending time on these apparently standard and innocuous issues? There was nothing really strategic about the plan. Just as everyone's New Year's resolution is to exercise more, every corporation's plan says, "Invest in the growing segments of the market." It was just business as usual. My next question is almost always of the form: "What about all this is difficult?"

I asked "Why is this difficult?" to shift attention from unsupported goals to recognizing obstacles and difficulties since that is the beginning of strategy. And the answers at QuestKo were slow in coming. Each executive had awareness of several problems, but it was not their habit to talk about problems very much. The company was profitable but not doing as well as in the past. There was a sense of decline.

The CEO believed that better integration among the divisions was needed. He had instituted an unpopular program of rotating certain staff members among the five divisions.

The CFO believed that QuestKo was overstaffed and that a staff reduction would increase profit. The vice president of human resources was concerned about the silos in the organization and wanted to move to an "open office" arrangement in order to foster coordination. A recent survey showed that the "customer experience" rating for QuestKo was poor—actually dead last compared to competitors.

Two competitors had merged, and that was a source of concern. QuestKo's products were deemed competitive, though its prices were a bit high. The market was growing, so sales revenue kept inching up as it slowly gave up some market share.

The company was installing a new computer system aimed at integrating disparate systems that had accumulated over time. That too seemed to be irritating employees and creating disconnects, as one had to use the new system to enter orders but the old system to see customer histories. Methods and systems still varied across the five acquired divisions. Younger customers wanted better access on their smartphones.

Looking at these difficulties was initially uncomfortable. These executives knew about problems, but as practical people they also knew that digging into difficulties could be an endless morass.

The QuestKo senior management group had a shared belief that "strategy" was a set of long-term objectives, like "being the leading . . ." Working with this group, the turning point came around the idea of a *critical winnable challenge*. Instead of looking at the difficulties as a morass, we began to zero in on which ones could be surmounted. Not at some distant horizon but fixed or dealt with in the near future—say, eighteen to thirty-six months. Given this reorientation, the group began to focus on customer satisfaction.

We found a crux when the CEO realized that attacking the customer satisfaction issue might be a way to better integrate the five divisions. More often than not, it is much less threatening to tackle a business issue than one of structure and functioning because issues of structure directly threaten power and position. With competent leadership, the changes in organization structure will come as people work out ways to tackle the common challenge.

The customer happiness issue didn't seem to have a single cause. Customers complained about error rates, slow response times, poor digital apps, and employees not taking ownership of problems.

In a strategy workshop the group developed a sharper and deeper view of the crux. The insight was to reorient the new computer system around customer satisfaction. The team called this "Two Birds" (because it was "Two Birds with One Stone").

In the past, QuestKo would have established goals about customer satisfaction and pushed to have them met without the critical how-to of effective execution. This time, the strategy group created an action plan.

1. It took the authority over defining the structure of the new IT software away from the consultants and put it into the hands of six customer-facing managers.
2. The new concept was that the overriding *purpose* of the new software was not to make IT happy but, instead, to enhance the customer experience.
3. Frontline managers in each business would gather biweekly to discuss problems with and solutions to customer satisfaction.
4. Much better records of customer complaints and interactions would be created.
5. Each biweekly meeting would include a written diagnosis of any customer-related problems and the actions to be taken to remedy these problems.
6. All employees would receive training in being more customer-centric in their jobs.

Over two years the change in orientation not only built better software but also changed the behavior of frontline managers. The company's customer experience evaluations rose to the best in its business. Market share and profits increased accordingly.

One critical change in point of view at QuestKo was from an essentially motivational view to one of problem solving. Top management had been setting financial and other related business targets and pushing for their accomplishment. They knew there were many problems and issues but did not like focusing on problems. By focusing on one critical yet winnable challenge—customer satisfaction—the company made a significant advance in performance, reputation, and coordinated competence. This didn't solve all their problems, but it developed habits of mind and organizational muscles that could move on to another challenge.

Creating a clearheaded diagnosis of the situation can be difficult when strategy creation is confused with motivational exercises or investment pitches to outsiders. Diagnosis requires facing hard truths. And strategy, as ever, is about action.

STEVE JOBS'S IPHONE

Diagnosing a challenge does not always mean one's own. In some cases, the problem is one faced by buyers or suppliers. I call this kind of gap a *value denial*, that is, something that should be for sale that isn't. Like on-time airline service, or reasonably priced home remodeling on a reliable schedule, or a phone that doesn't get scam calls from the "Social Security Office."

Steve Jobs's iPhone was based in his belief that people would value a mobile pocket-size combination Web browser and phone. But no such device was for sale in 2005. He also judged that the technology supporting such a device was just becoming available. And he judged that he could surmount the challenge of making such a product.

I once described how Jobs returned to Apple in 1997 and saved it from bankruptcy. The crisis had arisen in 1995 when Microsoft's Windows 95 operating system allowed the much less expensive PC clones to replicate much of the functionality of the Apple Macintosh. Then, in the summer of 1998, I asked Jobs a question. I said, "Everything we know about the PC business says that Apple cannot really push beyond a small niche position. The network effects are just too strong to upset the Wintel standard. So, what are you trying to do in the longer term? What is the strategy?" In response, he just smiled and said, "I am going to wait for the next big thing."

Building on the Hollywood connections he had from his stint at Pixar, the next big things for Jobs were iTunes and the iPod, released in 2001. Having the iPod in hand, one development project at Apple was to couple it with a phone. Another was work on Jobs's long-wished-for portable "book" computer. Jobs was more interested in the pad-like device than in phones. He saw existing mobile phones as uninteresting from a design point of view since their features were tightly defined and controlled by the wireless carriers who distributed them.

At the time, most mobile devices received their input from a physical keyboard or a stylus, used for poking at displayed letters. Could Apple develop a new type of screen for a pad device that responded to finger touch? And, importantly, could the screen be large enough to display a real Web page rather than a cut-down image of just some of the page's text? As part of these efforts, Jobs asked Apple engineer Bas Ording to work on a user interface that could smoothly scroll through a list of names. Ording was able to create and patent the inertia-like rubber-band touch screen scrolling that we now take for granted. Put your finger on a list, swipe it up fast, and the list scrolls several screenfuls down. Swipe slowly, and it only scrolls a few lines, bouncing when it hits the end of the list. Steve Jobs recalled the first time he saw that effect in 2005: "And when I saw the rubber band, inertial scrolling, and a few of the other things, I thought, 'My God, we can build a phone out of this.'"[2] With that, Apple switched its development focus from the pad to the phone.

At that time, the World Wide Web was about a decade old. On millions of desktops and laptops running Windows, people were surfing the Web, doing email, checking Yahoo!, Googling everything, and reading the news online. YouTube had just started, and Facebook was a year away from its public launch. But Web browsing on mobile devices was limited. The best phones of 2005 used

WAP browsers that showed only a short text summary of what a full-fledged desktop Web browser displayed. Steve Jobs's diagnosis of the situation was that the technology was close to being capable of providing a phone that could also be a real portable Web-surfing device (and an iPod too). No market research. He simply "knew" that this was something people would want and pay for. *The crux of the challenge was to create one now, while it was still hard, before technological progress made it easy.*

When Jobs initially demonstrated the iPhone to the public in 2007, he first showed how it was a better iPod. Strategically, he was disrupting his own best-selling product. He inertia-scrolled through lists of songs and high-resolution album covers. Then he showed how to watch a TV show on the phone and then a full-length movie (*Pirates of the Caribbean*). He turned the phone on the side and demonstrated how the movie instantly shifted to wide-screen display. He then demonstrated email and phone integration to contacts and finally turned to the Web. He showed full Web pages with the new pinch-to-zoom and tap-to-expand features. Then he showed Google Maps, with a search for nearby Starbucks coffee shops. Then he showed a map to the Washington Monument and then touched an icon to switch to satellite view.

The first stage of the rocket powering the new iPhone was how it put the Web in your pocket, not as a laptop or tablet, but in a small device stuck in the back of your jeans. The rocket's second-stage booster was apps, lightweight fast-starting programs that did specialized tasks. The first iPhone included a few apps like Visual Voicemail, the Safari web browser, the iPod music and video player, and Maps (powered by Google). Jobs initially did not want an app store; he wanted only pure Apple apps on the phone. The Apple team convinced him that was a mistake.[3]

When the Apple app store opened in 2008, it had five hundred apps. A year later, Apple's app store had fifty thousand apps. By 2015 there were two million. Cheap, plentiful, easy-to-buy apps made the iPhone very different from the PC world.

Also, in 2008, Google announced its "free" Android operating system that would enable phone makers to emulate many of the features of the iPhone, including a Google-controlled Play Store for apps.

In the old Monty Python TV show, the narrator would, at some point, say, "And now for something completely different!" In the smartphone world the third stage of the rocket was mobile social media, something no one had seen before. Facebook had one hundred million users in 2008, zooming to one billion by 2012. Instagram, Snapchat, WeChat, WhatsApp, Twitter, and more grew rapidly, in large part, due to smartphones. This new thing entranced billions. In Tokyo the pedestrians who walked while scanning Facebook on their phones were called "zombies." Even in my graduate MBA classes, students fiddled with their phones underneath their desks, unable to disconnect for an hour. Entering the main lounge of the Hotel Jerome in Aspen, I saw a huddled group of eleven teenagers looking like they were basking in the warmth of a small campfire. But the "firelight" was a single iPhone screen as one of them showed the others her social media posts.

Of course, Steve Jobs did not foresee all this. He simply wanted to put an iPod, phone, and the Web in your pocket with his trademark easy-to-use-and-learn interface. All of this unfolded in the way it did because Jobs had embraced the challenge of satisfying the as-yet-unseen demand for such devices.

THE WRONG CAUSAL MODEL

One of the most common tools of diagnosis is *analogy*—making connections to similar situations. The trick to using analogy well is access to more than one or two additional situations, to understand the logic in these other situations, and to check on how that logic maps to the current situation.

Analogy played a huge role in the success of Apple's iPhone because a bad analogy drove key competitors in the wrong directions.

When Apple introduced the iPhone in 2007, a number of industry experts predicted that it would not be a success. It would, they predicted, be a niche product, just like Apple's Macintosh PC, and, due to strong price competition, be profitless. This conviction rested on making an *analogy* between the smartphone business and the older PC business.

Microsoft CEO Steve Ballmer said:

> There's no chance that the iPhone is going to get any significant market share. No chance. It's a $500 subsidized item. They may make a lot of money. But if you actually take a look at the 1.3 billion phones that get sold, I'd prefer to have our software in 60 percent or 70 percent or 80 percent of them, than I would to have 2 percent or 3 percent, which is what Apple might get.[4]

John Dvorak was a much-followed columnist who specialized in technology. In 2007 he doubted that Apple could succeed in the handset business:

> This is not an emerging business. In fact, . . . it's in the process of consolidation with probably two players dominating everything, Nokia Corp. and Motorola Inc. . . . [M]argins are incredibly thin so that the small fry cannot compete. . . . There is no likelihood that Apple can be successful in a business this competitive. Even in the business where it is a clear pioneer, the personal computer, it had to compete with Microsoft and can only sustain a 5 percent market share. And its survival in the computer business relies on good margins. Those margins cannot exist in the mobile handset business for more than 15 minutes.[5]

At that time, Finnish Nokia led the mobile phone market with a 40 percent share. Nokia's chief strategist, Anssi Vanjoki, did not see the iPhone as much of a threat. In 2009, with Nokia still the world's leading mobile phone company, he said, "The development of mobile phones will be similar to PCs. Even with the Mac, Apple attracted much attention at first, but they have remained a niche manufacturer. That will be true in mobile phones as well."[6]

How could the CEO of Microsoft, a leading technology analyst, the chief strategist for the largest mobile phone company, as well as many others misapprehend the situation so badly? In short, they all used the same analogy—that smartphones were like PCs.

One can partly understand Ballmer—he wanted the industry to have a lot of phones all running Microsoft Windows Mobile. And he thought that Windows Mobile was up to the job. It managed contacts, made phone calls, did emails, and soon would allow businesspeople to see Microsoft Excel spreadsheets, view PowerPoint slides, and edit Word documents. Surely, Motorola, HTC, Nokia, and most of the rest would come around and all adopt the Windows Mobile system. With billions of units to be sold, and a Windows Mobile license fee of fifteen to thirty dollars a unit, the future looked almost locked in.

Ballmer also shared the then accepted wisdom in the tech industry that open systems beat closed systems. This rule of thumb came from the history of the PC business that was largely shaped in its early history by IBM. Its desktop personal computers were less elegant than the mouse- and Windows-based Apple Macintosh, but they were cheaper and also better for word processing. As millions of offices threw away their typewriters and adopted PC-based word processing, volume skyrocketed.

But IBM did not profit as it could have. Hubris led IBM to make two fundamental errors. First, in buying the IBM-DOS operating system from Bill Gates, it permitted him to sell his own branded copies (MS-DOS) to others. This seemed to them a valueless right because there were no other makers of similar hardware. Then, in building the PC, IBM created a copyright-protected bios (core firmware logic) that was written in such loose code that it was easy to emulate without violating IBM's copyright. These two errors ushered in a flood of IBM-PC clones running MS-DOS. Rising competition pushed down profit margins. In 1986 IBM chairman John Akers complained about the PC business, insisting, "We [IBM] are in the business of high margin sales."[7] In 2004 IBM sold the money-losing business to Lenovo. Note that there were no Apple Macintosh clones.

After developing the Excel spreadsheet for the Apple Macintosh, Microsoft used its new understanding of a mouse and Windows interface to construct the Windows operating system (OS). And in a second brilliant move, it bundled word processing, spreadsheets, presentation management, and database software into Windows Office, crushing stand-alone program makers like WordPerfect, Lotus, and dBase. From that point on, almost all the profits in the PC-clone arena went to Microsoft and Intel, whose x86 chip powered the machines. This business structure became known as the "Wintel" standard.

The Wintel standard was good for the world in general but bad for PC makers. Their boxes had to have an Intel-standard x86 chip, or else it wouldn't run Windows, and they had to have disks, keyboards, mice, displays, and so on, which Windows understood. All PCs contained the same basic internal components, sourced from the same suppliers. Branding provided access to distribution, but even then margins were very low. Within the Wintel cage of silicon and software, there was little differentiation.

When the iPhone appeared, people like Ballmer and Dvorak and Vanjoki thought that the mobile phone industry would evolve just like the PC industry. But the analogy to the PC industry did not apply. PCs became clones because IBM made mistakes in design and in intellectual property protection. And the PC market exploded because of the business demand for word processing. By contrast, business demand in the phone market was already sated by BlackBerry. It was the consumer demand for Web-enabled smartphones that would explode. And Apple had not made serious blunders in design or the protection of intellectual property.

Because this analogy was false, large firms like Nokia and Motorola were almost swept into the dustbin of history, and Microsoft whiffed its swing at the mobile market. And far from producing a profitless niche product, in 2015 Apple became the world's first trillion-dollar company.

AIRLAND BATTLE

The example of AirLand Battle shows the power of changing the frame. The original diagnosis was of an almost unsolvable challenge, at least within a reasonable period of time. Then a reframing of the challenge led to a creative response.

The October 1973 Arab-Israeli War started with simultaneous surprise attacks by Egypt and Syria, together using about 3,000 tanks and 350,000 soldiers. The Arab weapons were supplied by the Soviet Union, and their commanders had been trained in Soviet tactics. During the nineteen days of fighting, Arab and Israeli units engaged in a high-intensity melee not seen since World War II. The battle demonstrated the surprisingly effective power of the new range of portable missiles and rockets. The Arab forces, using Soviet weapons and tactics, dealt severe blows to the tough Israelis. The new weapons were surprisingly good at destroying heavily armored tanks and low-flying aircraft. The losses of tanks and aircraft to both sides were high. In particular, US analysts noted that both sides together lost more tanks than were in the US inventory.

Just six months earlier, the United States had stopped all combat operations in Vietnam. The US Senate's Case-Church Amendment guaranteed that the United States would not reintervene. (Two years later, the North Vietnamese army would take Saigon and reunify the country.) For a decade or more, the US military had been focused on low-impact battle in the jungles and rice paddies. Having lost that war, the US military was demoralized and disorganized. Then, the surprising events in the Mideast forced some US military thinkers to realize that they were not prepared for that kind of modern high-intensity fighting. After all, the United States had a treaty obligation with NATO to defend Europe from a high-impact attack by the USSR-led Warsaw Pact.[8] Additional alarm was supplied by the fact that, in the late 1960s, spies finally got their hands on the Soviet Union's war plans for invading Western Europe.

The original plan for defending Europe tried to deal with the very large advantage in force size possessed by the Warsaw Pact—19,000 main battle tanks versus 6,100 for all of NATO, 39,000 artillery pieces versus 14,000 for NATO, 2,460 fighter-interceptors versus 1,700 for NATO, three times the troops in place, and so on.[9] The original plan was a fighting fallback to the river Rhine. West Germany naturally resisted this sacrifice of its territory.

Translated Warsaw Pact documents revealed a war plan for the invasion of Central Europe based on the concept of a "double echelon." It envisioned an attack through Central Europe that would push to France and finally end at the English Channel. The first wave (echelon) would degrade the defense and identify the weak points. As shown in Figure 11, the second wave would strike through the weak points. In the words of the CIA: "The bulk of the forces of the first strategic echelon—those normally in the forward area—were expected to expend themselves somewhere near the Rhine. The second echelon would then come smashing through to complete the campaign against West Germany and the Benelux countries and push to the borders of France."[10]

FIGURE 11. CIA June 1968 Memorandum on Warsaw Pact War Plan

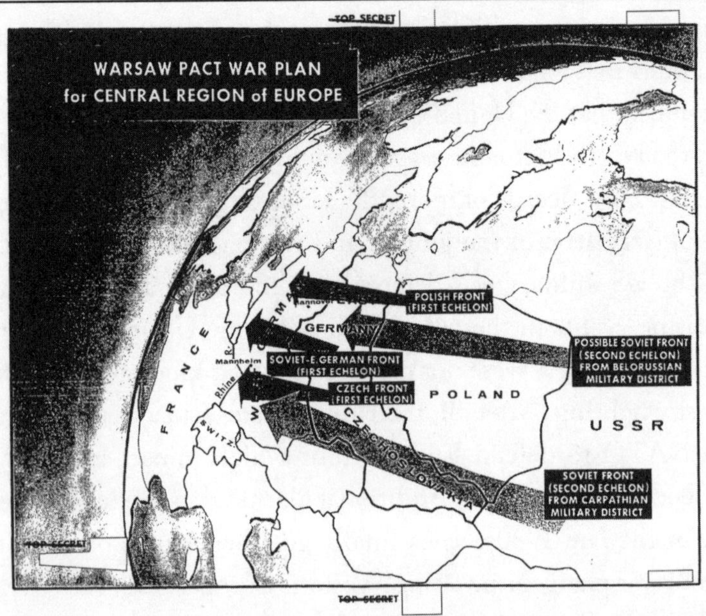

Source: "Intelligence Memorandum: Warsaw Pact Plan for Central Region of Europe," CIA, June 1968, 8, top secret (declassified in 2012).

The CIA was surprised by this plan for defeating NATO. They had long opined that the Soviet Union, like the United States, was mainly interested in deterring attacks, not in attacking.

After a bit of serious war gaming, some US planners believed that the new weapons revealed in the Arab-Israeli War, together with the "double echelon," would defeat NATO's fallback defense. They came to the uncomfortable conclusion that the NATO war strategy for defending Europe was doomed to fail.

Absent the Arab-Israeli War, and absent seeing the Warsaw Pact plans, it is not clear that this challenge would have been identified. After all, we had troops and equipment in Europe, and we had nuclear deterrence. But what if the Warsaw Pact could push NATO off the Continent without going nuclear . . . ?

National planning is especially hard because every agency has reasons it needs more resources. And, military planning is especially hard. As one colonel told me in 2000:

> Planning for the new century is very difficult. We have a reasonable handle on the evolution of weapon systems, but not on politics or even tactics. We have no idea where or when the president will ask us to go or what we will have to do. Maybe invade Greenland or defend Japan or save the penguins in Antarctica. How do you plan when you don't really know what you will have to do?

Pointedly, this colonel didn't mention invading Afghanistan.

Thus, even when this kind of competitive gap arises, not everyone notices it or raises it to critical importance. Many saw it as essentially unsolvable unless vast new sums were spent on new kinds of equipment. With Washington fixated on Watergate, top level leadership ignored the issue.

As happens in some organizations, some managers below the very top ranks begin to work independently on solutions to the challenge. They have different frames or different points of view. In this case, General William DePuy, then commander of the new US Army Training and Doctrine Command (TRADOC), believed that the competitive gap could be closed with revised battle tactics and much-improved training. He held that the United States would always be at a material disadvantage in Europe with respect to the Warsaw Pact. But he took heart from the Israeli win in 1973 where an outnumbered military outfought the other side. From that he diagnosed the crux of the challenge as being tactical—called "doctrine" in the military. His strategy for dealing with the defense of Europe was to change and modernize the US concept of how to actually fight—how to use existing resources to best effect.

DePuy had fought in World War II as operations staff (S-3) in the Ninetieth Infantry, serving in Normandy, France, and crossing the Siegfried line. He recalled that he learned a great deal from German infantry's tactics:

> We just had one line. The Germans had a little zone defense so that they had elasticity and resilience. You could not punch through it very easily. They didn't do things in a linear way. They took pieces of terrain and knit them together into a position from which they were able to fire in all sorts of directions. They used the terrain, they used cover and concealment, and they used imagination. In Normandy our people always lined right up on one hedgerow and then down another hedgerow. You know, one line. And, if you observe many units in the American Army today [1979], you will find that that still is exactly what we do.[11]

Later, in Vietnam, he commanded the First Infantry Division. There he also spent time on improving the direct fighting and concealment tactics of squads, platoons, and companies.

At TRADOC, DePuy developed a concept called "Active Defense." This was defense within a region by continuing tactical movement, exploiting the mobility of tanks, mechanized infantry, and close air support. DePuy emphasized that the United States had, historically, been unprepared in its first battles and that it could not afford to slowly learn how to deal with a sudden high-intensity attack in Europe. The most important action taken to implement these new ideas was establishing the Fort Irwin National Training Center in the California desert. Fort Irwin became a "Top Gun" center for the hands-on training of infantry and armor leadership in hard-hitting fluid tactics.

Committing the Active Defense concept to training manuals invited a vigorous debate within the military that expanded from tactics to strategy. Many voices felt that the concept was insufficiently aggressive. General Alexander Haig wrote that he "would personally like to see . . . a more explicit reminder that in general, the ultimate purpose of any defense is to regain the initiative by taking the offensive."[12]

Under the leadership of Lieutenant General Donn Starry, who had served with DePuy, a new doctrine was devised. First named "deep battle," it reached its full expression in the 1986 edition of the field manual of operations (FM 100-5). Renamed "AirLand Battle," the new doctrine expanded beyond DePuy's armor-centric view to one encompassing tight coordination between the army and the air force.

AirLand Battle aimed to leverage NATO superiority in communications, sensing, command and control, and operational flexibility, especially with regard to the fighter pilot–generals leading the air force. The key operational concept was responding to an attack very aggressively by counters deep into enemy territory. The old concept of using airpower and long-range artillery to "interdict" the enemy gave way to the idea of using these long-range strikes to confuse and disorient the enemy and then to actually shape his movements, channeling him into desired directions and even traps. The objective became one of winning rather than just defending. War gaming showed the new doctrine would work (with perhaps a 30 percent loss in NATO forces). Luckily, these scenarios never had to be put to the test.

The saga of AirLand Battle illustrates how a clear diagnosis of the challenge can be a strong lever for creating a new and better way to compete. It also shows the value of open debate among leaders on the shape of the solution. Finally, it shows the power of innovation in mind-set and practices. An organization cannot execute a brave new strategy if its people don't have the skills and mind-set to actually carry out the needed operations. The DePuy revolution in the US military doctrine of "how to fight" has business parallels in Lou Gerstner's campaign at IBM to move it from a machine-centered to a customer-centered doctrine and in Jack Welch's insistence on "speed, simplicity, and self-confidence," backed up by a strong GE training program at Crotonville. Less pleasantly, it also illustrates how much time it takes to make this kind of change in a complex organization.

9

Diagnose via Comparison and Frameworks

Measurement is always a comparison. We measure the distance to the moon by a comparison to the standard meter or to the Greek standard foot. We measure profit in comparison to last year or to revenue (net margin) and so on. In making such comparisons, the internal life and breath of most businesses is crowded with accounting statements, so that is where most diagnosis starts. Are sales growing faster or slower than last year? Are margins stable, shrinking, or rising? Then the subtler questions arise. Why are margins shrinking? Why are expenses rising? Why are we losing market share?

More interesting comparisons arise when activities or results are compared to those of competitors or a whole industry or those obtained in other societies. Reaching further afield for comparisons can strain the analogy but can sometimes lend unexpected insight.

LIGHT RAIL

In a reportorial coup, Brian Rosenthal, a *New York Times* reporter, published an article in 2017 titled "The Most Expensive Mile of Subway Track on Earth." The project he studied was the East Side Access tunnel, built to link Grand Central Terminal on East Forty-Second Street and Madison Avenue with Penn Station located on West Thirty-Third Street and Seventh Avenue. The objective was to create seamless access between New York's two major commuting lines, Metro North and the Long Island Railroad. The question was why costs had ballooned to $12 billion, or $3.5 billion for each mile of track, *seven times the world average* for subway tunnel track. Rosenthal wrote:

> For years, The Times found, public officials have stood by as a small group of politically connected labor unions, construction companies and consulting firms have amassed large profits.
>
> Trade unions, which have closely aligned themselves with Gov. Andrew M. Cuomo and other politicians, have secured deals requiring underground construction work to be staffed by as many as *four times more laborers* than elsewhere in the world. . . . Even though the M.T.A. is paying for its capital construction with taxpayer dollars, the government does not get a seat at the table when labor conditions are determined. . . . [The] construction companies meet with each trade union every three years to hammer out the labor deals. The resulting agreements apply to all companies, preventing contractors from lowering their bids by proposing less generous wages or work rules.
>
> Across the Atlantic Ocean, Paris is working on a project that brings the inefficiency of New York into stark relief. . . . while the Second Avenue Subway cost $2.5 billion a mile, the [Paris] *Line 14 extension is on track to cost $450 million a mile.*[1]

We all have heard hints about corrupt spending in our cities, our states, and at the national level. But to have a subway cost seven times as much as a similar project in other nations? The international comparison is biting. If New York City had more normal construction costs, it could spend less or do considerably more than invest in the political loyalty of a particular union.

Additional research by transit expert Aron Levy has shown that most US rail construction costs are inflated when compared to those in other industrial countries. In a 2011 study he provided the specific comparisons shown in Figure 12.

FIGURE 12. Aron Levy Data on US Light-Rail Construction Costs

Project	Cost per km in $ millions	Length in km
New York City East Side access	4,000	2
New York City Second Ave. Subway, phase 1	1,700	3
London Crossrail	1,000	22
London Jubilee Line Extension	450	16
Amsterdam North–South Line	410	9.5
Berlin U55	250	1.8
Paris Metro Line 14	230	9
Naples Metro Line 6	130	5

Source: Aron Levy, "U.S. Rail Construction Costs," *Pedestrian Observations* (blog), pedestrianobservations.com, May 16, 2011.

As in New York, there are unions in Paris. The difference lies in the rules and in who sets the rules about how many workers do a task. There are strong design review committees in Paris. Most US contracts go to the low bidder, who then renegotiates "change orders." To better understand the sources of these differences in practice and cost, one would have to dig deeper into this hard-to-collect data. The truth, right now, is that we don't really know the whole picture. But the international comparison brings to light issues that do not appear when we look only at local costs or costs versus budget. If you want to fix this, you have to know the contours of the problem. And, of course, you have to have enough executive power to do something about it.

In a similar vein, we do not really understand why national health care costs in the United States are double that of France while achieving worse average outcomes, or why our secondary school test results fall below those of many other developed countries. The standard know-nothing political response to these issues is "spend more." The next time you hear a politician calling for massive "infrastructure spending," remember Figure 12. Injecting more money into an inefficient system is just feeding the bloat. Fix it *before* you grow it.

REANALYSIS

Looking at existing data in new ways can reveal problems or opportunities. For example, most business firms have a cost accounting system that classifies products by type and has some way of assigning direct labor, raw materials, and factory-overhead costs to each class. Changing the logic of the classes can yield new insights. That was the case with 'DelPiro,' a Brazilian window manufacturer—systems of casement windows and external metal shutters—for upscale homes and condominiums. Unlike casements made by US companies, DelPiro's opened inward so that even with the outer shutters closed, air could come in through the open casements. The company produced smaller windows and shutters for inventory but only made the larger units to order. DelPiro's surface issue was declining profit margins. The deeper problems were that management did not have a clear view of the differences in profitability across its product line.

DelPiro's accounting tracked labor hours and direct materials costs for casements and for shutters. We reanalyzed their manufacturing activity, first placing the products into six different groups by size. After much work with the internal data, watching workers assemble windows and shutters, and initiating new record keeping over a month, we had data on labor hours and materials cost by size. Costs are tricky things. There is no such thing as "the" cost of making a casement window. There is the cost of making one more, the cost of a batch, the cost of processing an order for the window, the cost of setting up the work area for a batch, and so on. In this case, the accounting system had generated "cost" per unit produced by allocating everything to each hour of labor. To better understand the situation, we concentrated on understanding the costs of a batch. We analyzed the shop time taken to set up equipment versus actual assembly and finishing and looked at the costs of processing an order.

The results were eye-opening. The largest size windows had very high setup costs but were still much more profitable than management had thought. Seeing the high cost of setting up to make a batch of the larger windows, the company began to offer discounts for larger orders of the biggest windows. Moreover, the medium-size shutters were quite profitable. Given this new insight from the study, DelPiro began to push the marketing of these shutters, with newly designed mountings to fit over competitors' windows. This new push was a good success. Technically, the exercise at DelPiro was one of identifying "cost drivers," but the real spice was combining that with a segmentation based on size.

Strategy is often seen as product-market positioning and expansions into new realms. But these kinds of decisions ring hollow if the underlying systems and work practices of the organization are weak. Refurbishing battle tactics turned out to be strategic in the case of the AirLand Battle story recounted earlier. And for DelPiro, the cost project was the first step in building the muscle necessary for supporting more volume and subsequent moves into similar building products.

SoPretty

A reanalysis of data can, in some situations, turn an existing diagnosis on its head. 'Courtney' was the general manager of 'SoPretty,' a retail chain of thirty-eight stores that was a division of a larger corporation with activities in apparel, cosmetics, and accessories. The SoPretty shops had been started eight years before and expanded through the acquisition of another similar chain of stores. Courtney's background had been fashion, and she had successfully created a special aura around the SoPretty stores and their merchandise. One significant problem she faced in planning the chain's expansion was choosing store sizes.

The SoPretty shops varied in area from a tiny five hundred square feet to the largest at seven thousand square feet, with the average being four thousand square feet. Courtney focused on store profit by measuring profit before tax (PBT), which averaged $1.5 million for each store, varying from a high of $5 million to a loss of $1 million.

Courtney's staff had constructed the PBT measure to include rental expense that burdened larger stores with more expenses. Nevertheless, staff analysis showed that larger stores were distinctly more profitable. Accordingly, the staff made three recommendations:

1. Two smaller stores should be expanded into newly available space next door.
2. The space obtained for the next shop should be about six thousand square feet.
3. "Skill transfer" work—begin on moving know-how from the profitable to the unprofitable stores.

Trying to help Courtney, we looked at this data and expanded the analysis to include the population of the metro area, the median age and income in the area, and the number of competing stores within a few miles. It turned out that the number of competing women's apparel shops within a one-kilometer radius was by far the most important determinant of PBT. Surprisingly, the poorest-performing SoPretty shops had only zero or one competitor nearby. The shops with more competitors did better! Some further analysis and thinking showed why—more competitors signaled a shopping "district," with more foot traffic, since interested shoppers liked to visit several stores before deciding on a purchase.

We divided the stores into three groups corresponding to low-, medium-, and high-traffic locations. Courtney's analysts took as evidence that the larger shops were more profitable, but this original diagnosis that shop size was a key driver of profit was incorrect. Reanalysis of the company's data showed that the amount of traffic was a key driver. Yes, higher-traffic areas tended to have larger stores, but within high-traffic areas, being larger hurt rather than helped. This beginning insight was not a complete diagnosis, but it kept the effort from getting off on the wrong foot.

The MultiPlant Company

I worked with the 'MultiPlant' company on overall strategy. It operated sixty-three production facilities around the world, each making a variety of consumer food products. The company used so many facilities because the weight of the finished products (in bottles) made shipping expensive. The company was organized into marketing and production divisions, with each having geographic subdivisions.

Although MultiPlant faced a number of complex challenges, senior management was united in their belief that costs were much too high in some of the plants. The company had invested in an expensive SAP software suite that kept track of expenses and productivity at each facility. The lowest-cost plant produced a carton of product for $6.57, whereas the highest-cost plant produced a similar carton for $11.60. Detailed data showed the ages of equipment, the productivity of each line, the wages paid and employee turnover, and the costs of raw materials, energy, taxes, and packaging. The highest-cost facility was in Australia, and the lowest cost was in eastern Europe. Work was being done on cost drivers such as higher wages in Australia and the varied energy and raw material costs in facilities around the world.

To address the cost issue, the company had retained a consultant on transferring best practices from the low-cost facilities to the higher-cost plants. Process engineers from each geography had gathered to discuss what might be done. The top staff in the production division were poring over data on productivity differences. The analysis of scale showed no useful relationship between plant output and unit cost.

The MultiPlant head of strategy thought it might be a good idea to calculate the amount of gross profit lost from the operation of some of the high-cost facilities. Data on prices was held by the marketing department on Excel spreadsheets, separate from the SAP cost and operations information. Profit data was not calculated at the facility level but on broad geographies.

Bringing the price and cost data together, the result was surprising. There was *no relationship* between facility unit cost and gross margin per unit. The spread of profit rates among high-cost plants was just the same as for low-cost plants. This finding flew in the face of the widespread belief that the high-cost facilities were dragging down overall corporate results.

At first, senior executives did not really believe this result. They had made a significant investment in the idea that high-cost facilities could be somehow brought into line. The reanalysis triggered a special session on cost, profit, and strategy.

Gradually, an explanation emerged. The low-cost facilities tended to be in regions where retail prices were also lower. The high-profit facilities were located in areas with less competition from similar products. In explaining the spread of gross profit results, selling commissions were playing a role as were payoffs and side deals between local managers and customers.

MultiPlant had developed an erroneous belief about facility costs. It was supported by the organization's split between production and marketing as well as the SAP accounting system's single focus on costs rather than prices. That belief led them to confront the wrong challenges, seeking a crux in the wrong places. A reanalysis was triggered by an almost accidental request for a different look at the issues.

It is not easy to set aside long-held views about the nature of a challenge. But this group did so and refocused their diagnosis on a wholly different set of issues, ones that led them to higher performance over the next three years.

MAERSK LINE

In the early 2000s, Maersk Line (made famous by the film *Captain Phillips* starring Tom Hanks) was the largest container shipping company in the world and aggressively added new capacity, bringing ever-larger ships to market. It put the industry's first E-class ship to sail, carrying a record 14,700 TEU (twenty-foot equivalent unit). A few years later, it ordered twenty larger E-class ships with capacities of 18,270 TEU. A subsidiary of Danish Maersk Group, by 2015 Maersk Line operated about seven hundred ships serving more than one hundred countries.

Despite its size and market share, Maersk's profits were low compared to the enormous amount of capital invested in ships and offices. Looking at competitors, most also seemed to be in the same position. Despite the rapidly growing flow of containerized goods from China, the industry as a whole seemed profitless. Seeking the economies of scale from larger vessels, each company would buy new ones, adding to the overcapacity in the industry. And with too much capacity, vicious price cutting ensued. In many ways, the container shipping industry was an exemplar of the economist's "perfect" competition. Prices often dipped below the cash cost of operating a ship, yet the EU antitrust authorities were constantly threatening suit over price-fixing. Maersk was in a tough place with no easy answers.

The international airline industry had also faced profitless conditions. One step toward a solution was to have the United States and the EU agree to code-sharing alliances. For example, both American Airlines and British Airways belong to the Oneworld Alliance. This allowed American to sell a through ticket from Portland to Chicago with the Chicago to London flight on British Airways that cocarried (code-shared) an AA flight number. This also helped blunt the incentive for each airline to expand into the other's turf.

Working on the analogy to the airline industry, Maersk led an industry movement to form shipping alliances, gaining an antitrust exemption from the EU (renewed in 2020 for another four years). One of the main objectives of the new shipping alliances was to dull the incentive for new capacity additions by having alliance partners fill in when another partner did not have the immediate capacity to fill demand on a particular route. By 2017 there were three large shipping alliances, with Maersk Line and Swiss-Italian MSC belonging to the biggest, "2M."

Despite this maneuvering, by the end of 2019 it was clear that these attempts at coordination, some major mergers, and increased concentration among the eight major shippers, including Maersk, were not working. The container shippers were not breaking even. Capacity continued to grow faster than demand. The industry was projected to lose $10 billion in 2020.

The analogy between container shipping and the airlines was weak. To see why, notice how airline traffic has evolved. Under the old hub-and-spokes model, giant jumbo jets would connect key cities, while smaller jets would handle the regional traffic. But as passengers consider their costs of layovers, dealing with security at the large airports, and long walks from one airline to another, the industry has moved to point-to-point traffic using medium-size single-aisle jets. An airline cannot gain the economies of larger aircraft unless it can fill them up, which is one reason Airbus announced that it would quit production of its giant A380 jumbo jet.

In container shipping, by contrast, there remain sharp cost economies in ever-larger ships that constantly tempt companies into commissioning ever-larger vessels. This keeps adding undifferentiated capacity to the industry, making for fierce price competition.

In 2019, group CEO Soren Skou announced that Maersk's way forward was to use global scale and digital technology to integrate shipping with land-based operations like freight forwarding. "All the relevant participants in transportation can [digitally] track containers, and that wasn't possible 10–15 years ago," he was quoted as saying.[2] In other words, the new analogy was FedEx.

My own view is that the crux of the shipping-cost issue is land transport. Civilizations have grown around rivers, lakes, and inland seas because of the much lower cost of water-based transport. The highest costs in transport are moving products from key ports out over land to where people live and work. Companies like Amazon have made strides in optimizing these systems. Can Maersk carve out a position by integrating sea-based transport with land systems? Perhaps. My personal judgment is that such a breakthrough awaits a technology that breaks the key-port bottleneck and allows landing cargo at smaller sites.

INDUSTRY ANALYSIS

The case of Maersk fits nicely into one of the most popular tools for business analysis—Michael Porter's "Five Forces" industry-analysis framework. This framework is based on the economic theory of "industrial organization," or IO, which attempts to explain why some *industries* generate more profits than others.

Each of the five forces—the strength of competition, the ease of new entrants appearing, the bargaining power of suppliers, the bargaining power of customers, and the threat of substitute products—is a threat to an industry's profitability.

When employing the framework, you look in fair detail at each of these forces. Just looking at these facts about an industry can often help insight. But remember that the underlying model is about *industry performance*, not individual company performance. If the profit rates of firms within an industry are spread out over a wide spectrum, with some high and others low, then the five-forces framework is inappropriate. It is not that the model is wrong. It is a model of an industry of roughly similar firms. If your company is in an industry where almost all competitors are similar and are struggling with low profits and, especially, price cutting, then the five-forces framework is the right tool of analysis.

One issue with the framework is that most real industries contain firms with markedly different profit rates. Thus, the concept of "industry profitability" may have no meaning. In a careful analysis of Federal Trade Commission profitability data, I statistically estimated the relative importance of industry, corporation, and individual line-of-business effects on profitability.[3] Of all the variation (variance) in business-line profitability, only 4 percent could be attributed to stable industry effects. By contrast, 44 percent was due to stable business-to-business difference in performance. The locus of most profit performance differences is the line of business, not the industry or the corporation.

10

Use Sharp Analytical Tools with Care

There are a wide variety of tools available for help in analyzing business situations. Each tool gains its power by making assumptions and narrowing attention to just a few factors, or even just one, in a situation. The assumptions that give the tool its power may or may not be valid in a particular case. As you try to diagnose a complex situation, a sharp tool may help, or it may lead you astray to a misdiagnosis of the crux. These tools are double-edged—use with care.

The tools elaborated by top consulting firms are primarily focused on the diagnosis of competitive situations. They work by imposing a framework, gathering data, and then applying a frame of analysis or comparison to expose problems or missed opportunities. In this chapter I will treat a few common frameworks or tools used in analysis or diagnosis. In each case I will provide a heads-up about what can go wrong.

CAPITAL BUDGETING

It seems sensible, at first glance, to evaluate a proposed project or action by weighing its benefits against its costs. Capital budgeting is the financial tool recommended for making decisions on whether a large investment is worthwhile. The idea is simple: Calculate the pattern of future (estimated) cash flows. Then determine its present value—the current amount of cash that would be equivalent to those cash flows spread out over time. Accept the proposed project if the present value is positive. (More advanced methods begin to consider the riskiness of the future cash flows. And still more advanced subtleties are available.)

The puzzling thing about this lovely theory is that only a few companies do it this way. Most companies simply let managers shape a project and its expectations over time in discussions with more senior managers. The key issues discussed are not present values but competition, growth prospects, and judgments about timing and internal competence.

One reason for this enormous gap between theory and practice is that the risks considered in the theory are uncertainties about the levels of future cash flows due to economic, competitive, and project-related risks. But in the real world, the largest risk in long-term investments is that the people proposing the investment are incompetent or lying. One glaring example was 'Project T,' planned within one of the one hundred largest US corporations. The company's main business was mature and in decline, and Project T promised a youthful replacement, one that would restore the company's profits and prestige. Project T was big and was being managed directly by the senior vice president for new products, 'Bradley.' A fast-tracked forty-year-old manager, Bradley was smart and ambitious. As far as I could tell, he had an almost unlimited budget to spend on Project T.

My initial work with the company was on a smaller project, but I had wanted to get more involved in Project T, and, as it moved to a final decision, Bradley began to use me as a sounding board for his presentations.

The keystone of Project T had been a complex public test, enrolling hundreds of households in a trial rollout of the new technology. As I learned more and more of the details, I began to doubt. The market test results were odd. The data seemed to indicate that people didn't like the product very much. In the abstract, consumers expressed interest in the product. But in the test market, the estimate of participants' willingness to pay for the service was negative. That is, these people would pay a premium to cancel the service and get the product out of their homes.

Bradley's approach to this was to argue that willingness to pay would improve when ancillary services were provided and that the measured lack of price sensitivity would mean high future profits. Then there was the issue of competition. None of the ideas being deployed in Project T were proprietary, and most had actually come from outside firms. The financial projections were based on capturing most of the market and experiencing only price pressure from substitute products, not direct competitors. Was that reasonable?

It was a week before the presentation to a special committee of the board. Working late, Bradley, his closest assistant, and I were going over the slides and handout booklet. It was printed on vellum with a gray spiral binding and a dark-green cover. There were none of the technology analyses. The book showed pictures of the technology in use and estimates of the market-size potential. Cash flows were estimated and the net present value calculated—it was a positive $6 billion using a 10 percent discount rate and fifteen-year cutoff. Consultants had also calculated the risk-adjusted value of the project and even considered some real-options analysis. But Bradley was staring at the page he believed would get the most attention from the board committee.

The board, he argued, would focus on the projection of cumulative cash flow over time. As shown in Figure 13, cumulative cash flow showed a drop to about negative $2.5 billion as investments were made. Then, as profits accumulated over the future years, it climbed up, crossing the zero axis in the seventh year. Bradley said that the board committee would only look at payback—how soon the company would recoup its investment. And looking at the seven-year-plus crossing—over seven years to payback—Bradley was worried.

As we sat there at ten in the evening, Bradley took a pair of scissors and cut the payback line out of the page. He worked with scissors and some transparent tape and pasted a revised payback curve back on the page. The chart now showed a payback in five years.

FIGURE 13. Project T Projected Cumulative Cash Flow

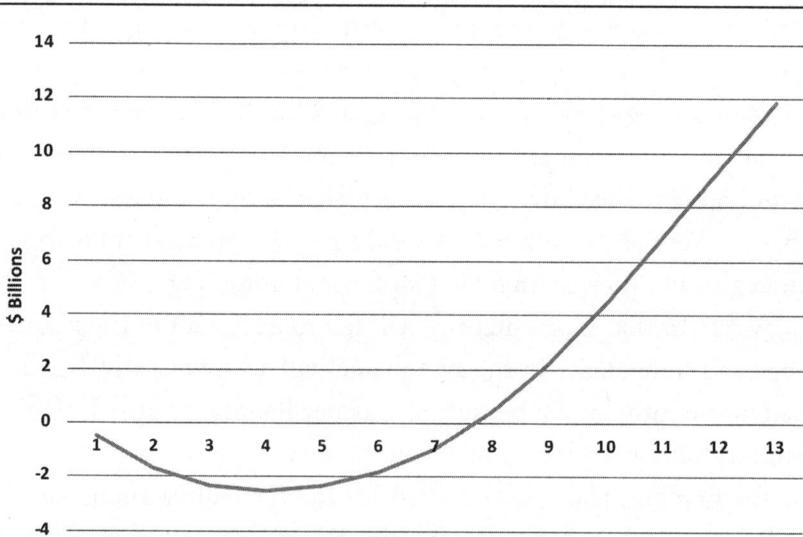

"Have this chart redrawn like this, and send the revision to the printer," he told his assistant and began to put on his jacket.

"Bradley," I said, "you have just tossed out $40 million in analytical consulting and test-market studies. What was the sense of all that if you are going to toss it out?"

"Professor Rumelt," Bradley said, "you do not understand strategic planning. Strategic planning is a battle for corporate resources. It is a battle I intend to win."

Despite Bradley's resolve, Project T never went forward. The board decided that the project was too risky, and, as Bradley had worried, they wanted an even faster kick. The next year, the company sold off two divisions and did a major acquisition. Bradley moved on to another senior position in another global firm.

The problem Bradley presents occurs whenever knowledge, resources, and decision rights are not colocated in the same individual. Once you have to ask someone else how to allocate your resources, there is a potential problem. And when you have to ask someone else to advise you on allocating a third person's resources, things get even stickier. Consequently, the quality of strategy work is limited by the amount of honesty and integrity in the system. Unlike Project T, the best strategy work is rarely delegated but is done by the senior executive, or a small group of very senior executives, in discussion with highly trusted advisers. In this case, the company was so large that the very senior executives would not comprehend the various strategies and projects that vied for favor and funding.

A system that lacks integrity will fail to utilize all of the knowledge and competence in the system and will act myopically. Bradley had an incentive to lie because it was not his money at risk. If the project did not work out, he would be first to know, and he would be the first out, blaming those left behind for fouling things up. If it did work out, he had much to gain. Winning such a commitment of corporate resources would be a feather in his cap and almost certainly lead to more power and pay within the company or elsewhere.[1]

Although the board committee members were not knowledgeable about the technology involved, they were not stupid. They were aware of the existence of behavior like Bradley's, and they knew that misrepresentations are most likely to be about the more distant future. They would, consequently, discount promises about more distant profits, forcing the company to behave myopically. Insisting on a four-year payback was, perhaps, a sensible response to a system that has actors like Bradley making proposals to a distant uninformed committee.

The board committee would know that the most likely way to misrepresent things would be buried in the more complex and sophisticated analyses. The cash flows Bradley forecast were the product of complex economic models containing hundreds of assumptions about consumer behavior, competition, future prices, and costs. Consequently, the board committee would tend to discount the results from these kinds of sophisticated analyses and overweight their own intuition. Their own judgments would be based on less information, but might also be less biased. Thus, a second form of myopia was created—an unwillingness to employ outside data and reasoning.

This kind of situation is called an "agency" problem, and a great deal of (mostly wasted) intellectual energy has been expended in trying to figure out how to produce good decisions in such messy situations. In the case of Bradley, there is no neat answer without some system of ex-post settling up—some way of holding him accountable for the outcome of the decision after six or ten years have passed. But any such system is incompatible with dynamic organizations and fast-track executive careers. In a few years, Bradley will have been promoted or moved on to another company, the project may have been reorganized, and subsequent decisions by other managers will blur the connections between outcomes and the original decision.

Thus, the formal theory of how to evaluate the financial returns from long-term projects is largely ignored by corporations. Instead of discounting at the "cost of capital," they look for rapid payback or use very high discount rates applied over short-term horizons. It is not that they are too ignorant to use the elegant theory developed by financial economists. It is that the theory ignores their real concerns with incompetence, lying, and deceit. And, of course, it ignores the tie-ins between their own bonuses and short-term corporate results.

TRANSCENDING ANALYSIS

Bradley's ultimate problem was that the people making the final decision about Project T did not trust his judgment and did not trust the inputs to his analysis. One method to cope with Bradley-type executives has been to transcend technical analysis by changing the language and rules of the game. An example of this was the development of the BCG growth-share matrix. With its vividly named quadrants of Dogs, Cows, Stars, and Question Marks, the tool had an oversize influence on thinking about corporate strategy in the 1970s and early 1980s. Today it still pops up from time to time.

The BCG matrix was largely the brainchild of BCG consultant Alan Zakon and arose out of a consulting project with Mead Corporation. The matrix placed each business in one of four quadrants depending on growth rates and the direction of cash flow. The axes, labeled market growth and market share, were created later for another client.

In the mid-1980s I had a chance to talk with William Wommack, who had initiated the project with BCG. He was just stepping down from the board of Mead Corporation. I asked Wommack about the challenge at Mead leading up to this way of thinking. He explained that Mead had diversified a bit into new businesses but that it had been still, basically, a forest-products company. He explained that the company had used a very sophisticated capital budgeting system. "The timber-mill people would come in with stochastic stoichiometric analyses about why we needed a plant expansion or a new facility," he said. Then the pulping and paper-mill people would produce equally sophisticated analyses explaining why they had to expand as well. "But," he complained, "these businesses never made any money! We just kept pouring in capital." Wommack indicated that he wanted a way to shift investment to newer, less capital-hungry, growing businesses. So they changed the language. The forest-based business "became a cash source whose role was to generate cash. Period." The cash would be invested elsewhere.[2]

The BCG matrix changed the framework for Mead and for other firms. The original framework was capital budgeting—a good finance committee accepts projects that pass the hurdle rate or that promise positive net present values. The revised framework transcended financial analysis through the image of portfolio balance—the role of some businesses is to generate cash, and others get to absorb cash. Each framework pulls attention to some aspects of the situation rather than others, and each alters the balance of power within the organization. Technical capital budgeting lends power to people who are skilled in finance and calculation. Portfolio balance frameworks redeploy power back to the top where they have the ability to label you a "dog."

Jack Welch used the same method when he became CEO of General Electric in 1980. Looking across GE's more than four hundred business units, he announced that each business should be "No. 1 or No. 2 in your industry." Otherwise, "Fix it, sell it, or close it."

Inheriting a complex multilayered "strategic planning" system, he transcended its intricate logic and began to dump businesses that did not lead in their markets.

A two-edged blade, the BCG matrix and Welch's number 1 or 2 system have been used by companies without acknowledging the underlying rationale—transcending capital budgeting systems. Being clearheaded means understanding the analogy or framework you employ.

DISRUPTION

The theory of "disruption" is a more recent commonly used strategy concept. Like the old BCG matrix, its careless use can create more fog than clarity. With overuse, the term *disruption* has come to mean almost anything that upsets an existing business or state of affairs. The idea, however, had a more precise meaning when it was first deployed by Harvard professors Clayton Christensen and Joseph Bower. Their focus was on the many leading companies failing to "stay on top" when competitors employed new technologies: "Goodyear and Firestone entered the radial-tire market quite late. Xerox let Canon create the small-copier market. Bucyrus-Erie allowed Caterpillar and Deere to take over the mechanical excavator market. Sears gave way to Wal-Mart."[3]

Why weren't previously successful companies responding effectively to these threats? Christensen and Bower's explanation was that leading companies were too focused on their existing customers, especially their largest and most demanding customers. Following these customers' desires for ever-larger, more powerful, or faster versions of products, companies lost sight of less effective but cheaper technologies. In the classic version of disruption, a maker of hard disk drives for desktop PCs had customers who wanted faster and faster drives with ever more capacity, so it would tend to ignore the new smaller two-and-a-half-inch hard drives. The existing customers weren't interested in them. But as the smaller drives became more capable, they went into laptops and actually became more cost effective than your traditional larger desktop drives. In this story, the company is "disrupted from below."

Clayton Christensen's vivid descriptions of disruption from below in the hard-disk industry, the excavator market, and steel mini mills terrified a generation of executives. Executives worried that they were too focused on their successful products and their best customers. Should they respond to every competitive product that was not as good as theirs? How helpful is this framework in understanding the dynamics of competition?

The Christensen theory had disruption coming from a low-price, less capable product. But there were glaring examples of the opposite. The iPhone was high priced, yet was clearly disruptive to RIM's BlackBerry and Nokia's phones.

BlackBerry (Research in Motion [RIM]) was specialized around the enterprise, both businesses and government agencies. In 2003 it received certification for a private high-security network for government customers. Its email network pushed past congested public data networks and saved customers the then costly data charges for data on telco networks. The handsets were controllable by corporate IT departments, who could remotely wipe them clean if lost or stolen.

Corporations and agencies loved to control the BlackBerry ecosystem. BlackBerry Enterprise server push-email would cost about $37,000 for five hundred users, whereas a comparable Microsoft system would cost $107,000. And BlackBerry's private email servers offered two strong encryption standards. In 2008, one year after the iPhone appeared, Morgan Stanley opined that RIM "had the best secular growth story on telecom equipment." Consultants urged BlackBerry to continue concentrating on the enterprise market where it had a lock rather than the hypercompetitive consumer phone business.

Users liked the fact that companies paid for everything—the handset was simply given to employees. In early 2010, Morgan Keegan & Co. opined that BlackBerry was doing, and would do, better with price-sensitive and message-centric business customers.

What directly destroyed BlackBerry was that during 2010, companies quickly, and surprisingly, began to adopt the "bring-your-own-phone" approach. Email was getting cheap, and people were bringing their own personal smartphones to work anyway. With iPhones and Androids appearing everywhere, security was lost. The rapid disappearance of the enterprise market killed BlackBerry. More precisely, it was the enterprise model of control over employees' phones that fractured, and BlackBerry along with it.

The BlackBerry example shows that there are more ways to be attacked than from below—a business can be attacked with better, more expensive products as well. A number of people have studied whether there really is a significant amount of disruption "from below."

- Historian Jill Lepore in a *New Yorker* article looked again at the hard-disk-drive industry. She found that, over two decades, "victory in the disk-drive industry appears to have gone to the manufacturers that were good at incremental improvements, whether or not they were the first to market the disruptive new format."[4]
- Researchers Sood and Tellis looked at the rise of thirty-six new technologies from 1879 through 2000. Their detailed economic analysis did not find a strong pattern of low-price, low-performance disruption.
- Mitsuru Igami reexamined Christensen's original hard-disk industry data set. He found that incumbents had cost advantages but delayed response to new entrants because of an "unwillingness to destroy old sources of profits."[5]
- Josh Lerner also reanalyzed the hard-disk-drive industry and found that it was the followers who made the most innovations over time.[6]

In sum, follow-on research has not supported the Christensen story of companies being too focused on main customers and missing the rise of low-performance, low-price disruptors. Since we do see powerful firms occasionally pushed aside by smaller rivals or newcomers, or new technology, what is happening? Some insight can be gained by looking at a few dramatic examples of real disruption.

The decline of Kodak is often used as a warning about the fate of those who ignore the warning signals of disruptive forces. But there was no low-cost, low-performance "product" disrupting it. What would you have done had you owned Kodak? It made 70 percent gross margins on a large, slowly declining film business. It wisely sold off its intellectual property in chemicals and actually built a digital camera nearly fifty years ago, in 1975. Its executives knew digital was coming, but they imagined a world where digital photos would be printed and put in albums or hung proudly on the wall. So they invested in digital photo storage and fine printing. In 2000 could you or they foresee people sharing low-resolution selfies on their small screen phones? If you were to invest millions or billions in digital, in what device or system or product? Cameras? Printers? CDs? Personal computers? Screens? Photo-processing software? Phones? Kodak was disrupted, but not by a competitor. It was disrupted by an entire ecosystem.

Kodak's demise is also mirrored in the downfall of the *Encyclopedia Britannica*, done in by computers and the Web. For several generations, the *Encyclopedia Britannica* was sold, often door-to-door, to parents as an investment in the education of their children. The price was thousands of dollars and normally included a handsome bookcase to house the thirty-two volumes. In print for more than two hundred years, it was written by more than four thousand separate contributors and edited by a staff of about a hundred.

It offered a CD-ROM version, but sales did not compensate for the loss of hard-bound book placements. It tried an online subscription version, with little uptake at its prices. It wasn't Wikipedia, or Encarta, or Scholarpedia, or Digital Universe, or tablets, or phones that "disrupted" *Britannica*. It was the entire ecosystem of personal computers, phones, the Web, Google, bloggers, Google Books, and more. As with Kodak, there was no one product to counter, no clear competitor to parry, no acquisition that could save the day.

How to Deal with Disruption?

The real challenge of "disruption" is not that you don't see it coming. The real challenges are:

(A) that it costs more profit to respond than it seems to be worth
(B) that your organization lacks the necessary technical ability, financial strength, or organizational skills to respond
(C) *that it is the destruction of the whole ecosystem in which you live*

If you do not face any of these three sharp challenges, then you do not really have a disruption problem. You have a fairly standard strategy problem. For example, in 1980 the rise in oil prices had damaged Monsanto's large asset-heavy petrochemicals business. Still, it had the skill and resources to redeploy into agricultural genetics and build a profitable, growing new business that helped alleviate world hunger. This was, of course, a long-term strategy not offering the kind of stock-price pop that interests the "activist investors" of the world.

In case (A), where a new technology could hurt a current profit pool too much to warrant an immediate response, the cost and benefits of waiting should be assessed. It just might be that letting the existing business slowly decay is best. To do this gracefully, it is wise to make it part of a more diversified firm's portfolio. If one tries to run a public firm in gradual decline, Wall Street, activists of all stripes, and funds will make your life miserable. If your company is not diversified, it might be best to sell the business to a company that is.

Letting the business decline for a while, then acting later, is the other option in case (A). That is what most telephone companies did when the Internet threatened to disrupt their very profitable T-1 data lines renting to businesses for $1,500 a month. They waited, letting the DSL business mature, and then waited some more as optical fiber was installed everywhere, and then, after WorldCom went bust in 2002, they finally began to offer cheap high-speed data services.

In case (B), if you lack the technical skill to respond, the usual path is to acquire a company that does have the skill. This is by far the standard reaction to technically disjunctive disruption. Many of the "poster-child" stories of disruptive collapse occurred because there was no one to buy. There was no decent smartphone company for BlackBerry to acquire. Nor was there a facile maneuver for Kodak to either save its film business or enter the super-competitive camera and smartphone industries. In such cases, it seems best to seek out a joint-venture partner who has related skills, to sell the business to someone who is up to the task, or to run out the clock on the declining profits.

More often, a company lacks the organizational flexibility to respond, its structure long specialized around something else. Or the firm has a large sclerotic "blob" at its center that specializes in committees and PowerPoints rather than problem solving. In such cases, acquisition might be the solution, but it would normally be best to leave the acquired company apart from the central blob whose inability to be flexible was the motivation for the acquisition. There is more on this in Chapter 13's subsection "Inertia and Size."

In case (C), where the entire ecosystem collapses, there is not much you can do unless you have a crystal ball and can get out before the deluge. There is no denying that major changes in technology, tastes, and regulation can disrupt and kill off a business. There is no managerial trick to make a business immortal.

TOOLS LIKE CAPITAL budgeting, the BCG matrix, and disruption theory can be helpful in analyzing situations. And there are many more—value-chain analysis, willingness-to-pay modeling, multinomial logit models of competition, McKinsey's 7S framework, the Blue Ocean Strategy Canvas, scenario development, benchmarking, product life cycle, root-cause analysis, and more. Each narrows attention to just a few factors or issue, or even just one. And each tool is built on assumptions. Ignore those assumptions at your peril.

PART III

Through the Crux

Part I introduced the idea of challenge-based strategy and the crux. Part II described methods of diagnosing challenges, especially those arising from competition. Part III provides a focus on overcoming the crux of a challenge after it has been identified. Here we look at the sources of "edge" or advantage, issues arising when trying to innovate, and the complexities of working through a crux when it points to dysfunction in your own organization.

11

Seek an Edge

Two equally matched fighters meet in the ring. Which will prevail? In competition, we seek advantage, and it can come only from some asymmetry. Perhaps one fighter has a longer reach or more stamina. We build business or military strategies around such things, the better strategist having a keener eye as to which asymmetries can be turned to advantage.

THE FUNDAMENTALS OF ADVANTAGE

Edward Mark was a friend of a friend. At forty, his job in a lighting design boutique had ended, and he was looking for a next career. I was asked to look at his business idea. Over coffee, he handed me a short document: a business plan for an aerobics studio. Edward had noticed that aerobics studios were all the rage. With a smile, he told me that he had always wanted to live in Mammoth, California, a ski town and entryway to the high Sierra. His idea was to borrow money from his family and start an aerobics studio in Mammoth. There would be a good demand, he guessed, in such an active athletic town. And, he thought, there would be instructors available at good prices because of the many active people living there who were always on the lookout for work. His business plan projected revenues, costs, and profits for the next five years. He had no prior experience in aerobics or in service businesses.

Edward Mark's business proposal was a hypothesis—a guess about what would work. One way to test the hypothesis is to simply try it. Just as competition in the natural world eliminates poorly adapted species, the marketplace test will reveal bad business ideas and select in favor of "what works." But running to the marketplace with every new idea would be extremely costly and wasteful. As Karl Popper eloquently pointed out, it is better to let "our theories die in our stead."[1]

In business competition, one cannot *expect* to make a profit without some source of advantage. We look for advantage in four basic places: in information, knowing something that others do not; in know-how, having a skill, or patent, that others do not have; in position, having a reputation, brand, or existing market system (for example, distribution, supply chains) that others cannot readily imitate or push aside; in efficiency, whether based on scale, technology, experience, or other factor that others cannot easily attain; and in the management of systems, whether bridging complexity or moving with speed and precision, that others do not have. In each case, we look for an important asymmetry, one that can be turned to advantage, between you and competitors.

In the case of Edward Mark's proposed aerobics studio, there was no visible source of advantage. Unhappily, a neutral adviser should recommend against it. Edward did not have any special information: his view of the opportunity was garnered from public information and newspaper reports. He had no scarce resource: his skills had no connection with either aerobics or service retailing. Given the lack of special knowledge or resources, the financial projections were just wishful thinking.

This conclusion upsets some people. They say, "But it might work!" Yes, it might. Edward Mark might have hidden skills at service retailing. Or perhaps the Mammoth City Council will block additional aerobics studios a month after he opens his studio, leaving him in a protected position.

Note that advantage is about "expecting" to make a profit. A gambler might win in Las Vegas, but one cannot *expect* to win in games created by casinos. To *expect* to make a business work under competition, you need to have an advantage in knowledge or resources or both.

What kind of advice should one give to Edward Mark? More to the point, what words of counsel was he willing to hear? I softly praised his entrepreneurial élan, but not his business plan. The trick, I said, is that "you need to know something special about this business, to have an approach based on a special appreciation of the situation or on special information. To develop this appreciation, you need to decide which is the more important focus, aerobics or Mammoth. Then, immerse yourself in that subject. Learn about the people, the issues, the various approaches, the locations, the politics, and so on. Opportunity, like the devil, is in the details."

When you are looking for a source of power or leverage to punch through the crux of a challenge, it is useful to remember the basic elements of advantage. Unlike Edward Mark, most operating companies do have special information and resources. Managers in a company with any history know more about its products and its system of creation and production than anyone else. And they should know more about its customers and how they use its products and services. We start our search for performance concepts in those asymmetries—in the special know-how and knowledge acquired over time.

DON'T GO BERTRAND

It is all too easy for companies with histories of success and large pools of assets to slide into brute price competition. The outcome is never attractive.

The logic of fierce business rivalry was developed in 1883 by French mathematician Joseph L. F. Bertrand. He imagined two local springwater companies, each tapping into the volcanic rock of the Auvergne in central France (where Volvic water originates). Customers know that all the water is identical and prefer to buy at the lowest price. Each competitor, he observed, should notice that it could gain sales by a price cut. In particular, he reasoned that each water company would try to adopt a price just under that of the other firm, thereby getting all the customers. This process of action and reaction would inexorably slash prices down to cash cost, which is just about zero in the case of springwater. In Bertrand's world, what matters is the willingness of competitors to slash prices. And that, in turn, depends on the buyers' reactions to lower prices.

Bertrand competition occurs when the market responds quickly and decisively to price cuts. Competitors have plenty of capacity, prices are easily communicated to buyers, and products are standardized so that quality differences are minimal. In Bertrand competition, prices are driven all the way down to cash costs.

The only way to win in Bertrand competition is to drive out competitors and monopolize the supply of springwater or have real costs of doing business that are significantly lower than anyone else's, a very rare situation. For, example, the world of online stock brokering looks increasingly like Bertrand's world, and one cannot recommend investing in the infrastructure to support it.

Most real-world successful strategies are built on supplying better quality or performance than competitors or better than others are perceived as offering, or by specializing in a market segment where your skills match buyers' needs and tastes, or by counting on customers' lack of complete attention and lethargy. The mortgage industry, for example, is protected by homeowners' lack of instant attention to their outstanding loans and new rates. As one Goldman Sachs analyst told me, "We tried to model consumer behavior with economic concepts. It did not work. The average mortgage borrower acts as if they are asleep and only wake up every four years to glance at rates. If they were awake all the time, the business would be much less profitable."

KNOWING YOUR EDGE

In early 1982, I was invited to spend a week with Shell International's planners at Runnymede, England. During the week, Group Planning had provided a vivid and sophisticated overview of several possible futures for the international oil industry, covering political, social, and economic issues. Late in the afternoon of the fourth day, a number of executives were asked to sum up what they had heard. One reported, "We are making a great rate of return on the upstream. But we are losing money in downstream operations, especially in Europe. We are clearly better at the upstream than the downstream." (By upstream, he meant exploring for petroleum and pumping it out of the ground. By downstream, he meant refining petroleum into gasoline, diesel fuel, and other final products.)

The executive's quick summary was mistaken. Yes, Shell made more money on upstream than on downstream operations. But the difference had little to do with them being "better at" one than the other. In the upstream, OPEC had more than doubled the price of oil over five years. Anyone with preexisting oil properties was making money. On the other hand, the higher prices had cut the demand for oil in Europe by 19 percent. European refining capacity far exceeded the reduced demand. The excess capacity in refining meant that competition among refiners had pushed margins to historic lows, and refineries began to lose money at a rapid rate. It was temporarily a case of Bertrand competition. A spate of closings was in progress. Shell planned to shut a huge refinery in the Netherlands as well as one in Germany. Texaco, Gulf, and BP also announced closings and shutdowns.

If there are, in fact, reasons to invest in and operate facilities that put commodities into direct price competition with competitors, one should not be surprised at Bertrand results. It doesn't mean you are not "good at" or advantaged in the business.

As you examine a proposed solution to a crux, the solution is almost never more price competition or more investment in Bertrand markets.

CLOSE COUPLING

One of the subtlest sources of advantage is the close coupling of activities, especially a new inventive coupling. When facing a tough competitor, the crux often lies in maneuvering around the main market with a new and better appeal to a somewhat different set of customers. This new market is often reached by coupling your existing technology with something else, something the tough competitor will not immediately imitate.

Most of the time existing products and services are already composed of coupled components. At first, the new coupling is typically seen as an innovation. Afterward, it is typically taken as the natural order of things. A GE turbofan jet engine is an amazing tight combination of engineering, materials, and construction. Steve Jobs's iPhone was a close coupling of hardware and software that was deeper than had been accomplished elsewhere. Amazon's distinctive competence remains the unusually close coupling between an online shopping experience and extremely efficient warehousing and logistics. No one else seems to have come close to this tight fit between different skill sets. These familiar couplings remain hard to duplicate and are the basis of continuing advantages.

To create advantage, one has to bring together and couple skills and ideas that have not yet been combined. That normally means combining or bringing together activities that have different knowledge or experience bases. Can you combine the ancient trade of beekeeping with modern data on crop locations, crop genetics, and weather?

In the late 1970s, Seymour Cray pushed the envelope in high-speed computing, earning the title of "father of the supercomputer." His particular skill integrated three bases of knowledge not normally coupled. He understood basic computer design, the problems of solving differential difference equations, and Maxwell's equations governing the propagation of electromagnetic signals. His machines combined very high-speed operations with vector processing capabilities to offer 40X to 400X improvements over standard IBM hardware.

For the Wright brothers, the crux of the problem was moving from gliders to powered flight. Others had gliders, and still others had gasoline engines. But no existing gasoline engine was light enough to power the Wright glider. The Wrights studied existing engines and then designed a very simple yet very lightweight four-stroke, four-cylinder, gasoline-powered engine. They built it in their Dayton bicycle shop. The first powered flight in 1903 would not have been possible without that engine. And it could not have occurred so soon without the Wrights' amazing coupling of aerodynamic intuition, lightweight airframe construction skills, and gasoline engine design and construction.

Today, one of the most ambitious strategic couplings being attempted is Santa Clara–based Nvidia's acquisition of UK-based ARM. Since I wrote about Nvidia in *Good Strategy/Bad Strategy*, the company has developed one of the world's strongest positions in the growing AI, or artificial intelligence, market. It got there because its graphics processors, while as complex as most of Intel's x86 microprocessors, work on a different principle.

A standard Intel processor is a general-purpose machine and does anything its program requests. A "core" is what used to be called a CPU or processor. Today, a modern Intel core has 200 to 500 million transistors, and the whole processor has 4 to 12 cores. In the most advanced applications, all cores can be tasked by the software at once, but if all were fully loaded at once the heat would melt the device. So careful power balancing is required. Most desktop and laptop programs get along just fine with 1 core.

By contrast, an Nvidia graphics processing unit, or GPU, has much simpler cores. Each has to do only a few simple multiplication, division, and other arithmetic operations. A GPU core has only 10 million transistors, and the most recent consumer GPU from Nvidia has 2,176 cores. It is this ability to run simple simultaneous operations that make Nvidia GPU-based chips so useful in AI pattern training. Nvidia's most recent high-end AI chip, the A100, has 54 billion transistors and 43,000 cores.

ARM is the owner of the processor architecture design that underlies most mobile devices and is beginning to invade some of Intel's cloud-processing space. ARM architectures are a bit simpler than Intel's and may use less power. ARM does not design processors per se but has a flexible set of designs and standards that enable a great deal of mix-and-match play by designers as they decide to add touch-pad interfaces or cameras to a system.

It was ARM's entire ecosystem that attracted Nvidia. Under CEO Jen-Hsun Huang, Nvidia has developed deep engineering skills at very high-speed parallel operations on its processors, high-speed memory-access architectures, and a freely available language (CUDA) that drives its cores. The crux of this strategy will be to use ARM-supported designs around Nvidia cores to serve cloud-based specialty areas like encryption, image analysis, and some type of machine learning. And what if this growing competence at tight integration of processing and memory lets it overtake the Intel architecture? Like any business strategy, it is a bet. In this case, it's one with a huge upside if it pays off.

THE BEST FRENCH restaurants are rural with reliance on fresh local produce. In the United States, this coupling is very rare. It took Alice Waters, working out of her Chez Panisse restaurant in Berkeley, to put food fresh from a local garden at the center of a new American cuisine. Waters's passion for fresh farm-to-plate dining inaugurated a revolution in thinking about good food. In 2009 she received the French Legion of Honor for her contributions.

In many consumer products, the challenge is creating models or brands with differences coupled to different customer groups. The crux of such challenges is gaining a realistic understanding of real customer behavior, wants, and needs.

The first consumer products company to take customer research seriously was Procter & Gamble. In the late 1920s the company was experimenting with "brand management." The idea was to have, for example, Camay soap differentiated from Ivory soap and have a brand manager for each. In this context, Paul Smelser, with a PhD in economics, inaugurated serious market research, making P&G a leader in understanding its customers. Smelser would prod executives with questions like "What percentage of Ivory soap is used for face and hands and what percentage for dishwashing?"[2] When no one knew, he became convinced that the company had to find out things like that.

Smelser's research department's most well-known innovation was its corps of field researchers. Mostly young women, these employees were trained to visit consumers in their homes and find out how they used cleaning products. No notes or clipboards were permitted. The field researchers had to have good recall and write down what they had learned after the home visit. P&G leveraged this and other market research data to become one of the great consumer products companies in the world.

Intuit's successful Quicken, QuickBooks, and TurboTax products lead in their categories. Like the old-time P&G, Intuit has what it calls a "follow-me-home" policy. Going into users' homes, Intuit managers found that the users of the original Quicken checkbook balancing program were actually using it as an accounting tool for small businesses. However, most had little familiarity with formal accounting terms. Intuit then built QuickBooks to minimize the appearance of double-entry bookkeeping. Brad Smith, Intuit CEO from 2008 to 2018, said, "What you get from a follow-me-home you can't get from a data stream. You've got to look somebody in the eye and feel the emotion."[3]

'Indego Materials' faced a threat and handled it with an intense focus on coupling with key customers.

Powdered metals are used to fabricate a wide variety of items, ranging from toys to jet-engine blades. Indego Materials was an important manufacturer of powdered metals, specializing in tungsten, tungsten carbide, titanium, and thorium. Known as refractory metals, they have a hardness that makes them difficult to shape with traditional cutting or metal-removal methods. The preferred method was to put powdered metal into a mold and then use either very high pressure or heat (sintering) to create the finished shape. Tungsten carbide was, in particular, a very hard substance, typically used to cut other metals.

Beginning in 2010, Indego had enjoyed a competitive advantage in the tungsten and thorium markets because of the proprietary additive it had developed. With the additive, smaller and more detailed elements of the final shape could be reliably created. Without the additive, producers had to limit the fine detail that could be incorporated into the sintered end product. There were about twenty major customers for its powdered metals around the world.

But there were problems. As CEO 'Ron Herwaith' explained in 2016, "We are experiencing new competition from Korea, which has been able to pretty much match our performance. Margins are in decline. One of our big problems is that we don't know exactly what other treatments our customers apply before molding and sintering, and we are not completely sure what their final performance requirements are. They tend to simply ask for a price quote and delivery specifications."

The Indego executive team decided to try working with a key customer, one who had asked for help on several issues the previous year. In the ensuing four-month engagement, Indego found that the customer liked the hardness and small-feature properties of Indego's powdered tungsten, but was also interested in porosity—microscopic holes or channels in the material to allow self-lubricating bearings. Indego engineers worked the problem and found that adding trace amounts of powdered tantalum and another additive solved the customer's problem.

Based on this experience, Indego built a small pilot fabrication facility where it could try out some of the fabrication methods being used by its customers. It then created a skilled team of sales-engineers who worked with key customers to help them improve and differentiate their products. By taking customer issues to the pilot facility, Indego was able to help customers use powdered metals much more effectively. Over a few years, margins improved as the product transformed from being seen as a commodity into a specialty material.

UNCOUPLING

Tight coupling is an individual entrepreneurial act. By contrast, *uncoupling* is normally an industry phenomenon, occurring when previously combined or integrated activities are taken on by specialized firms. Here the advantage comes from taking one of the newly specializing positions early, leaving behind those trying to preserve the old integrated system.

For example, once upon a time IBM and a few much smaller competitors offered totally integrated computer systems to industry and government. They system-engineered and constructed the memory, processors, card and tape readers, printers, terminals, and more. The advent of the microprocessor deconstructed this system. As each device became smart, sporting its own microprocessor, separate vendors for disk drives, keyboards, main processors, monitors, memory, software, and more appeared. In this vast uncoupling, there were huge pools of profit in online selling (Dell), huge profit in the cross-coupled Intel microprocessor and Microsoft's Windows and Office, and good profits in the decoupled hard-disk-drive industry, even as former returns to engineering the whole system vanished.

INTEGRATION AND DEINTEGRATION

Integration concerns activities where an "upstream" stage supplies inputs to a "downstream" stage, like trees to mills and then mills to lumber, notebooks, and paper towels. There is an array of challenges wherein the crux points to actions of integration or deintegration.

Between 1909 and 1916 the Ford Motor Company reduced the selling price of a Model T automobile from $950 to $360, thereby hugely broadening its base of potential customers. This success was not, as many believe, due to the moving assembly line. There was no more than $100 of labor cost in a 1909 Ford. The greater savings was reducing the cost of materials from $550 per car down to $220 per car.[4] This came from a unique setting for industrial engineering that integrated backward into making the automobile's components. At that time most of its suppliers, for seats, windows, wheels, and so on, were unsophisticated mom-and-pop garage operations. Ford's industrial engineers figured out how to produce these items in volume, in good quality, on time, and at low cost. That powered the amazing cost reductions in the Model T.

While the logic of integration still applies, it is much rarer to find such opportunities, and deintegration is more likely to pay off. Suppliers of parts, services, and components have become better at their specialties than the integrated company. It is the obverse of the Model T story. Deintegration is the force behind the huge wave of outsourcing to "supply chains," with both manufacturing and knowledge-based skills such as coding moving offshore to lower-cost locations. An important example is the deintegration of most semiconductor production to specialized chip makers. Originally, companies like Fairchild, Texas Instruments, IBM, Motorola, and others designed and produced their own memory and processor chips. Today, by contrast, only Intel and Samsung maintain strong in-house chip-production facilities.

Integration and deintegration decisions will differ within a company depending upon the product line. For Bata, a Pakistani shoe company, it made sense to stop making its own sandals, outsourcing to the vibrant local fabrication industry. Its more complex "sneakers," by contrast, continued to be made in-house as they required specialized know-how in the vulcanization of rubber to fabric.

'GamaGee' is a Swiss financial services company that is expert at creating a specialized type of insurance product. It does only the design of the financial instrument. The actual insurance function is handled by specialists in that area, marketing is subcontracted, and distribution is via financial advisers. In the modern financial sector, integration tends to be restricted to the sharing of hard-to-get customer and market information.

SCALE AND EXPERIENCE

The most easily thought-of mechanism to achieve greater efficiency or market control is scale. If a business is bigger, won't its costs be lower?

Yes and no. Samsung produced 295 million smartphones in 2019, compared with runner-up Apple at 197 million. Since Samsung is more vertically integrated into chips and screens, you might think that its greater volume and integration would give it a strong "scale" and integration edge. But Samsung sells 150 different model phones, while Apple sells only 3 models. Most of Samsung's so-called scale is spent on making very low-cost, low-profit phones for the developing world. Consequently, Samsung grabs only 17 percent of global phone profit, whereas Apple gets 66 percent. So in this case bigger does not seem to be better.

There are clear economies of scale in many activities. The strategic issue is the scale or size required to be efficient. If good efficiency is obtained at a scale of one-tenth of the whole market, then there is room for ten efficient firms. That means that scale will not be a source of advantage or edge.

Countervailing scale are the costs of shipping and customers' desires for differentiation. For example, if the costs of running a restaurant fall with the amount of seating and number of meals served, it still makes little sense to build a thousand-seat restaurant. Customers are looking for more than just a meal. There are economies of scale in airliners, with the Airbus A380 delivering the lowest cost-per-seat mile. It was designed to unseat Boeing's 747 as the grand airliner of the skies. But it operates at a low cost only if an airline can fill all the seats. Airbus canceled production in 2019.

Similarly, in the global automobile business there are significant pure-cost economies of scale in production. Yet in the world market of 75 million cars in 2019, the very largest producer, Toyota, had a 10 percent share, followed by Volkswagen at 7.5 percent and Ford at 5.6 percent. So something else was at work. If scale was really important, the largest automakers would totally dominate the market.

The economies of scale in automobile production were not determinative because everyone does not want the same automobile. Buyers' desires for different features and for just being different counteract the pure economies of production. The issue each producer faces is not just unit cost but the variety of buyer social norms, needs, tastes, and incomes.

There is a large logical gap between production economies of scale and those that simply have a larger organization. In fact, larger organizations will generally require more layers of managers and committees to coordinate the whole. For this reason, many of the mergers based on the hope for "economies of scale" fail. After the deal, it often turns out that the hoped-for gains were illusory, as the roles, skills, pay scales, and tasks in the merger partners were too dissimilar for effective combination. Obvious examples of this were the disastrous Daimler & Chrysler, Alcatel & Lucent, and the AOL & Time-Warner mergers.

Issues of scale play a role in advertising and research and development, as these activities are more sensitive to the expenditures of competitors. This is a very complex set of issues that must be carefully analyzed. In general, one attacks a larger competitor through an initial focus on part of the business from which they will probably retreat.

Experience

Everyone knows that you get better at something after doing it a number of times. The classic research on learning by doing was on the wartime production of B-17s at Boeing's No. 2 plant.[5] The first batch of aircraft, assembled in 1941, took about 140,000 labor hours for each airplane. One year later, the same aircraft were taking only 45,000 labor hours each to assemble. Labor hours per aircraft dropped to 15,000 by the time the B-17 was discontinued in 1945.

The causes of this reduction in labor hours per B-17 remain instructive. Careful research has rejected scale economies as a cause. Nor did the workers get "better" at working; the workforce started as skilled craftspeople. But as the plant expanded, relatively inexperienced workers were brought aboard. What did change markedly was the organization of the work. There was a sharp reduction in rework as "bad" parts were pulled before going to assembly. Plus, there was a movement to just-in-time production, eliminating the central stock room in favor of local stock and the reorganization of work into subassemblies that were then added to the airframe.

The Boston Consulting Group, led by Bruce Henderson, renamed "learning by doing" as the "experience curve" and used it to catapult BCG into a leading position in strategy consulting. I saw my first experience curve in Henderson's office in 1976. BCG analysts had studied cost data from client Texas Instruments' semiconductor business. The log-log plot showed unit costs falling as cumulative production rose; cost per unit dropped about 20 percent for each doubling of cumulative output. Henderson's argument was that the experience effect meant that once a firm got into the lead, it could stay there. It seemed to explain sustained success under competition.

Today, with hindsight, one sees that curve as basic semiconductor economics. With a given production setup, unit costs fall as yield (the fraction of good parts) rises. Yield, in turn, rises as sources of defects are identified and corrected. Much more important, over time, producers were able to pack more and more transistors onto each square millimeter of silicon—the process now dubbed "Moore's Law." But the critical element, one missing from Henderson's presentation, was that Moore's Law applies to the industry as a whole, not the individual competitor. Texas Instruments discovered this hard fact when, after racing down the hand-calculator "experience curve" in search of a protected position, it found not a pot of gold but a host of Taiwanese competitors with equivalent costs. Most of the cost reductions shown on Henderson's curve were not proprietary and could not be the source of sustained performance differences.

Experience does matter. The more stable the activity, the more complex the process, the more continued operation can lead to increases in efficiency. In aircraft production, one still forecasts that the labor cost of the twentieth airplane will be much less than that of the first. And, of course, experience isn't restricted to manufacturing. Google, one supposes, gets better and better at improving its search results.

The strategic issue with experience is the degree to which it can drive an advantage over competitors. Just as is the case for simple scale economies, beyond a certain point, factors other than accumulated experience become decisive.

NETWORK EFFECTS

"Network effects" is the technical name of the huge "edge" giving us giant tech quasi-monopolies like Microsoft, Google, Facebook, Twitter, and, to some extent, Apple. If you can hook into network effects, you can launch a product or business from nowhere to somewhere in record time. Or, like a young couple who announced a party and no one came, you can fail to catch the network effect and be left in the competitive dust.

Whereas economies of scale drive down unit *costs*, network effects drive up the *value* of the product. For a network effect to happen, the value of a product or service has to rise as more and more people use it.

In 1974 the young Bill Gates took an economics course at Harvard that covered network effects in telephone systems. Excited about the new microcomputers, he dropped out of Harvard and wrote a program named Microsoft Altair BASIC. The actual program was mbasic.com and was widely copied by hobbyists. Games were written in the language, like Scott Adams's text-based adventure games. Bill Gates railed against the piracy of his product but came to realize that its wide use blocked the purchase of better versions of BASIC by competitors (for example, TDL BASIC). Yes, he didn't get paid for the copies, but it became the de facto standard for the CP/M systems of the era. In the future, network effects for Microsoft's Windows and Office products would help make Bill Gates one of the world's richest people.

If you can create a new product with potential network effects, it may zoom (like Zoom) to success in a very short time. Still, the strength of the edge can be cut when there is a change in the underlying system. For example, the first spreadsheet, VisiCalc, was totally dominant on early Apple computers. Then, on the PC, Lotus 1-2-3 replaced it and became dominant. Then, with Windows, Microsoft Excel was the winner.

The combination of the Internet and network effects pushed many companies into giving their services away, potentially a Bertrand competition trap. The question in such a business is "How will it get paid?" The term of art, *business model*, arose as a way of answering this question. In essence, a business model explains where revenue will be earned when services are provided free of charge. The basic Internet business models are on-page advertising, advertising based on user information, free use with premium paid tiers of service, and pure subscription.

The powerful positions held by Google, Facebook, Twitter, and other Web-based platforms are some of the strongest network effects seen. This leverage derives from being able to provide users with more tailored content and provide advertisers with a targeted audience and to provide immediate feedback about users' responses. Facebook's social network now encompasses 2.5 billion active users. Without a significant change in technology or law, it is very hard to disrupt it.

PLATFORMS

The most recent explosions of new firms have arisen on "platforms"—businesses with two-sided network effects. A Web-based platform works to serve both buyers and sellers, becoming a marketplace. Whereas Facebook could first build the user base, a platform like Airbnb is of little use to customers unless there are renters and little use to renters unless there are customers.

For the platform strategist, edge arises from having network effects on both sides, a moderate "lock-in" of both buyers and sellers.

The early crux issue is deciding which side to build first, later adding the other side. The decision depends on the specifics of the situation and the ingenuity of the owners. Airbnb attacked this crux by first building a listing of apartments. The company raided Craigslist for listings as well as newspaper listings and other online vacation and for-rent notices. They subsidized these early listings by paying for professional photography of the apartments. This not only encouraged property owners to list, but also made their listing appear comparable to good hotels rather than the bare-bones Craigslist format. Over time, as renters began to use the platform, Airbnb no longer had to pay for photography—property owners hired their own to keep up with the look of other listings.

Uber is a platform connecting drivers and their cars with people wanting a ride. At Uber its ride-sharing prices are low enough to pull business away from taxicabs and black cars. There is controversy over what it pays drivers. It is obviously easy enough to get people to drive for Uber, though the turnover is reported to be on the order of 60 percent per year. The company spends a great deal on marketing, on paying fines, and on making political contributions around the world. The big question as of this writing is whether there is a "pathway" to profit. Uber lost $6.77 billion in 2020, an improvement from its $8.5 billion loss in 2019. The company claims it will break even in 2021, though that claim has fine print—it does not include depreciation expenses, stock-compensation expense, regulatory reserves, goodwill impairments, financing expense, COVID-19 expenses, and other carve-outs. The big unknown is whether the company had been "investing in growth" or whether its pricing structure is basically unsustainable.

One important aspect of Uber is that it enables drivers to start their "business" with very little setup cost and with very flexible work hours. This movement toward lowering start-up costs and time flexibility is a strong draw for many people. It is the basis for platforms like Etsy, which provides crafters with a place to easily sell their wares.

Specializing in handmade or vintage items, Etsy was started by Rob Kalin, Chris Maguire, and Haim Schoppik, all graduates of New York University. They studied the getcrafty.com and Crafster .org message boards, where individuals shared information on their projects and methods. Many of those posting on these boards were interested in selling their wares but hated eBay. To get started, the founders offered the message-board posters several months of free listings on Etsy. The first sales were typically to other crafters. Etsy pushed the seller side by providing premade shops, edit tools, credit-card facilities, handbooks, and meet-ups. Its existence was also publicized by feminist bloggers who saw crafting as a way of rejecting mass commercial culture. The buyer side grew rapidly.

Etsy's 2005 IPO raised $287 million, giving it room to invest in more growth. While Wall Street's intense focus was, as always, on quarterly growth numbers, one consequence of Etsy's growing size was a loss of some sellers to alternative platforms like ArtFire and Amazon Handmade. As Etsy began to expand, the definition of "handmade" was loosened to allow a "hand-designed" product to be contract manufactured. Growth also had some buyers complaining that it had become too big. One writer exclaimed that "Searching for 'mermaid' in the wedding gown category of Etsy returns 1,299 results, ranging from a $6,882 gown made by Project Runway's Leanne Marshall to one purportedly handmade lace dress going for $65."[6]

Nevertheless in 2020, Etsy was valued at $6 billion on earnings of $76 million. It shows growth in merchandise revenue of more than 20 percent per year. Its revenue comes from a 5 percent charge on sales, a 3 percent charge for payment processing, and a 20-cent listing fee for four months.

WHEN WE THINK about edge or advantage, we tend to look at search costs as well as stickiness, or switching costs. That is, how well does the platform meet the buyer's need to easily search for a desired category or item? And how easy is it for a buyer or seller to switch to a different platform?

With Uber, search is fast and easy, though one can get caught with fares three times normal if there is a rush. There is some concern about the lack of stickiness on both sides of Uber's market. A large portion of its drivers also drive for competitors like Lyft, and its ride-hailing phone app is fairly easy to duplicate. Some of those concerns also apply to Airbnb.

The craft platform space sees buyers and sellers willing to move to alternative platforms, but it is somewhat costly for a seller to do so. This is chiefly due to the cumbersome structure of code underlying websites and the slightly sticky nature of a Web link to a shop. I expect that, in five years, it will become much easier to move the logic of a shop from one platform to another, making the platform market more competitive. An additional complexity of the craft platforms is quality control. Etsy lists twelve million different jewelry items of which some are handmade and some obviously come from Alibaba. Photos vary in quality, and the company has a hard time policing its "handmade" rule. At ArtFire photos are even more varied in quality. There remains plenty of scope for value-increasing innovation in these sorts of platforms.

12

Innovating

To be a strategist on technology-based issues one must be aware of how technology progresses. Inventive genius does, of course, play a role. Our whole patent system, for example, is built around the idea of the lone inventor. Yet invention is rarely out of the blue. It typically comes as new insights and findings are "in the air" and being talked about and developed. Jack Kilby at Texas Instruments and Robert Noyce invented integrated circuits within months of one another. Elisha Gray filed for a patent on the telephone on the same day as Alexander Graham Bell. Researcher Mark Lemley's conclusion on this topic was that "the history of significant innovation in this country is, contrary to popular myth, a history of incremental improvements generally made by a number of different inventors at roughly the same time."[1] And most inventions build on an infrastructure already in place. Thus, Edison's inventive genius came after electricity was understood. Google's clever search algorithm came after the Web and other search engines had been built. The World Wide Web developed on the architecture of the Department of Defense–funded ARPANET, and its packet-switching base had been under study since the mid-1960s.

Technologies advance in waves, layer upon layer, each building upon the infrastructure and knowledge laid down in previous layers. The strategist needs to have an appreciation for the long wave—one that extends over a century or more—and for the shorter waves that are generally driven by reductions in the costs of delivering particular new benefits. For a large corporation that draws its strength from underlying technologies, the long wave must be appreciated, even as current profits draw on short-wave products. For the smaller or newer company, or the product division of a larger company, the strategist focuses on the shorter wave, as it is the mechanism for revealing the benefits of technology and innovation.

THE LONG WAVE

One long wave that seems, to most people, to have run its course is fabric making and clothing manufacture. For example, before the Industrial Revolution (1760–1860), most people were, by modern standards, poor and wore clothes until they fell apart. Before 1700 the time of most ordinary married women was taken up with making thread, fabrics, and garments. Single women were "spinsters" because they mostly spun thread for sale to others for garment making. Eve Fisher has calculated the hours taken to make a man's shirt by hand: "7 hours for sewing, 72 for weaving, 500 for spinning, or 579 hours total to make one shirt. At minimum wage—$7.25 an hour—that shirt would [today] cost $4,197.25."[2] As manufactured shirts came onto the market, the cost reduction was not so much from some prior ordinary shirt (there were none!) but from the implicit costs of making one at home. Today an ordinary men's dress shirt can be bought for under $20, a savings of 99.5 percent. From 1760 to 1900, similarly large price reductions can be seen for clocks, tableware, and the other basic components of everyday life. That was the revolution.

Despite the fact that fabrics are one of the oldest products, innovation continues. Today most clothing is made from cotton or polyester or both. As an example of a new wrinkle in this long wave, ecological concerns are driving customers to ask for fibers grown without pesticides and synthetics that do not form micropellets. This joining of social trends with technology is prompting the adopting of Piñatex, a fiber made from pineapple-tree waste and

MycoTEX, a fabric that is grown from the cells and filaments of mushroom mycelium.

The most significant long wave of the past two centuries has been the harnessing of electricity. It was 1820 when Örsted saw that an electric current made a compass needle deflect—the first indication that electric current could move physical objects. By 1840 electric motors were being developed for lathes and other tools. Soon, electric motors began to appear in factories, replacing the complex systems of pulleys and leather straps that distributed steam power. During the revolutionary 1880s, the first electric power stations appeared in New York and other towns. By the 1890s, electric cable cars began to replace horse-drawn carriages in American cities, the first being Cleveland. By the turn of the twentieth century, homes were adopting Edison's electric bulbs, replacing candles and gas.

It was the wide availability of home electricity that allowed companies to commercialize the new electric appliances in the 1920s—electric washing machines, refrigerators, and radios. The next twenty years would see IBM perfect electric tabulating machines and researchers build the first primitive computers. The first transistor was demonstrated in 1947 at AT&T's Bell Laboratories, and within a decade IBM was creating complex computers using transistors. During the 1960s, the technology of integrated circuits was developed, leading to semiconductor memory and microprocessors. The first "home" computers appeared in the late 1970s.

To build the modern Internet, it took the confluence of inexpensive small computers and high-capacity fiber-optic cables, developed in the 1970s and 1980s, and the existing cable-TV signal-distribution systems. Mobile phones harnessed radio, integrated circuits, and the growing mastery over managing cellular networks. Layer after layer, branch after branch, electrical technologies built upon new science and, importantly, preexisting infrastructures. And the story is far from finished.

These long waves can be observed but are hard to predict. I once participated in a "futures" forecasting exercise in 1967. Herman

Kahn, the famous futurist, led the group. Scientists, business leaders, and a sprinkling of government people began to imagine what the world would look like in thirty years—2007. Barring a nuclear war, the group forecast that we could cure cancer, have colonies on Mars, have one-hour rocket-based travel from anywhere on the planet to anywhere else, have cheap clean energy from fusion, and, maybe, would achieve automatic language translation.

What the futurists predicted was really a wish list, as if technology was some sort of magic machine granting our desires. Of the forecasts, only language translation is close to being accomplished, and that, still, imperfectly. We did not get cheap clean power, cure cancer, or have colonists on Mars. What we got is something the group did not forecast—we got computers everywhere, carried in our pockets, and hooked into a worldwide network. We got the ability to find out almost anything quickly.

As the Internet first appeared to the public as the World Wide Web, it was forecast that a new age of shared information and human freedom had arrived. And, to a large extent, this has happened, transforming work and our culture. Still, no one predicted that attention spans would fall or that the network would amplify and inundate the world with the wildest speculation. Even a decade past, no one predicted that social media like Twitter would become bullying mechanisms viciously enforcing ever-changing social norms. We did not get what we wished for. In this case, we got what technology delivered, regardless of our wishes.

One lesson is that the strategist needs to know the nature of the long wave being considered. Some advance greatly over time, while others, like ship propulsion, seem to reach natural limits. In general, the further into the future one looks, the more unpredictable technology becomes. The somewhat predictable technological future seems to be about five to seven years off. Beyond that, the strategist has to take a portfolio point of view, making bets on a variety of possibilities, some of which will conflict or compete with one another. Such views tend to be the province of large firms, governments, and subsidized research laboratories.

SHORT WAVES

Within a long wave of change, technology progresses in shorter steps. These steps occur when the costs of doing something new become low enough to permit commercialization. For example, Philips and others had developed dim light-emitting diodes in the early 1960s. Then, the first dim LED bulbs appeared on calculator displays in about 1970. In the mid-2000s the LED bulbs became bright enough and cheap enough to begin replacing incandescent bulbs. The next short wave in electrical lighting will probably be laser-diode lighting with potentially large benefits in outdoor applications.

In a case where costs will come down with scale or experience, the strategist normally seeks out the least-price-sensitive buyers for early versions of a product. This has a dual payoff. First, the company gets at least some sales and some feedback from customers. Second, because the initial market seems so limited, managers in other firms may be loath to push for entry into such a small market. When Corning first developed fiber-optic cables in the 1970s, signal losses limited the useful distance to less than one mile. Who would buy a short communications cable? The US Department of Defense did. Fiber-optic cable is immune to the electromagnetic-pulse waves created by atomic explosions. In 1975 early Corning fiber-optic cables connected the network of computers linked underground at NORAD in Colorado. Today, of course, with the problems of signal losses solved, fiber-optic cables undergird the global Internet.

The fastest adoption of fax machines was in Japan because of the odd system of addresses used in Tokyo. There, buildings are numbered in the order of their construction, not their position on a street. This makes it extremely difficult to tell someone how to visit your office or shop. The fax machine provided a nice solution to this difficulty—after inviting someone to a meeting, the inviter faxes a map showing their location to the invitee. Today, this custom still remains, though now mostly by email and instant-message transmissions of maps.

Many marketing "experts" tell us that early adopters of new technologies tend to be "influencers." Perhaps, in some cases. Early adopters of cell phones in the United States tended to be drug dealers who used them to connect street sellers with the hidden supplies in nearby buildings. Because their needs were so local, this cemented the analog AMPS system in the United States, while Europe moved to develop digital technology. In the same vein, early adaptors of the first Altair personal computers were hobbyists, not influencers.

In the short case examples that follow, I will detail how individuals and companies saw a cost savings or benefit potential and some of the steps taken to commercialize the idea. In each case, I will suggest what the early crux issue was or what it might be today.

Intuitive

Gary Guthart was a teen when he got a job at NASA Ames writing software for evaluating the flight performance of combat jets. After gaining a PhD in fluid mechanics, he landed a job at the Stanford Research Institute. He reported that while standing at a basketball game at SRI, a researcher asked him if he knew anyone with skill in a certain kind of nonlinear equations. Guthart said that he knew about that topic and was soon working in the surgical robotics research lab. There, he was asked to sew the femoral artery of a rat and then try it again with a jury-rigged robot prototype. He saw and appreciated the incredibly fine scale at which work must be performed in many surgeries—a scale smaller than most human eyes and hands can reliably master. He saw the difference the mechanical aids could make and became convinced that this new technology would save lives.

When venture capitalist John Freund, surgeon Roger Moll, and scientist Robert Younge formed Intuitive Surgical (1995), buying SRI's intellectual property, they took Gary Guthart and his software skills into the company. The SRI technology had been funded by the Department of Defense in the hope that battlefield wounds could be treated by surgeons over a remote link. Intuitive pushed in a different direction, specializing the technology around a surgeon working alongside the patient in an operating room. The company's first prototype added wrist-action movements to the surgical manipulator and a 3-D vision system to the display. Early laboratory trials showed that the 3-D display vastly improved the operator's ability to perform complex surgical tasks.

The next prototype (Mona) added interchangeable instruments to permit easy sterilization. The Mona system was used in the first human trial in Belgium, a gallbladder removal. The next model, da Vinci, incorporated multiple improvements, including greatly improved 3-D imaging and manipulators. The US FDA gave approval in 2000 for general surgery.

After several bumps in the road, Intuitive is today the world leader in physician-guided robot surgery. Thousands of surgeons around the world have now been trained on Intuitive's da Vinci robot systems that generate large benefits—mainly in cutting the complications associated with surgery. Gary Guthart's and others' skills were just the right thing at just the right time to ignite this wave of change. He became CEO of Intuitive in 2010.

Today, in 2021, Intuitive faces a number of challenges and opportunities. Guthart is investing in a technology for doing biopsies deep in the lungs and in stomach-shrinking surgery. On the competitive side, giant Alphabet (Google's parent) has announced a robotic surgery effort, as has medical device maker Medtronic. One overall larger issue is that robotic surgery remains limited by the lack of tactile feedback to the surgeon. Most surgeons rely on touch to determine how much pressure to put on a blade or how to manipulate soft tissues, and robot systems lack this sense. If this issue could be solved, the market would become many times larger. If it were solved by Alphabet, it might sorely damage Intuitive. Taking this issue to be the crux, and were I Guthart, I would seek a "good-enough" solution. That is, I would bet that AI researchers at Alphabet would seek a total solution and that I could prevail with a system that gave good-enough indications of tissue density and nodule location. Of course, I would keep this confidential.

Zoom

In 2016 I was in Europe working with a multinational tech company. The senior officers had gathered in a conference room to have an Internet-enabled conference with other officers in the United States and Asia. They brought up the Cisco WebEx connection on the local computer and tried to connect with their compatriots abroad. There was a picture with some, but no sound. A technical support person was called (in a high-tech firm!), and he got the picture but lost the voice. Turning the system off and rebooting did not fix the issues. That was hardly my only experience with failed conferencing efforts. In general, it seems that corporate security systems and video conferencing systems do not play well.

Cisco had acquired WebEx in 2007 for a bit more than $3 billion. One of the employees who came along with WebEx was Eric Yuan. He had come to the United States from China in 1997, having studied mathematics and computer science there. He had been on the team that developed WebEx. As WebEx expanded its customer base under Cisco's ownership, Yuan rose to become vice president of engineering, directing a cadre of more than eight hundred developers.

The challenge Yuan faced was that the WebEx product had not improved over time. Initially innovative, by 2010 its software base had not been upgraded, and it still required a complex multistep installation procedure. Interviewing customers, Yuan commented that "when I talked with a WebEx customer, after the meeting was over, I felt very, very embarrassed because I did not see a single happy customer."[3] Velchamy Sankarlingam, who had worked with Yuan at WebEx, observed that at Cisco it was "a completely different mindset. . . . Cisco just sells the gear. . . . [I]f a company's network goes down, nobody's going to go blame Cisco."[4]

Yuan quit Cisco in 2011, taking a clutch of engineers along with him. The new company, Zoom, was based on building a video-centered conferencing tool, one that would be much easier to install, use, and maintain than WebEx.

The crux of the technical and commercial challenge was to eliminate the complexities involved in signing up, opening an account, and downloading a program and then an app for your phone for WebEx, Skype, Microsoft Teams, TeamViewer, and other offerings. Plus, creating easy-to-use high-quality video conferencing was not easy—the engineers had to make it work in any browser, regardless of firewall settings, and the video had to be separately compressed for screen sharing, with adjustments for each user's computer speed. Yuan's team powered through this crux through a combination of focusing top-notch engineers on all the friction points—and on insisting that the product "make customers happy."

Zoom was free for up to one hundred attendees for forty minutes. Because it was free and easy to use, and because it was, by definition, a communication device, it began to spread like wildfire. With the COVID-19 lockdowns, Zoom traffic increased by 3,000 percent in May 2020. To "Zoom" became a verb. Students Zoomed to school. The product's security was criticized, the Zoom team made fixes, and public health experts began to worry about the effects of back-to-back Zoom meetings on locked-down people.

As much of the world moves past the COVID-19 emergency, the obvious challenges for Zoom are a reduction in video meetings combined with jealous competition from Google, Microsoft, and others. Some competitor will undoubtedly also solve the high-quality, ease-of-use combination of features that catapulted Zoom to leadership. Whereas the stock market will be focused on obvious and predictable reductions in use as lockdowns fade, a strategist should be looking at the next opportunity. One way to proceed is to look around for applications that are, today, as clunky as WebEx was in 2011. Most current versions of "team" collaboration tools fit the bill.

Dropbox

Dropbox is an example of software that couples reducing implicit costs with free use and a network externality. In early 2015 I was discussing the future of Dropbox with Drew Houston, the company's

CEO and one of its two founders. He explained that he had been traveling in 2006 and forgot his thumb drive. There was not an easy way to keep a laptop in synch with the computer at home. The episode triggered the creation of the Dropbox file-synching program. By 2015, Dropbox was widely used. Its carefully engineered features let the user assign desktop files to Dropbox, and the system would constantly scan for any changes in the file and then backup sectors (chunks) of the file as necessary. If a user had two or three or ten computers, Dropbox would keep chosen folders or file in synchronization on them all.

Dropbox was free to users who needed less than two gigabytes of storage and had a tiered pricing scheme for those who needed more. Its fast growth had been powered by the free tier and Dropbox users offering to share folders with other users—all they had to do was also sign up for free. This network effect is less powerful than Google's, but it is coupled with the fact that once you have many files on Dropbox, it becomes costly (implicit costs) to move to another solution.

The issue worrying Drew Houston in 2015 was competition from Google, Microsoft, Box, and others. Drew told me, "Competition from these heavyweights is worrisome," but then he went on to say that he remained convinced that Dropbox would endure and grow by offering the simplest, easiest, and most glitch-free file-synching service.

Dropbox went public in 2018, and today, as of this writing in 2021, its market value is $10 billion, with more than six hundred million users. Drew Houston's identification of the crux as hassle-free file synchronization across multiple devices remains valid. There is certainly the issue of storage cost, but the seamless way in which Dropbox works means that there is little or no maintenance, dramatically reducing implicit costs of fiddling with individual file movements. Competitor Google offers Drive, which can synch files, but it does it a file at a time, not a sector at a time. The user interface is not obvious, and if you change a large file, and have several devices, there is a lot of uploading and downloading. Plus, its file sharing is oriented around pushing users to adopt its own versions of word processing, number crunching, and presentation routines. Many users cite the fact that Dropbox is not one of the tech giants as a reason for choosing it.

Still, as in 2015, the drive among the tech giants to commoditize cloud storage remains "worrisome." Like the springwater in the Auvergne, storing a megabyte online will become close to a perfect commodity, and participants will be playing a destructive Bertrand game. Dropbox has, in my view, the best offering, and switching costs will keep its user base from rapid evaporation. Still, the challenge of imitative competition in the longer term is substantial. The crux challenge for Dropbox (in the longer run) is to develop more proprietary products. Its recent integration of DocuSign (an e-signature tool) and HelloSign are steps in this direction. Another step might be the creation of a virtual "deal room" that investment professionals use to hold and view deal-specific documents. Specialized document storage for law firms and lawsuits would be more along this line. An easy-to-use version-control service is another interesting opportunity.

THE COMMONALITIES AMONG the stories of Intuitive Surgical, Zoom, and Dropbox are not accidental. Successful innovations typically enjoy a time in the sun when competition is somewhat muted and growth is rapid. Still, that very success whets the appetites of larger and older firms, each looking to maintain their vitality by ingesting younger upstarts. The crux problem for the younger innovator is to use its agility and lack of bureaucracy to outmaneuver the competition.

Tech Giants

Couple dramatic cost reductions, or benefit increases, with strong network effects, and you have the giant tech companies that currently stride the world. For example, the ease and simplicity of online search are now almost taken for granted.

The appearance of these giant information-based tech companies—Google, Facebook, Twitter, and Apple—was not anticipated. In the beginning, the Internet was seen as an information highway that all could travel. What should have been seen, but was not, is that the sharp reduction in implicit consumer costs was delivered by systems with huge network effects. That is, Google search dramatically reduced the cost of finding information, and the more people who used Google search, the better Google search got, so that its value to consumers became higher and higher even as the price remained zero.

In 2003 Mark Zuckerberg, a Harvard sophomore, wrote software for Facemash, which provided photos of female students, side by side. The game was to decide which one was "hotter." Soon after, he wrote TheFacebook, an application that allowed Harvard students to post their own photos and information about themselves. By 2007 Facebook had burst out of the college scene and had millions of users and one hundred thousand business pages.

Zuckerberg had not anticipated any of this. It happened because of the complexity of the Web's underlying markup language—it was difficult and costly to create a personal Web page. Providing an easy way to create a personal website, coupled with the network effects of social media, Facebook became the monster that it is today. Still, the complexity and cost of setting up your own website outside of Facebook remain (see Sharon Thompson and the "WebCo" story in Chapter 6).

To the extent that Google and Facebook and Twitter face large challenges, they stem mainly from the public and governmental perceptions of monopoly and especially their power to shape speech. It also remains somewhat surprising that the tech giants have so successfully bypassed issues of copyright, so assiduously enforced in most publishing and entertainment businesses.

COMPLEMENTARITIES

An important, often critical, issue in innovation is the presence or absence of what Professor David Teece calls *complementary assets*.[5]

These are skills or resources that are necessary to bring the new invention or product to market and to provide whatever ancillary services it needs. If, for example, your new innovation is a better blood-pressure metering device, the existing systems of distribution into hospitals and doctors' offices are complementary to your invention. You will probably have to share much of the benefits your invention creates with existing powerful complementors. On the other hand, if you have invented the iPhone, which every network operator wants to carry, the shoe is on the other foot.

I have always found the story of Philo Farnsworth to be instructive with regard to intellectual property and complementary resources. Born in a remote cabin in Utah in 1906, Farnsworth moved with his family to Idaho in 1918. The farm there had an electrical generator and some motors, and Farnsworth began to take them apart and figure out how they worked. He read everything he could find about electricity. In high school he showed his chemistry teacher his ideas for an "image dissector," a vacuum tube with an electron gun, deflector plates, and a cesium oxide screen. The teacher took notes. Seven years later, a student at Brigham Young University, Farnsworth filed a patent for a "Television System." He was twenty-two years old.

By 1929 Farnsworth was able to demonstrate the transmission of an image of his wife. But a problem arose because RCA, leading the radio revolution, had acquired a 1923 patent application by Vladimir Zworykin, for an "iconoscope," a design for a TV camera. The application was denied by the patent office because there was no evidence that the device worked. (It didn't, yet.) RCA offered to pay Farnsworth $100,000 for his patent, and when Farnsworth refused, RCA challenged Farnsworth's patent in court. Farnsworth lost two rounds but won when the patent office granted him priority. (His chemistry teacher's notes were evidence.) Farnsworth went to work with competitor Philco.

Zworykin, working for RCA, had by then improved his design and patented the kinescope, which became the standard for the early television industry. Farnsworth would try his hand at producing his own complete television system but could not sell many sets. He continued to invent, collecting more than three hundred patents, including one for a tabletop nuclear fusion device, the Farnsworth-Hirsch fusor. He died at sixty-four of pneumonia after being bankrupted by his last, unsuccessful, business venture.

One lesson of the Farnsworth story is that you may be the first with a new idea, but technology moves in waves, and the sparks that lit the idea in your mind are flashing in other minds as well. If you are truly first, establish strong intellectual protection. But at the same time, be aware that others' ideas are also developing and improving. In so many cases, the success of a new product or idea depends on complementary assets. In this case, RCA had the R&D labs and budget, the broadcast technology and systems, and the strategic patience to make television work. Neither Farnsworth's nor Zworykin's concept was television. To get television started as a business, RCA had to perfect the cameras and TV sets and obtain licenses. It wasn't until 1939 that RCA began to broadcast from the Empire State Building on channel 1, sending shows out into the ether to a world that wasn't yet watching. By 1945 there were perhaps ten thousand TV sets in America. There were six million by 1950, and by the 1990s they were ubiquitous. In retrospect, RCA's complementary assets were decisive. Farnsworth should probably have worked with RCA, negotiated a better deal, and gotten access to their well-funded research laboratories.

13

The Challenge of Organization Dysfunction

Sometimes the problem is us. It is not so much the competition, or changing technology, but an organization's inadequate ability to respond. Either the required skills are not there, or something is wrong with the organization's leadership, structure, or processes that keeps those skills from being identified and applied. The crux of such problems always lies with how leaders have designed the organization or with how they manage it.

The most common problems created by the organization itself arise from its history of specialization and, usually, success. What worked in a certain era, especially the era of growth and success, becomes "the way things are done around here." Arnold Toynbee named this the "idolization of ephemeral technique," seeing it as one reason for the breakdown of civilizations. An outsider like myself can often see this anchoring in things ranging from the design of offices to the structure of internal reports and to how people talk about the business. Visiting General Motors in 1985, it was a bit like time travel back to 1956 when it strode the earth like a colossus. Take some navy captains to drinks, and you have a good chance of hearing about the 1942 Battle of Midway. The Benetton Group was a leading fashion company in the 1960s. Its headquarters north of Venice, Italy, are in stately sixteenth-century buildings with interior decor constantly featuring its dated "united colors" and "global" themes. Revenues have been falling for a decade, and its fashion offerings today seem a bit stodgy and dull.

SEEKING A POINT OF LEVERAGE AT GENERAL MOTORS

INSEAD is an international school of management in Fontainebleau, about fifty kilometers from Paris. In 1993 I left my perch at UCLA in California and spent the next three years on the INSEAD faculty, a midlife stir to life's stew.

One session of my INSEAD strategy course was on General Motors or, more generally, about excellence. Not that General Motors could then be considered excellent. The sad truth was that the company that had been Peter Drucker's exemplar of excellence in the 1950s had become moribund, lagging ever further behind upstart Toyota and a revived Ford and Chrysler. No, in that session we were in Zen mode, looking for excellence by studying its absence. What was keeping GM from learning from its Fremont joint venture with Toyota, or extending the important lessons of Saturn to other divisions, or simply cutting its design-cycle time below four years, or even making automobiles with fit and finish up to international standards?

As part of the preparation for class discussion, students had read a number of reports, articles, and histories of the company. Best of all, we had a flesh-and-blood GM executive with us. The executive, Alan, was the father of an INSEAD student and visiting Fontainebleau (and Paris) that week.

Alan described the General Motors situation with grim precision. Like a pathologist identifying the signs of a terminal disease, he ticked off items on the fingers of his hand: honest analysis replaced by spin doctoring, rampant careerism, insufferable bureaucracy, lack of trust together with its twin, checks and rechecks on every plan. "There are a lot of talented people," he concluded, "but it feels as if all their energy is directed inward, dealing with each other, rather than outward, dealing with the marketplace."

Alan had brought with him a copy of Maryann Keller's *Rude Awakening*. "This describes the situation in about 1982," he said, and then read aloud: "The employees were not prodded to be more efficient or more innovative. The structure of the company and the corporate culture which valued conformity more than creativity prevented that from happening. The reward system functioned on automatic pilot. Put in the years, support the party line, and you'll be protected from harm."[1] Raising his eyes to the class, he concluded: "Over a decade later, the characters have changed, but the plot remains the same."

Student comments were slow in coming; they were not sure how to deal with this message. Finally, a French product manager said, "It's the leadership. It's senior management. Every manager takes their cue from the top about what is acceptable. If you have a dishonest culture of conformity, it comes from the top."

In France the educational system of *grandes écoles* virtually guarantees leadership positions to those who excel in their studies, especially mathematics. The French students tend to see organizations as extensions of the leader. German students tend to focus on technical competence. Americans frequently emphasize the importance of incentives. True to the stereotype, an economics major from Michigan said, "There is an old saying about the folly of rewarding A while hoping for B. If you reward conformity, it isn't surprising that creativity is lacking. It seems to me that the problem is simply one of incentives. People do what they are rewarded for doing. If GM needs more creativity, it needs to reward risk-taking and bold new strokes."

Other comments focused on bureaucracy and the lack of a clear set of guidelines for behavior. A British finance specialist said, "General Motors is just too bloated. You can't change an organization of that size. It has to break up into smaller pieces."

I turned to Alan and asked for his reaction. Did he disagree with anything that had been said? Did he agree with anything? Alan's response was daunting. Addressing the class, he said, "It's everything you have said. And more."

The class was vaguely disappointed. They wanted a crisp resolution—if not an action plan, then at least a clear diagnosis. The problem couldn't be "everything." Surely, there was a way to unravel the knot. They saw the mass of problems, but did not see a crux—a point of leverage that, when pressed, could cause the various pieces of the puzzle to fall into place.

A point of leverage for GM finally came fifteen years later, in 2009, through bankruptcy, the largest ever for an industrial firm. At that moment it had $82 billion in assets and $173 billion in liabilities. The bankruptcy allowed GM to cut wages, break away certain large liabilities, and get US government investments of about $50 billion (later repaid).

The next point of leverage was the ignition-switch fiasco, unfolding from 2006 through 2014. Eventually linked to 124 deaths, the faulty ignition-switch design appeared on the Chevrolet Cobalt and Pontiac G5s. It allowed shocks, or knee strikes, or large swinging key chains to turn the ignition from "Run" to "Accessory," thus cutting power to the airbags. An internal investigation, overseen by Anton Valukas, a former US attorney, revealed that engineers knew about the switch's problems but failed to connect that to the airbag-deployment issue. Even though an accident report by a state trooper had made the connection, the GM engineers just didn't link the known ignition-switch problem to the known airbag-deployment problem. The Valukas report expressed surprise that the GM engineers had so little understanding of how the cars actually functioned as a system.

In addition, the Valukas report raised the issue of culture at GM: a manager "said that, if an employee tried to raise a safety issue five years ago, the employee would get push back."

> Engineers, too, failed to elevate the issue. Starting in mid-2012, there were three high-level managers brought in as "champions"—Woychowski, Federico, and Kent. The very reason they were brought in was to help resolve an unexplained pattern of airbag non-deployments in an expeditious manner. But they did not elevate the issue to their

> superiors, and the common thread was to hold more meetings and refer the matter to additional groups or committees.[2]

The report also documented common knowledge of the "GM Salute" and "GM Nod." The "Salute" was crossed arms with fingers pointing to others, indicating that responsibility was someone else's problem. The "Nod" was agreement in a committee but with no real intention to follow up.

CEO Mary Barra presided over the recall of millions of GM cars due to the ignition-switch problem. GM paid $900 million to the US government as a criminal fine for not getting to the problem and its solution with dispatch. GM set aside $600 million for compensation for victims.

This experience seems to have pushed change at GM. Barra killed the matrix and flattened the organization. She fired fifteen employees for cause. She has put together a team of executives at the top who would model problem-solving behavior. GM has dropped brands and whole divisions. It has new electric cars and is researching self-driving cars. The company has returned to profit.

After the 2009 bankruptcy, General Motors dropped four famous (North American) brands: Saturn, Hummer, Pontiac, and Saab. Since the ignition-switch crisis, CEO Barra had gotten the company out of Western Europe, Russia, South Africa, and India. It stopped assembling cars in Australia and Indonesia. Once the world's largest automaker, GM is gradually rethinking the logic of scale economies that drives so much of the industry. Among traditional marquees, it continues to do well with full-size trucks, crossover SUVs, and Cadillac brands. Its new focus is on all-electric vehicles, which Barra sees as the growth market of the future.

INERTIA AND SIZE

Mass has inertia. The greater the mass, the more force will be needed to change its speed or direction. Organizational inertia is normally the problem of large organizations.

One has to respect a large organization. When successful, it means that it has solved the substantial problem of governing at scale. As scale increases, so do managerial problems. Size increases the difficulty of coordinating large groups of specialists; size makes it more difficult to move information from its source to the locations where it can be best used. Size dilutes the effects of each individual's efforts and thus makes motivation more difficult. Size insulates and buffers the organization as a whole against isolated and local challenges, thus making responsiveness more difficult. Size increases the span of activity beyond that which even the most skillful senior manager can be familiar, making the intelligent direction of the enterprise more difficult. Thus, a *successful* large corporation is one where managers have found structures and processes that address these difficulties. These difficulties are never solved or eliminated, but successful firms have found ways of managing that have brought the costs of size under control.

ORGANIZATION AND INERTIA AT NOKIA

In 2007 Nokia was preeminent in mobile phones, shipping more than half of the industry's units. Five years later, its share had stunningly collapsed to under 5 percent. For many, the explanation for Nokia's fall from grace was clear. A *New Yorker* article's summary was short and sweet: "What happened to Nokia is no secret: Apple and Android crushed it."[3]

Yes, but there is more to the story. What happened to Nokia's vaunted engineering skill, to the people that produced the industry's first smartphone in 1996? Nokia's decline was hastened by clinging to its outmoded Symbian operating system, and that inertia was, in turn, a result of the way it was organized and led.

Nokia's position in mobile phones came out of a 1991 deep strategy study. The Finnish telecommunications equipment company determined to leverage the then new GSM digital standard and to concentrate on mobile communications. The timing was propitious, and Nokia's GSM carrier equipment and mobile phone businesses both grew rapidly. The company prided itself on its agile "can-do" style and culture.

Its Communicator was the world's first smartphone. Launched in 1996, it had a horizontal folding case and a small but complete keyboard. In 1998 the company developed Symbian, to provide an "open" operating system for its and others' smartphones. Symbian was designed to be efficient. It was written in a special subset of the standard C++ language and used specific instruction sets on the host microprocessor. With demand soaring, and Moore's Law driving down the costs of digital circuitry, Nokia's business boomed. By early 2002 Nokia's products made up 36 percent of worldwide mobile phone sales.

The company's basic strategy was to drive down manufacturing costs of phones through huge global volume. It released Symbian through a foundation as open-source software, available to any developer in the world, cementing Symbian as the pre-smartphone standard. This was the idea that Google's Android system successfully implemented for the smartphone world.

CEO Jorma Ollila expressed concern that Nokia's rapid growth had come at the expense of its agility. In 2003 he began to reorganize Nokia into a matrix structure. Part of the idea was to separate mobile phones from "Enterprise Solutions" and other businesses. Another motive was to keep the mobile phone business from becoming too politically dominant within the company. Symbian would be the common software platform across all phones.

The new structure immediately began to create problems. The key operating executives were those in charge of specific classes of mobile phones, and the management system held them to strict measures of profit and time-to-market for new models. Conflicts over resources were resolved by politicking and many—slow—committee meetings.[4]

Not only did the matrix slow decision making, but it also helped insulate top management from the truth on the ground. A policy of segmenting the market into smaller and smaller pieces generated a proliferation in products. By 2004 Nokia had brought to market thirty-six different mobile devices and introduced another forty-nine in 2006. This presented a problem because the Symbian OS was deeply integrated with the host processor, so it had to be reengineered for each new mobile product. Its lack of modularity made improvement very difficult.[5] R&D work on specializing Symbian began to grow, and top management quixotically responded by capping R&D expense at 10 percent of revenue.

Despite Apple's supposed secrecy, Nokia engineers knew about Apple's finger-touch design plans in late 2005. Nokia had built stylus-operated touch-screen devices since 2004, and Nokia top managers made the development of finger-touch technology a priority. A manager reported that in 2006, the CEO "felt it was the next big thing. . . . He brought it up with the executive group every way he could . . . followed up on it in every single meeting."[6] Yet no such phone appeared until 2009.

It is easy to conclude that Nokia's strategies of clinging to Symbian and constantly proliferating new "lifestyle" products caused its downfall. But the deeper question is why no one acted to fix the situation. What was the source of this deadly inertia?

The answer is fourfold. First, the industry shifted the locus of excellence from making hardware to writing software that integrated with the hardware.

Second, the leadership had little knowledge of software. Although the company had its roots in clever engineering, over time the top management became financially oriented. Jorma Ollila's background was in investment banking. His successor as CEO, Olli-Pekka Kallasvuo, had been corporate counsel. They could call for various results but had little or no comprehension of what software was or how it was created. Top management set performance goals but utterly failed to understand the crux of the internal problems of structure and software the company faced.

Third, the matrix so diffused responsibility that there was no one in charge of creating a new finger-touch phone—at least no one with the authority and budget necessary to carry out such a task. Once the company had rapidly scaled, engineering became routine, and managers were busy hitting financial and time-to-market goals. No one with technical know-how had the authority to abandon Symbian and develop a better OS, as Google did with Android.

Fourth, the leadership style at the top was very interpersonally aggressive. Researchers who interviewed seventy-six Nokia managers found that middle managers and engineers felt bullied into making optimistic promises they knew were false. One top manager admitted that, unlike competitor Apple, "there was no real software competence" in top management. Other managers reported that top managers gave direction but did not want to hear bad news. Targets were set by the top without regard to feasibility. Managers who questioned the feasibility of targets were pushed to the side and eventually out. Top managers seemed to believe that more pressure would make anything work. Several emphasized that Ollila, who was chairman from 1992 to 2006, was "extremely temperamental," shouting at people "at the top of his lungs."[7]

ORGANIZATIONAL TRANSFORMATION AND RENEWAL

The good news is that organizational issues such as those affecting Nokia and General Motors can be resolved successfully using the principles of crux-strategy problem solving: diagnosis, reduction to a crux, performance concepts, and coherent action. In many new Internet digital-based companies, change can come quickly since they lack the factories, fixed assets, unions, and huge managerial structures of more traditional companies. That makes change somewhat faster, though no less painful for those set aside or let go.

For many organizations, however, real change seems out of reach. Well-educated and well-intentioned managers sit on top of complex organizations started generations ago by talented entrepreneurs and grown labyrinthine over time. Many have only limited acquaintance with the technologies or processes they oversee. Managing by studying reports of operating results, they can only create "strategies" that are no more than demands for better results.

It can take years to make fundamental changes in traditional firms. When I was on the faculty at INSEAD, in France, for a while I headed the Corporate Renewal Initiative. We tracked in detail about ten "transformations" where fundamental changes in structure and function had been undertaken by fairly large companies. The average renewal took over five years. And when you looked at the before-and-after photos of the senior leadership team, most of the names and faces were different. Transformations implied a change in senior leadership.

There is a large literature on organizational change. Here, I want to emphasize certain aspects that I have personally found to be important.

The senior leadership must commit to change, not just the words, but discomfort and outright pain of wrenching loose traditions. Those who cannot commit cannot be part of the team. In a company of any size, the core team at the very top is five to eight people. They will manage and direct a group of twenty to forty managers who work the change process. Without these groups leading the charge, both intellectually and with daily follow-up, not much will happen other than slogans on the wall.

Complex organizations must be simplified before real change can be engineered. The first step is weeding out unnecessary activities, outsourcing them, assigning them to subcontractors or to the dustbin. Then, further simplify by removing superfluous layers that filter information without adding any substance. Then one must break large units into smaller ones. This disrupts political baronies and reduces the comforts of businesses losing money being subsidized within a larger business. This, in turn, exposes more units to the weeding process. Further simplification can be achieved by reducing diversification and trimming the number of products made and market niches served.

Once simplification has taken place, it is easier to see and comprehend the basic operations of a business. This is when actual renewal can take place. The most common approach is to bring together midlevel managers into teams, each assigned to solve a specific issue facing the company. These issues are not usually organizational per se, but are business performance issues that will undoubtedly require the teams to seek both policy and organizational remedies. Teams that can do this work well will form the nexus of the new generation of leadership.

RENEWAL AT IBM

Founded in 1911, IBM's enormous success in tabulating and then computing had been due to the brilliance of key engineers and its ability to manufacture complex machinery. By 1963 it had become clear that the costs of creating software for its many different models were beginning to equal hardware costs. The crux problem was the need to have a single operating system for its wide range of hardware. The solution was to reengineer its whole line of machines to be software compatible. The new line—the 360s—would all have compatible instruction sets. Pushing through this change was one of the great transformation efforts of the era, taking the company close to insolvency.

In 1967 I was writing a case on IBM and met with IBM president T. V. Learson who had been one of the ramrods for the 360 project. He told me: "We knew we were betting the company." He wanted a set of compatible machines so customers could upgrade without buying wholly new software. There were radically different engineering ideas about how to get there. The business-machines engineers had very different views about compatibility than did the high-performance scientific-computer engineers. "I basically pitted them against one another in a cage fight, with very experienced judges," he exclaimed. Out of that came the idea of adding microcode to the business machines so that they would run the new software yet be compatible with the old.

In 1964 the line of six new computers and forty-four new peripherals was announced and showcased. In the next month close to one hundred thousand new systems were ordered. IBM's growth rate accelerated.

With fast growth came a larger and larger headquarters staff. In 1972 T. V. Learson, now the CEO, complained, "One of our top facility managers recently told me that no subject of any consequence could come up in his location without somebody's calling a meeting and having thirty people show up." Nine years later, CEO John Opel complained that "a growing bureaucracy is affecting the performance of our business." One study found that a development group had to wait eight weeks and get thirty-one signatures in order to buy a small piece of equipment needed to work on a critical business problem.[8]

An early hint of issues was the way the IBM PC was developed during 1980. Don Estridge, who headed the PC project, learned his lesson about IBM's creaky software development in an earlier failed project. Called System 1, it was to be a smaller main computer, and it needed an operating system. Literally thousands of programmers appeared, laboring first in writing detailed specifications and then to slowly work on the code.[9] That experience was why, when he was later tasked with creating a small personal computer (the PC), he went outside IBM to Bill Gates for an operating system.

By the early 1990s, a trio of researchers reported that the company had a heavy reliance on an "army of corporate staff" and that decision making was slow.[10] Divisions were powerful baronies, and a "nonconcur" from one could kill an idea. Profits were vanishing, and the downward spiral seemed unstoppable. The advice from Wall Street was to break the behemoth into parts and sell them off either as independent companies or to others in the IT world.

In early 1993, IBM sought out and hired Lou Gerstner as the new CEO. Before being chosen to lead IBM, he had been a McKinsey consultant, worked at American Express, and had been CEO at RJR Nabisco. The changes he made at IBM over the next three years are one of the classic cases of organizational transformation.

Gerstner's key insight was that no other firm had IBM's breadth of technology and boardroom customer access. But splitting its organization into product and geography fiefdoms was preventing these skills and resources from being deployed to customers. In addition,

IBM had a strong culture that resisted change. In a very insightful interview Gerstner remarked:

> It's very hard to change a culture, and you can't impose it. You're dealing with people's beliefs, people's commitments, so it tends to be a multi-year process. You gotta talk about it a lot, you gotta give them a reason why they should behave differently, you have to connect it to the strategy of the institution, their own personal benefits. And we did that, over a period of about four or five years.[11]

From a cultural point of view, Gerstner invested a great deal of time and energy in writing down and distributing his view of how the company should be acting as a coherent whole: "One IBM" was the slogan. Still, the dominant culture was set by the "nonconcur" process, an official system where any important action could be vetoed by any important executive. Gerstner wrote: "This unique brew of rigidity and hostility often landed on my own doorstep. I discovered that just because I asked someone to do something, that didn't mean the task got done. When I discovered this, days or weeks later, I'd ask why. One executive said, 'It seemed like a soft request.' Or: 'I didn't agree with you.'"[12]

Very early on, Gerstner inaugurated a benchmarking study. He found that IBM's equipment prices were too high and that its expenses were four times the level of competing firms. He cut mainframe prices and then had to find ways to cut something like $7 billion in expenses. In 1993 75,000 people were let go. Many businesses were sold or closed—the weeding process.

Most telling for the leading company in IT was the existence of 128 chief information officers presiding over 125 different data centers, worldwide. The reduction in IT departments and data centers, down to 3, generated at least $2 billion in savings.[13]

With regard to driving change, the most innovative approach Gerstner developed was the creation of the Corporate Executive Committee, or CEC. It had ten members plus Gerstner. Each member of the CEC was given full executive power over a particular change program: procurement, sales, IT, product development, manufacturing, and so on. These executives' full-time job was just change. Like a viceroy in the old world of kings, they had plenipotentiary power to hire, fire, reassign, and reorganize in order to push through the reengineering of the company.

At IBM culture was slower to change. But with forced change and turnover, eventually it did. Once, at UCLA, I was interviewing a young, innovative cultural anthropologist who was thinking about working at a business school. He explained to me the huge differences across cultures in norms of cooperation. Over lunch, I asked him about his thoughts on inertia and change in organizations, a subject on which I was writing at the time. He said, "The only way to change a group's norms is to change the alpha. In all human groups, the alpha person defines the 'right' way to think and act. Change the alpha, and you change behavior." Importantly, an alpha is not necessarily the person in formal charge. It is the person everyone respects and wants to emulate. At IBM culture gradually changed as new alphas appeared.

When Gerstner was followed by Sam Palmisano in 2002, the new CEO put very strong emphasis on the company's "values." His exhausting "ValuesJam" involved 320,000 IBM employees in a several-day online debate and discussion of the company's values. In addition to the obvious praise for innovation, it became clearer that IBM would make "client success" its first priority, a large change from the product-first history of the company.

Today, in 2021, IBM is a major actor in the information-processing industry. Yet despite its renewal, it has not yet regained its former leadership. Its software business has grown more slowly than the overall enterprise and the SaaS (software-as-a-service) market, and it has lost share in IT outsourcing to Accenture and Infosys.

Gerstner's transformation saved IBM, and putting the client first helped reshape the older product-based method of operating. Yet he and Palmisano also wedded it to "client success" for its large corporate customers, so IBM has been slower than others to grasp the swarm of new, smaller, customers the Web and cloud have empowered. And the embedded IT departments of its large clients have been slow to move operations to the cloud, so IBM has played third fiddle to Microsoft and Amazon in the cloud space. Its strategic challenge is classic. Its range of skills combined with being actually "plugged into" so many major corporations and organizations give it an unparalleled resource position. But those very customers are not the nimblest or the ones pushing the frontiers of information technology.

Success leads to plenty, which leads to laxity. That diminished alertness allows old structures and practices to persist long after their sell-by date. Talented executives are called in to transform and renew the company and install new systems and an updated managerial logic. Then, after a time, things change again, and those structures and processes become problems . . .

It is amazingly hard to keep a large, successful, profitable company focused on both productivity and change. Can it be done?

Organization and culture are strategic issues. When they support the basic competitive position of the firm, they are a source of advantage. When they impede efficiency, change, and innovation, they become strategic issues. Grand statements about "our vision" and "the Strategy for Growth" that ignore festering organizational problems are part of the problem. Good strategic leadership should confront internal issues with the same vigor it uses to advance its external purposes.

PART IV

Bright, Shiny Distractions

Modern leaders of companies and agencies are tempted by a host of distractions. They are told that the company must have a "mission" from which all other decisions must flow. They are liable to begin their strategy work with an attempt to explicate their goals in the belief that a strategy can be deduced from goals. They may confuse, as have many influential leaders and speakers, strategy with management. The two are related, but different. We can sympathize with their being distracted by the ninety-day chase after quarterly earnings, both guidance and results, but we should not let them think that strategy is chasing short-term results.

14

Don't Start with Goals

It is common to believe that strategies are plans for attaining certain goals. But who specifies the goals, and how do they do this? When a leader sets a goal, it is actually a decision about what is important and about where resources and energy will be allocated.

But a goal set arbitrarily, without an analysis or understanding of a critical challenge or opportunity, is an *unsupported goal.* By contrast, a good goal is the result of effective strategy work that targets certain *actions* that will move the organization forward. To avoid confusion, it is best to call this an objective to distinguish it from an unsupported goal. Unsupported goals, like hitting a specific profit target in the next twelve months, are Dilbert-style corporate management, because such goals are disconnected from the reality of the situation.

CURTISS-WRIGHT

My thinking about strategic goals first clarified many years ago during a strategy meeting led by Ted Berner, then the CEO of Curtiss-Wright. He contacted me because of my research book on diversification.[1] Berner had guided the company since 1960, and he wanted an outsider with expertise in diversification to help shape the corporate strategy. He asked me to work with a small top-management team.

The company's cofounders were the stuff of legend. Glenn Curtiss had been a motor designer, motorcycle racer, and test pilot. Curtiss rose to national fame in 1907 when his V-8-powered motorcycle achieved a speed of 136 mph, giving him the title "the Fastest Man Alive." He was the first to fly an airplane on a takeoff from a naval ship (1910). During World War I, Curtiss supplied thousands of easy-to-fly "Jennys" and N-9 seaplanes to the military.

Wright Aeronautical had been created by the Wright brothers and became an engine manufacturer. On its nonstop flight from New York to Paris, Charles Lindbergh's *Spirit of Saint Louis* was powered by a Wright Whirlwind engine. Two years later, in 1929, Curtiss-Wright was formed as a merger of the Wright and Curtiss interests.

Curtiss-Wright became a major manufacturer of aircraft engines and propellers during World War II and in the 1950s. The rise of jet engines in the 1960s almost eliminated that business, and Curtiss-Wright diversified into other aircraft components, nuclear control equipment, and components for the automobile and construction equipment industries.

Curtiss-Wright had been deeply involved in bringing the rotary (Wankel) engine to market. After German NSU Werke built the first working rotary engine in 1957, Curtiss-Wright bought an exclusive US license to develop and build Wankel engines. In the automotive industry there was great excitement about the rotary engine. The Wankel ran smoothly with no reciprocating pistons. It hummed rather than roared and fed power smoothly to the drivetrain. The first production cars to use the Wankel were the 1967 Mazda Cosmo, followed by its popular RX-7. American Motors' vice president of product, Gerald Meyers, said that the automaker could "convert 50 percent to rotaries by 1980 and 100 percent by 1984."[2] Wall Street loved the story, and in 1972 Curtiss-Wright's stock price soared to sixty dollars on earnings of thirteen cents.

The Wankel, however, was not fuel efficient, and its promise began to evaporate in 1973 after the sharp rise in the price of oil. In addition, the US government began to clamp down on emissions standards, and the Wankel had emissions issues. General Motors canceled its Wankel development program, and no other automakers seemed willing to sign a contract with Curtiss-Wright. Its stock price fell to five dollars in 1974. The company continued to produce military nuclear components, nuclear systems and devices, turbine generators, and various aircraft components. It was also expanding its ability to produce components for the new wide-bodied airliners. Despite the collapse of its stock price, it remained relatively debt free and had good cash reserves.

CEO Ted Berner began the Friday strategy meeting by asking the group to clarify the company's goals. I recall his injunction that "We should first agree on what we are trying to accomplish. Once that is clear, we can dig into how to get there."

The morning's two-hour discussion of goals was painful. The executives offered broad goals like "grow" or "diversify" or "increase return on capital." No one could argue with these broad goals, yet these kinds of aspirations had no bite unless they became more specific. Then, if someone were more specific, arguing, say, that the company should seek to enter the pollution-control equipment business, such a "goal" was obviously an extremely powerful decision about what to do.

The rest of the day was committed to a review of the company's businesses. As we broke, Berner told me that we would revisit the topic of goals the next morning. He asked me to lead off with a quick summary of what constituted a "good strategic goal."

I did not sleep that night. I had come prepared to discuss the pros and cons of various approaches to diversification, not the problem of goals. The question "What should a business strive to accomplish?" is, logically, not much different from the question "What should a person strive to do in life?" And that question has bedeviled philosophers for twenty-five hundred years. Should people seek faith, honor, truth, justice, power, wealth, balance, or simply happiness? Or are we free to define our own goals and values, as existentialists hold? And what does any of that have to do with what one does tomorrow? I borrowed a typewriter and, overnight, created a brief presentation that has, for me, stood the test of time. Forty-six years later, I continue to find it helpful in thinking about fruitful strategy work.

> What is a good strategic goal? It is obvious that a business should try to survive and to increase profit. Yet, these aspirations do not translate into specific actions. So, we meet to create a strategy---an answer to the question "What shall we do?" Answering that question creates the goals the organization will work to accomplish. Good strategic goals are the outcome of strategy, not its input.
>
> When we work on strategy it is natural to remind ourselves of our broad ambitions and values. But ambitions, desires, and values do not tell us what to do. For example, values like liberty and security are shared by almost all Americans, but they do not tell us whether or not Social Security should be backed by real savings or simply be a pay-as-you-go commitment. And, they do not tell us exactly how much security we are willing to give up to gain an increment of liberty, or vice versa.
>
> Specific goals, like earn more than 15 percent on capital, or reduce military and aircraft sales to less than 50% of the total, may seem more useful because they are concrete. Critically, declarations of specific goals like these are actually decisions. They are sharp choices about what will be done. Specific "goals" like these determine where senior executives will spend their time and

energy and where corporate resources will be allocated. Seeking goals to guide our decisions, we wind up making decisions masquerading as goals.

A business organization competes. It competes for revenues, it competes for skills, it competes for reputation and recognition, and it competes in the capital markets for funds. A strategy is a decision about how and where and with whom it will compete. Unfortunately, there is no magic calculator connecting strategic choices with financial or other metrics of success. Consequently, there is no way to work backwards from broad goals to strategy. And, narrow goals are no more than strategy in disguise minus any supporting analysis.

Strategy should be based on judgments gained by examining changes, problems, skills, resources, and opportunities. Strategy may act in the service of desires, but its practical shape is determined by insights about what has changed, about skills and knowledge that are both protected and special, about the skills and resources of other agents, and about what resources can be mobilized.

Today, this year (1974), the price of oil has risen from $3 a barrel to $12. This will have large implications for many industries. We should start our work on strategy by looking at these consequential changes and how Curtiss-Wright can weather them and use them to its advantage.

Strategy is a considered judgment about what to do. It cannot serve all of our desires

```
at once. Our strategy defines which broad in-
terests can be advanced and which cannot in
the current situation. Having decided on a
way forward---a strategy---we can then fash-
ion the specific goals that will guide its
implementation.
```

The next day's meeting started off with passing around Xerox copies of my short note. (In those days we didn't have PowerPoint, and people would actually read blocks of text.) There was not thunderous applause. The group did turn to some of the issues I had highlighted. They began to pay some attention to the implications of the dawning oil crisis. They began to express the view that the company was good at high-performance-equipment design and construction for difficult environments. But it was not very good at anticipating government-contract dynamics. They would like to put their skills to work in more stable businesses.

I did not work with Curtiss-Wright beyond that two-day session. At that moment the firm's total value was about $10 billion.[3] Subsequent events showed that Tim Berner's "strategy" for the company was conglomerate growth—the acquisition of unrelated businesses. Within a year, Curtiss-Wright began buying the stock of Cenco, a semiconglomerate making pollution-control equipment and medical equipment as well as operating nursing homes. Two years later, Ted Berner launched a proxy battle for control of Kennecott (copper). Then conglomerate Teledyne began buying shares of Curtiss-Wright. The company's total value sank to $2.9 billion over three years. Over the next twenty years, Curtiss-Wright gradually returned to its original center of supplying sophisticated parts and assemblies to commercial aircraft and defense companies. Today, in 2021, Curtiss-Wright is a medium-size diversified provider of flow and motion-control products for the aerospace, nuclear, and oil and gas industries and of metal-treatment services for aerospace, automotive, and industrial markets. Its total value is about $6 billion.

GOALS ARE DECISIONS

Misunderstanding the relationship between goals and strategy, as was the case at Curtiss-Wright, is the origin of wheel-spinning frustration in many strategic retreats and planning meetings. As at Curtiss-Wright, executives want to develop strategy but first seek agreement on the goals of the company. This is the most common pop-culture advice for setting strategy.

At the strategy retreat, agreement on broad universal values seems easy. The company should make more profit, it should be larger, it should be better than competitors, and it should engender respect and treat its employees well. Few will disagree with such values and aspirations. But the instant a value is expressed as a specific goal, especially a metric, it implies a stream of actions. *Setting a specific metric is deciding what is important.*

If a goal—a decision—is set based on an understanding of the forces at work in the central challenge being faced, then it can be useful in guiding action. But if a goal is simply proclaimed, absent a diagnosis of the forces at work, then it, by itself, is a decision about what is important, a decision lacking a foundation in sound diagnosis. By contrast, a good goal, or good objective, flows out of a process of problem solving. A good objective has the form of a task—set up operations in Australia, work with a particular customer to solve a product quality problem, create a breakaway team to focus on developing a better waterproof coating, and so on. Starting with unsupported goals—like gain market share—lacks entrepreneurial insight and tries to get performance by flogging the system.

Ted Berner asked me, "What is a good strategic goal?" The answer is that good strategic goals are an *outcome* of working the gnarly problem of strategy, not an *antecedent*. When organizational leaders face the issue of strategy, they are building a bridge between general desires and ambitions and the specifics of action in the here and now. If they do their job well, one outcome will be good strategic objectives.

Goals are important instruments of management. They are created by leaders and managers as tools for guiding action. A good objective

- resolves ambiguity, defining a problem that is simpler to solve than the original overall challenge
- is one the organization knows how to achieve or can be expected to work out how to achieve
- represents a clear set of choices, narrowing focus, resolving conflicts, and helping define what shall be done and what shall not be done
- is not always something on which everyone agrees

ARBITRARY UNSUPPORTED GOALS

Bad strategic goals come in two eye-catching and distracting colors. The first is an unsupported goal set without an analysis or even recognition of the underlying problems. I recall CEO John Akers's 1985 goal for IBM to increase its revenues from $46 to $180 billion over the coming decade. Like today's Apple in smartphones, IBM then dominated the computer industry, taking in almost two-thirds of the industry's profits. But the sun was setting on the time of the mainframe and on the isolated IT departments that operated them. Akers's unsupported goal led IBM to grossly overinvest in staff, taking it near death as its central business collapsed. Goals like Akers's dodge the responsibility to lead—like a coach who shouts "Win the game!" instead of giving advice on how to play.

As an example of a large global unsupported goal, consider 'Sendia Products.' Sendia was one of the five hundred largest companies in the United States. Its board of directors indicated that its growth had not been up to par and wanted to "take the company to the next level." The new CEO was responding with a strategy entitled "On to the Next." To make that slogan concrete he had set a goal of doubling revenues from $50 to $100 billion over the next five years.

The goal of doubling revenue in five years was unsupported. Even though Sendia completely dominated its market, that market wasn't growing very rapidly. The CEO's intent was to enter two adjacent markets. The positive element in the first adjacency was growth. The negative was that Sendia had already failed at offering products in this market in the past. There was also a very strong dominant successful competitor. In the second adjacency, there was less growth and no clear product winner among the scattershot of offerings.

The senior executives of the company were gathered in a room dominated by a large screen on one wall. The screen displayed the PowerPoint slides being prepared for the upcoming board meeting. The keystone slide was the financial projection that took revenues from $50 to $100 billion in five years—a complex waterfall chart. Its message was that two new areas would add $40 billion to revenue. The remaining $10 billion would come from growth in existing areas. The supporting slides offered data about the company's products and the industry situation with a focus on the two key initiatives that would achieve the growth goal.

The key slide on the first new initiative showed losses for the first few years followed by soaring profits as volume built. There was a note that the present value was positive. The CEO asked, "What is the market-share implication of those projections? Shouldn't we include that on the slide?"

The chief financial officer looked over her notes and said that the projection was for an 85 percent share in five years.

"That doesn't seem reasonable," observed the CEO. "After all, there is a serious competitor in this market. We are starting from zero."

The senior vice president for product development spoke up. "We are good at the technology. Once the producers realize the performance we can offer, they will switch over to our product."

The CFO visibly winced, possibly recalling the previous failed attempt at entry.

"What if we plan for a 40 percent share? Isn't that more reasonable?" the CEO asked.

The CFO responded, "Then we only hit $74 billion instead of $100 billion in five years."

The CFO's assistant then pointed out that the lower market share would drop the present value into negative territory. The CEO asked about the lowest-share assumption that would keep the present value positive. The analyst said it would be about 50 percent.

The CEO sighed. "Let's put the expected share at 50 percent, and make our plans for the second initiative more aggressive. We will meet tomorrow at the same time to finish this up."

Despite having a solid core business, Sendia did not have a strategy. There was no discernible source of advantage or even potential future advantage to back up the ambition to double revenue in five years.

In the three years after the meeting just described, both new initiatives failed and the CEO was terminated.

Why did this CEO focus on manipulating numbers on slides rather than a clear-eyed appraisal of technology and competition? One driving force was the board of directors, which had been reshaped over a decade to meet goals of independence and diversity. Each outside board member was respected and competent, but only one of them had an even superficial knowledge about the complex technology the company employed. The only language external members of the board had in common was financial accounting. The board pressed the CEO every quarter to deliver projections of growth.

At Sendia the unsupported growth goal corrupted top management. I believe that, in their hearts, they knew that their PowerPoint slides were hogwash. But the pressure of "On to the Next" had them making up numbers and promises that couldn't be kept. More courage would have helped. It always amazes me when executives taking down millions of dollars a year lack the courage of the average fireman.

The pop-psychology belief is that goals motivate. Stupid arbitrary goals don't motivate achievement. They motivate cynicism and fabrication.

MISAPPLIED GOALS

A second type of bad goal addresses the wrong problem when diagnosis is lacking or restricted by politics or myopia. In such cases, there is a problem statement, together with policies, actions, and goal setting. But the goals focus energy onto the wrong activities, missing the real problems. Most of the time, these bad goals are a collection of short-term measures that fail to address the critical underlying issues. An example was the efficiency goals at Dean Foods.

Created by the 2001 merger of a Chicago-based dairy company (Dean) with Suiza Foods, a fast-expanding roll-up of regional dairies, Dean Foods came to be a very major player in the US dairy industry. After the merger, Dean processed more than one-third of the fluid milk in the United States, about the same as its three largest competitors together.

Dean's constituent parts were forty to sixty small milk processors. Some were mom-and-pop operations; some were larger. The processors gathered milk from dairy farmers, pasteurized it, homogenized it, and performed varying degrees of separation. The fresh milk sold in most grocery stores was only twenty-four to thirty-six hours from the cow. The roll-up gave Dean Foods more than sixty different brands of milk and butter, some fairly well known and some very local. Among its name brands were Alta Dena, Creamland, Foremost, Meadow Brook, and Swiss Dairy.

Since the late 1990s, fluid milk consumption in the United States had been gradually declining, on average about 2–3 percent per year, with ups and downs along the way. The US government subsidized dairy farmers ($22 billion in 2018) and administered a complex system of price controls. Dairy farmers as a whole generally produced excess milk that was often just poured into the ground. Milk prices varied with demand, the size of the herd of cows, and the price of feed. Demand was pushed and pulled by fashions for cheese, yogurt, and protein powders.

The fundamental problem faced by Dean Foods was that it wasn't really a national company. Competition was local. Supermarket,

Walmart, Kroger, and Costco buyers pitted one local processor against the other, seeking the lowest price. About 80 percent of all fluid milk sold was private-label products with no national brand names. Having a national footprint did nothing to increase bargaining power. Dean Foods management had long sought a strong national milk brand but was hampered by the product's basic commodity nature, the difficulty of long-distance shipment, and their lack of sufficient profit to finance a $200 million advertising campaign.

To deal with this set of issues, the company sought to increase its operational efficiency. It closed some processing plants and adjusted supply routes. It established a system of "key performance indicators" (KPIs) that measured performance and progress weekly and monthly. The KPIs covered volume, revenue, sales discounts, expenses, elements of cost, and customer margins by district.[4]

Unfortunately, most of the costs in the dairy system are related to feed prices and herd size. Feed prices, in turn, swing with oil prices as they drive the demand for ethanol and, consequently, the price of corn. Milk prices are usually capped by surplus production. Pressing the existing system for efficiency was not going to solve these fundamental challenges.

Dean Foods did have three interesting brands that were not commodity fluid milk: Horizon Organic, Silk, and Alpro soy milk, all parts of a company named WhiteWave that had been acquired in 2002. In a move that seemed prescient, the company split them off and performed an IPO in 2012, essentially selling the WhiteWave company for $2.9 billion. On the other hand, perhaps the move was impulsive: five years on, Danone acquired WhiteWave for $12.5 billion.

Beginning in 2014, Dean Foods faced a trifecta of problems. China cut back sharply on its milk imports, and the EU lifted its milk-production quotas. Russia banned milk imports. Surplus milk was spilled into ditches in the United States even as consumer demand took a downward step. The company doubled down on its efficiency goals. Seeking some branded product, it bought Friendly's

Ice Cream in 2016. Chief operating officer Ralph Scozzafava advanced to the CEO job in January 2017 and implemented a strategy of even stronger cost pressure and aiming more squarely at being a private-label producer.

Over the next three years, sales fell by 5 percent, and net income fell from $62 million to a loss of $500 million. Despite the constant public pronouncements of cost rationalization, cost of goods sold rose from 72 to 79 percent of sales. Scozzafava was let go in mid-2019 after the stock price had fallen 87 percent in a year. Dean Foods declared bankruptcy in November 2019. News media blamed the drop in milk consumption and Walmart's decision to develop its own dairy supply. But, even as farmers complained, milk was still being dumped because of surplus production.

What could Dean Foods have done differently? It could have kept the $2 billion it spent in 2007 on a huge dividend and used those funds to buy or acquire some brands in categories that were growing and unregulated. It could have kept WhiteWave and used it to anchor more brands and a national distribution system. Or it could have expanded into being a distributor of other grocery products. It could have recognized that the business was local and moved, region by region, to be a contract processor for Walmart. It could have made Friendly's Ice Cream into a quality product instead of another box of airy frozen foam for kids.

Rolling up dairy processors did not solve the problems of excess production or declining demand. Nor did it magically make a national business out of forty to sixty local processors. Dean Foods' raft of KPIs could not make fundamental improvements in a host of local patched-together businesses. Measuring something doesn't always mean it can be improved.

Had the product been pickles or corn chips, the original roll-up might have worked. But hard-to-brand, locally processed, private-label fluid milk?

15

Don't Confuse Strategy with Management

It was a cool November day in 1966. Secretary of Defense Robert McNamara arrived to give a brief address at the Harvard Business School. He was a "whiz kid" who had taught at the Business School, served in the US Air Force during World War II, been the president of Ford, and been picked by President Kennedy to be the secretary of defense. At that moment, in 1966, McNamara was in the middle of the ramp-up of the war in Vietnam. I stood with a small crowd just outside the auditorium in Baker Library, listening to his amplified comments. I remember his key argument. It was one he made elsewhere as well.[1] His point was simple: "As a technology, management has rapidly developed in the last thirty years. We now know how to manage anything—the Ford Motor Company, the Catholic Church, or the Department of Defense. You break the overall objective into parts which can be measured. You put someone in charge of each part and measure their progress, holding them accountable for results."

I have never forgotten the claim that "we now know how to manage anything." McNamara's formula was a form of management by objectives. You establish measurable goals and track progress along those dimensions. At the time he spoke in 1966, McNamara was supporting General William Westmoreland in a goal of killing more Vietcong and North Vietnamese than they could replace.

It turned out that the North could and did replace troops faster than the United States could kill them. The dogged pursuit of this goal turned the American public against the war. Writing thirty years later in 1995, McNamara said: "Looking back, I clearly erred by not forcing—then or later, in either Saigon or Washington—a knock-down, drag-out debate over the loose assumptions, unasked questions, and thin analyses underlying our military strategy in Vietnam. . . . I doubt I will ever fully understand why I did not do so."[2]

As argued in Chapter 4, given the political and value constraints, there was very likely no strategy solution in Vietnam. Managing by measuring progress didn't work. The "progress" led into a trap—a war of attrition and combat of wills. McNamara's dilemma in Vietnam is a vivid illustration that management work and strategy work are two different things. A collection of goals or metrics is not a strategy. A strategy is a reasoned argument about the forces at work in a situation and how to deal with them. Don't let the metrics drown out thought.

Clark Clifford, who replaced McNamara as secretary of defense, wrote this about him: "In reforming the Pentagon, his talents had served him well, but . . . Vietnam was not a management problem, it was a war. . . . [T]his man, who was probably our greatest minister of defense, was not well suited to manage a war—yet this was precisely what was required by the circumstances."[3]

Robert McNamara was a very skilled manager. But his failure at strategy work put a scar on our society that lives on today.

DRIVING RESULTS

A few years ago, a phone call was an apt reminder of McNamara's Harvard speech. The voice on the telephone was an executive at a large financial services company. She was asking if I would be willing to design and teach two sessions on strategy for a new senior-level executive program. When I asked about the purpose of the program, she said, "We have the marketing and finance sections of the program covered. What we want from the strategy sessions is a focus on driving results." I demurred and suggested someone else for the assignment. "Driving results" is important, but it is not strategy work. McNamara worked hard to drive results in Vietnam, but, as we've seen, he did not have a strategy.

Motivating and measuring performance is the vital heartbeat of organizations that "keeps the trains running on time." You cannot improve most operations without measuring efficiency. To better the customer experience, you need to know what is happening. How long does it take to install our software on a client's system? Having a concrete goal can be a powerful motivating device. "Get some exercise each day" is vague. "Thirty minutes a day on the treadmill" is concrete and more likely to be followed.

It would be a simpler world if all one had to do to achieve great purpose was to get people to hit their targets. Leaders would just set or negotiate higher and higher targets every year and "drive results" to their achievement. In that simpler world there would be no need for strategy. But "driving results," as McNamara discovered, is management work, not strategy work.

Strategy work *defines* the goals and objectives to be sought. Good strategy work begins with recognizing a challenge and in understanding the difficulties in overcoming it. Good strategy work produces policies, actions, and objectives.

Management work—accomplishing given objectives—is often called *execution*. It is a popular trope to argue that execution is much more important than strategy. Rosabeth Moss Kanter wrote, "The game is won on the playing field. When a strategy looks brilliant, it's because of the quality of execution."[4] She is not correct. Success is the outcome of both good strategy and good execution. If either fails, things don't work out. They are both important. The issue is not relative importance, but that they are different. Strategy and management are different kinds of work. "Driving results" in the absence of a clear strategy is putting the cart before the horse.

METHODS OF MANAGEMENT

Before about 1840, most businesses were small and family owned. The economy was mostly farming and trading. Traders did the buying, transport, and selling themselves or with the help of two or three others. It was the railroads that forced the need for full-time administrators. Railroads generated the first-ever organization charts and a constant flow of both planning and record keeping. After the 1870s, true departments and hierarchies of administrators began to appear.[5] As the large companies of the 1900s started to emerge, new structures of managers who managed other managers were devised.

In 1954 Peter Drucker set out to describe this new world of managers managing other managers. His influential 1954 book, *The Practice of Management*, tried to systematize the task of managing a modern complex organization having layers of managers. He eschewed the older model of the manager directing work by giving orders. With managers managing other managers, he taught that each manager's objective had to be set in an informed negotiation, considering the limitations and opportunities of the situation. People, he held, should understand why certain objectives were important. The system became what is now called "management by objectives."

Drucker's "management by objectives" soon became systematized as a formal goal-setting process—essentially a negotiation over budgets and goals, together with top-down information about overall purpose. This system of management is now fairly universal. Most modern organizations run to the drumbeat of quantifiable targets.

The current approach to this is called the Balanced Scorecard, a system popularized by Robert Kaplan and David P. Norton.[6] This system divides goals into four categories: financial, customer, internal process, and learning innovation. A significant improvement over simple budget goals, the Balanced Scorecard is currently in use in many large firms. Kaplan and Norton explain that "any changes made at the annual strategy-planning meeting get translated into the company's strategy map and Balanced Scorecard."[7] This makes it clear that the Balanced Scorecard is a management work tool, designed to manage, or implement, or help execute a strategy.

DELKHA

'DelKha' is a nice illustration of the difference between management and strategy. Well managed, it still faced a challenge its management system could not handle.

In 2010 I received a call from 'Felicia Kha,' who wanted help with "tying strategy to the Balanced Scorecard." Her mother had started the business as a trading company linking Vietnam to Singapore and the United States. By 2010 the company had expanded into supplying many mechanical and electrical components for computers (personal, business, and servers). Its stock traded on the Singapore exchange. DelKha had stayed away from active electronic components like motherboards and instead focused on power supplies, boxes, connectors, wiring harnesses, and cooling components; it manufactured cooling fans that were used for computer cases, CPU cooling, and video-card cooling. Most other components were sourced from a variety of suppliers in Asia.

Felicia Kha had pleasant offices in San Francisco overlooking the bay. On her office wall hung a nicely printed Balanced Scorecard, shown in Figure 14 without the colorful artwork and minus the numerical targets.

Felicia explained that she liked the scorecard idea. The point was to have a balanced set of objectives instead of just a budget. She said, "Our people need to believe that if they do their jobs well, everything will work out." Her difficulty was declining prices and slowing unit sales.

The larger problem was that PCs, in general, were topping out. Laptops were still selling fairly well, but most were built by integrated manufacturers who either made or sourced components directly. And with pads and smartphones booming, the future did not look bright for a PC component trader and maker. Felicia was concerned that the company would not survive the rising crush.

FIGURE 14. DelKha Balanced Scorecard

THE MISSION	
To be the most successful computer-components company in the world, delivering the best customer experience in the markets we serve	
GOALS	**KEY PERFORMANCE INDICATORS**
Financial:	
Beat the STI Index in share price appreciation	Net margin - Operating income per customer
Sales growth of 10% per year	Return on equity
Gross margin above 35%	Sales growth rate
Customer:	
On time all the time - Quotes in 2 days - Be ready for the new products and versions	Sales and sales growth per customer and product class
	Customer retention
	Cost and revenue per sales visit
	Satisfaction score
Internal:	
Maintain at least two sub-contractors on each item	Turnover of key supplier-relations people
Keep moving fast	External hiring ratio
Inventory parts not fans	Satisfaction scores
	Time to deal with design changes
Innovation and Learning:	
Work with lead customer to keep abreast of new designs	New product types adopted
Consult with customers on design choices	Hours/salesperson product training
	Hours/supplier person product training

DelKha's Balanced Scorecard, together with the more detailed operating information and budgets, had kept the company on track. It was a reasonable system of management, but what Felicia needed in 2010 was strategy work, and statements of mission and basic goals were not helpful.

We formed a strategy working group of five and began to meet regularly, first focusing on the challenge of DelKha's declining fortunes. We started by looking at her customers' problems. What challenges did PC makers face? Felicia answered that "these guys are some of the most sophisticated buyers in the world. Guys like Dell and HP [Hewlett-Packard] carry almost no inventory and can assemble a computer to order in less than an hour." She went on to say that Sony monitors were drop-shipped direct to business customers. "These guys don't need anything from us except low prices and on-time delivery," she continued. Overall, their business problems were slowing demand and margins being squeezed by competition with each other.

The head of sales offered that there were makers who specialized in the PC-gamer segment. Those companies had a demand for higher-quality components, especially high-power cooling systems. Everyone felt that it would continue to be a niche business.

At a subsequent meeting, one senior manager suggested that plenty of customers outside of the PC business had supply-chain problems. They had not developed the sophistication of Dell, HP, and so on. Could DelKha help them solve their problems? There was a good discussion about becoming a supply-chain adviser and manager for non-PC companies. The obstacle in that direction was that DelKha's skills and knowledge were limited to PC components. Felicia committed to using her network of Vietnamese American businesspeople to seek out a potential customer. Two other executives would also sound out people they knew.

A month later, the networking had not indicated opportunity in supply-chain advice or management. There were existing firms doing this with better depth than DelKha. What did turn up was a potential customer for DelKha's brushless cooling-fan motors.

The potential customer, 'FlyKo,' wanted a high-power brushless fan for a flying drone. The French company Parrot had just released the first Wi-Fi based consumer drone, and it was a big hit. FlyKo sold a line of radio-controlled (R/C) model airplanes and wanted to make an even better radio-controlled drone that could fly well beyond the range of Wi-Fi.

DelKha bought a Parrot drone, brought the head of fan engineering into the strategy group, and discussed the challenge. He was excited by the idea and thought that DelKha could meet or even beat the performance of the Parrot fans.

In a traditional motor, the electricity sent to the central rotating element had copper contacts through which the current passed via carbon "brushes." On a brushless motor, there were no brush contacts, just an air gap. The sequence and timing of the magnetic fields was managed by a microprocessor timing the feed of DC electric power to coils.

DelKha put together a task force to work with FlyKo. The DelKha engineers were able to deliver the fan, and FlyKo built a prototype drone. Unfortunately, its inventory of regular R/C airplanes was not selling, and FlyKo had to invoke Chapter 11 bankruptcy.

The strategy team at DelKha liked the idea of building on the company's brushless-fan abilities. There were surely other customers whose problems could be solved by DelKha. Felicia decided to buy the now fire-sale-priced radio and electronics assets of FlyKo for $100,000. A key FlyKo engineer began to work for DelKha as a consultant.

With this new capability in place, the senior executives realized that their challenge had changed. Three months ago, the critical challenge seemed to be the declining PC industry. Now it had become taking a position in the growing brushless-motor industry. Brushless motors were being used in robotics, medical tools, and drones and would, they hoped, be used in cordless power tools.

DelKha's first successful consumer product was an R/C model car produced in partnership with a toy company. It was much simpler to operate than a flying device. Distributed through toy outlets, it was quiet yet had amazing range and speed. Clubs formed to race against each other in parking lots on Sundays.

Focusing on solving customers' problems, DelKha next built a very high-powered yet quiet fan for a company making portable vacuum cleaners. Again, the combination of cordless battery power and the quiet yet potent brushless motor helped make the customer's product a success.

By 2014 DelKha was an established player in the high-performance brushless-motor industry. Its stock had quintupled in value, and its employee count had quadrupled.

DelKha's strategy quest had started by looking first at the seemingly mortal challenge of the declining PC-parts business. We then began to look at the challenges of others that had some connection to its skills and knowledge. There were false starts in supply-chain services and airborne drones. Yet a new business did emerge based on its brushless-fan capabilities.

In 2019 DelKha's Balanced Scorecard looked very different than it did nine years before. There was now much more emphasis on innovative engineering and on motor-performance parameters. Its own distribution and partner relationships got much more attention. It remained a useful management tool, though with very different goals and KPIs.

Still, in DelKha's strategy quest, the scorecard had not been helpful. Its use is in managing a business. It is not much help when the challenge is not a failure of efficiency in current operations. It did not help in redefining the business or in building a new business. If you are under the illusion that strategy is about pushing people to meet top management's goals, then stick to your scorecard. But good strategy work is not management work. You need both, but don't confuse one with the other.

16

Don't Confuse Current Financial Results with Strategy

The 90-Day Derby is the cycle of consensus quarterly earnings estimates, corporate guidance about earnings, and the intense attention paid to these numbers by both Wall Street and the leadership of many public corporations.

How did this happen? In 1976 the Institutional Brokers' Estimate System (IBES) began to collect estimates of future annual earnings of US corporations. Over time, this evolved into average, or "consensus," estimates, and the estimates' horizon shortened from annual to quarterly earnings. In reaction to this dynamic, many companies began to offer "guidance" on their earnings in upcoming quarters.

By the mid-1980s, whether a company hit or missed the consensus estimate became an important issue. As this measure grew in popularity, many firms got better and better at hitting the earnings targets. Some observers claimed that in the new logic, missing by a lot could be better than missing by a little: "In the growth stock fraternity, 'missing by a penny' now implies the height of corporate boneheadedness—that is, if you couldn't find that extra penny to keep Wall Street happy, then your company must really be in trouble, and since missing by a penny is already going to send your stock plummeting, you're better off missing by a dime or two and saving those earnings for the next quarter."[1]

CEOs who are caught up in quarterly 90-Day Derbies spend a great deal of time and energy preparing guidance and then trying to live up to it. This creates an inevitable focus on accounting results and on trying to keep short-term earnings predictable.

If the point of business is to make money, what is wrong with trying to keep earnings as high as possible and growing consistently? The problem is severalfold. First, current earnings are the harvest of investments and actions taken in the past, sometimes by generations long gone. Today's profits are not simply the result of hard work by today's managers and employees. They come from past cleverness, luck, and the outcome of past strategic battles. Microsoft's high current earnings come because its software products have become standards that almost everyone must have to be productive and to work with others. In the same vein, costs borne today may well be the key to future harvests of profit.

And, of course, it works the other way around. Once great Boeing has been struggling with design flaws in its 737 MAX, with an overenthusiasm for international outsourcing, with overheating lithium batteries, and more. All of these depress earnings, but the lower earnings are not due to how hard or skillfully today's managers, engineers, and employees work. They are almost all due to the culture brought in by its "merger" with McDonnell Douglas in 1997. The McDonnell Douglas approach to finance and cost-cutting overwhelmed Boeing's traditional engineering culture. A GE-trained general manager, McDonnell's Harry Stonecipher remarked, "When people say I changed the culture of Boeing, that was the intent, so that it's run like a business rather than a great engineering firm."[2] Getting costs down in the short term pleased Wall Street but may have damaged Boeing for generations.

The second problem is that current earnings do not determine the value of a corporation. The value of a corporation depends on all the future dividends or other payments it may make to shareholders, adjusted down for the risk of default, and adjusted upward for its possible acquisition by an optimistic buyer. The value is about the future—this quarter's results are hardly a reliable indicator of that long-term stream of future payments.

To see this most clearly, consider a company like Amazon. Since its IPO in 1997, Amazon has never paid a dividend, yet its stock price has grown greatly. So its value is all about future expectations. Like other stocks, its price vibrates intensely because of the great uncertainty about how far in the future those dividends may lie, their potential size, inflation, and other factors.

Suppose you were the CEO of Amazon, working to expand the company's offerings, to speed their delivery, to manage the hugely physical job of storing and moving millions of packages each day, building its cloud-services business, and beginning to expand its international footprint. On an early April call with Wall Street analysts, one asks about your new shipping center: "Isn't that going to hurt earnings in the fourth quarter?"

Reflect for a moment on that question. Amazon's value depends on its earning power over the next five, ten, twenty years, and more. Its stock price vibrates from hour to hour over uncertainty about that future. Looking to that future, just how important is the earnings-per-share number in the fourth quarter? Should Amazon adjust its investment plans to make it a little bit higher? Should you go out of your way to predict fourth-quarter earnings per share to the nickel with the understanding that this analyst, and others, will call you into account if you miss?

Where in the world is that question coming from? To see, consider the analyst who is asking. I have known a few and watched them work. Probably trained at Wharton or New York University or UCLA, they learned to discount future cash flows and how to build an Excel spreadsheet to forecast those cash flows. I have seen analysts with beautiful and complex ten-page spreadsheets that estimate the value of a company based on thirty to forty key growth factors, ratios, and industry parameters. That "model" of future cash flows and, ultimately, dividends will estimate the value of the company differently when any input number changes. So if fourth-quarter earnings turn out to be a bit lower than the model forecasts, the spreadsheet does that wonderful thing that spreadsheets do and changes all its forecasts about the future, quarter after quarter, on out forever. And that, of course, changes the model's prediction of the company's value and reduces its estimate of the "correct" share price.

To do this analysis, the analyst is using tools that mostly assume certainty. That is why a blip in earnings in the fourth quarter percolates into the future. But this is nonsense, an artifact of the mechanical nature of the spreadsheet model. In reality, earnings are like any other economic measure. They contain a strong random element. Track your monthly spending on groceries. A blip upward does not mean your finances are out of control, and a downward blip does not signal coming starvation. However, to insert proper logic into their estimates of value, the analysts would need PhDs in advanced Bayesian statistical modeling and certainly would not use spreadsheets. By construction, their fairly primitive estimating tools grossly overreact to blips.

A third problem is that the "true" value of a company is very hard to know. Fischer Black, coauthor of the famous 1973 Black-Scholes option-pricing formula, was a believer that market prices were unbiased estimates of true value.[3] But, over drinks, he also told me that the "true" value of a company was anywhere from half to twice the current stock price. Although unbiased, stock prices are very uncertain estimates of true values. That fact is missing from most conversations during the 90-Day Derby.

A strong point of view on this general issue was recently voiced by Warren Buffett and Jamie Dimon. Writing in the *Wall Street Journal*, they argued:

> The financial markets have become too focused on the short term. Quarterly earnings-per-share guidance is a major driver of this trend and contributes to a shift away from long-term investments. Companies frequently hold back on technology spending, hiring, and research and development to meet quarterly earnings forecasts that may be

affected by factors outside the company's control, such as commodity-price fluctuations, stock-market volatility and even the weather.[4]

The fourth problem is that the pressures of the derby induce some CEOs to make wasteful decisions. Anyone who has worked closely with the top executives to public corporations does not need academic research to know what is going on. Here are two quick examples from the many I have personally witnessed:

- 'Softways' software products occupied a growing segment of the market. The company lacked a key component of the systems that its main competitor was bringing to market. It was estimated that it would take about a year of programming effort to bridge the gap—an expense of about $20 million. The CEO demurred, being unwilling to damage earnings by that amount. Instead, the company went ahead and bought a firm that had the technology, paying $175 million for it. Half of the capital came from new debt, and the other half had come from their offshore private-equity backers. The expressed rationale had nothing to do with speed and everything to do with not reporting lower earnings. The acquired technology was capable but did not interface easily with Softways' existing software. It took almost two years to integrate the two technologies, twice the estimated time of developing it internally.
- 'Zotich' was a chemical company delivering a special input to five key customers. In recent years, customers' demands for performance were increasing, and Zotich's strategy was to excel at R&D aimed at customers' needs. In the summer of 2017, a downturn in industry demand for its customers' products rebounded to hit Zotich's earnings, and the stock price fell. In response, the CEO promised a quick upswing in earnings. He achieved that by cutting R&D staff significantly. At the same time, competitors were ramping up their R&D efforts. This was a strategically disastrous move. Over the next two years the stock price fell by 60 percent.

For companies that do not make these kinds of foolish choices, the 90-Day Derby still distracts management from more strategic concerns that actually affect the value of the company.

SHAREHOLDER VALUE AND INCENTIVES

The rise of shareholder value as the North Star of corporate purpose came of age in the 1980s. The idea that directors and managers should act to maximize shareholder value arose with special impetus from Harvard professor Michael Jensen's agency theory of the firm. "Corporate managers are the agents of shareholders," he wrote, and stressed that shareholders were often hurt by managers who refused to pay out cash to shareholders, instead investing in poor projects.[5]

Making shareholder value and return the North Stars of corporate purpose was an expression of economists' newly formed *agency theory*. This starts with the assumption that managers (agents) will not work very hard (they will "slack") and will make self-interested decisions unless there are incentive arrangements to align the interests of owners and managers.

Unfortunately, agency models don't address issues more complex than motivation—issues of belief, diagnosis of the situation, and judgment about importance. If the critical issues are obvious waste and abuse, then incentives can help reduce inefficiency. But incentives go only so far. Einstein spent the declining years of his life trying to create a "unified field theory." Would a $100 million bonus have sped the work to completion? If the problem is to win the war against the Nazis in Europe, would it have happened more quickly had Eisenhower been promised a $100 million bonus for an early win? Do the US Marines run toward rather than away from rifle fire because of promised bonuses? The problem is that the model assumes that incentives are all that matters.

Agency theory's incentive program does not solve the strategy problem. Strategic ability is not necessarily induced, nor is strategic incompetence blunted by pay for results. We can see that in privately held companies. There the interests of the owner and the manager are conjoined. Yet issues of strategy—of what to do and how to compete—remain. Incentives can motivate attention and energy, but the question of what to do remains.

In practice, "incentives" for top managers are constructed by contractual bonus payments, direct grants of stock, and stock options. The modern trend has been to tie compensation directly to share prices rather than accounting results. During the 1980s, options became the biggest component of top executive compensation. After the dot-com crash, the role of options was replaced by restricted stock grants. By 2019, performance-based stock awards were more than half of CEO compensation in the S&P 500 and about 40 percent of compensation in the broader Russell 3000.[6] This large increase in incentive pay has been concomitant with the rise of active institutional and individual investors. As Keith Hammonds at *Fast Company* magazine commented:

> What's different is the sandbox that today's CEOs play in. The sand started shifting in 1993, the year that professional managers took on investors—and lost. In the same week, the CEOs of American Express, IBM, and Westinghouse all resigned under pressure—basically because their companies' financial results were lousy. In the years that followed, executive pay was increasingly tied to company performance: More stock; more options.[7]

These compensation plans are designed by well-paid consultants who insist that these incentives are necessary to "align" the interests of CEOs with those of shareholders. What they do not admit is that this is not possible. These payments are conditional on certain events happening. That makes them into options.

An option is any contract permitting the holder to get or buy something at a fixed price, no matter the actual market price or worth. Today, Apple stock is $130 per share. You can buy an option contract for $20 that guarantees that you can purchase a share of Apple stock *one year from now* for exactly $130 a share. It the stock price doesn't go up, or if it goes down, you are out $20. But if it goes above $150 per share, your option contract will give you a profit. If Apple goes up to $170 a year from now, you will have doubled your original $20 investment. With more uncertainty, stocks tend to drop in value. Options, on the other hand, tend to rise in value with more uncertainty because the downside is limited. The bottom line is that you cannot make managers face the same situation as shareholders with option-like payments. Shareholders own shares, not options.

Research on incentive pay and corporate performance does not show any strong connection. Of course, it is hard to untangle the fact that rising share prices induce higher payments to executives regardless of the cause. If the CEO of a fairly well-managed company is lucky enough to work within a generally positive macro economy, and even better in an exciting industry, the stock price should be rising, providing valuable payouts unrelated to actions taken at the top. During most times, about 30 percent of individual stock-price movements are explained by the overall market results. In buoyant times, like the first half of 2019, 60 percent of individual stock movements are explained by the overall market. Thus, top managers and board members may receive large increases in wealth without outperforming rivals.

The basic problem with the shareholder-value goal is that senior executives don't know how to achieve it. Spending more time at the office won't help. Cutting costs as Boeing unwisely did after the merger with McDonnell Douglas had a long-term adverse impact. There are few if any reliable links between actions and share value. Of course, we believe that higher expectations about future earnings will drive up share value. But what creates these higher expectations? Should Walmart expand or slow its investment in China? Should Apple bring out its own streaming service? Should GE stick with its coal-fired energy business or sell it to someone else?

When I was a doctoral student in 1967, my adviser set me the task of interviewing professors in the various subject areas and writing down their conceptual schemes. Marketing had the "Four Ps," finance had the debt-irrelevance theorem, and so on. In accounting, Professor David Hawkins grinned and said, "Every business case has the same solution: increase sales, cut costs, and make the bastards work harder." Skip ahead more than a half century to 2020, and consider the instructions of the CIO Wiki: "In order to maximize shareholder value, there are three main strategies for driving profitability in a company: (1) revenue growth, (2) operating margin, and (3) capital efficiency."[8]

To see what is going on here, imagine you are the general manager of the Los Angeles Rams football team. You are interested in winning more games and hire a consultant. After six months of study, the consultant comes back and reports: "Your goal is to maximize the number of wins per season. Our research shows that the number of wins is driven by the metric *net yards gained*. That is, in turn, driven by *gross yards gained* minus *gross yards lost*. You need to manage to increase yards gained and decrease yards lost." Your consultant's advice is just as helpful as "increase sales and cut costs." His problem and your problem and the problem of senior corporate executives is that winning in business and football is a matter of subtle skill, not pressing buttons and winding cranks.

WHAT CAN BE DONE?

One way to have a CEO's financial incentive align with those of investors is to make him or her a longer-term shareholder. That would mean a grant of stock on hiring of sufficient size that it becomes a key source of wealth to the CEO. There could be no performance conditions attached except loss on negligence or crime. The stock would be owned outright by the CEO and his or her heirs but would not vest for seven years.

Owning a good chunk of stock with a horizon of seven or more years, a CEO would be able to make sounder judgments about actions to benefit the company's value versus those aimed at bouncing its current accounting earnings.

An example of a plan that moves in this direction is ExxonMobil's:

> The design of the compensation program helps reinforce these priorities and links the majority of compensation granted over multiple years to the performance of ExxonMobil stock and resulting shareholder value. This is achieved by using stock to pay a substantial portion of a senior executive's annual compensation and restricting the sale of the stock for periods of time far greater than the restrictions required by most other companies across all industries. The objective is to grant more than half of annual compensation in the form of restricted stock, half of which must be held for 10 years or until retirement, whichever is later. The other half must be held for 5 years.[9]

Another way of reducing the din of the 90-Day Derby is adjusting the company's clientele. Senior management's clientele is its board of directors, the key pension and mutual-fund investors, the analysts who follow the firm, and, of course, the ordinary investors who choose to buy its stock. Speculators don't count. They have a lot to do with stock-price gyrations, but their interest is in price movements, not the company's value.

Build and attract a clientele that believes in the company's commitment and ability to create long-term value. If pension-fund managers need a quick 12 percent return to bring their underfunded pension plan back from insolvency, tell them to buy another security. Constantly remind your clientele that the economy is uncertain, that there will be ups and downs, and that stock prices are noisy, uncertain measures. Tell them that to build long-term value, there will be experiments that don't work. Tell them that you and your team are building value for the decades to come and that if they are looking for a quick hit, look elsewhere. Creating new value is not a smooth process. Tell them that if they see very smooth corporate performance, someone is either fudging the numbers or milking the cow.

The financial press calls all who buy and sell stock "investors." But most stock trading is by speculators, not investors. To quiet the

90-Day Derby, you want a clientele who are investors, not speculators. There is nothing illegal or immoral with speculating on share prices. But you should not confuse such "owners" with those who are interested in the value of the company rather than the fluctuations in its stock price.

In a 2001 study, Brian Bushee found that among institutional investors, what he termed "transient" investors were associated with overweighting the near-term earnings.[10] By "transient" he meant very diversified portfolios with high portfolio turnover. Institutions with narrower, more focused holdings seemed not to have this short-term bias. In another interesting study, Kim et al. found that when a company stopped offering earning guidance, its clientele shifted to longer-term investors.[11]

The board of directors can be crucial. If you want to stimulate a longer-term view, don't crowd your board of directors with deal makers or investment bankers. Try to build a board of directors that understands the business well enough to look beyond each quarter's and even each year's results. If they don't understand the business, or technology, or how the industry really works, all they can do is watch the quarterly results.

An electrical engineer distinguishes between the "signal" and the "noise." The signal is the message, and the noise is the corrupting static and error that make it hard to hear or understand the message. It is important that your clientele accept the "noisy" view of security prices—that the message of intrinsic value is often masked by random noise. Long-term managers like Warren Buffett and Jeff Bezos write annual letters to their investors stressing this fact. In his initial 1997 letter to shareholders, Bezos famously wrote: "When forced to choose between optimizing the appearance of our GAAP [generally accepted accounting principles] accounting and maximizing the present value of future cash flows, we'll take the cash flows." In a 2009 letter, in the midst of the world financial crisis, he wrote:

> In this turbulent global economy, our fundamental approach remains the same. Stay heads down, focused on the long term and obsessed over

> customers. Long-term thinking levers our existing abilities and lets us do new things we couldn't otherwise contemplate. It supports the failure and iteration required for invention, and it frees us to pioneer in unexplored spaces. Seek instant gratification—or the elusive promise of it—and chances are you'll find a crowd there ahead of you. Long-term orientation interacts well with customer obsession. If we can identify a customer need and if we can further develop conviction that that need is meaningful and durable, our approach permits us to work patiently for multiple years to deliver a solution.

Warren Buffett has always emphasized that his investment horizon is the very long term: he doesn't buy with an intent to sell. He constantly advises his investors, and anyone else who will listen, that investors should own a diversified equity portfolio, bought over time. For these investors, he argues, "quotational declines are unimportant. Their focus should remain fixed on attaining significant gains in purchasing power over their investing lifetime."

If investors are to stay with you through ups and downs, they must have trust in you as a person, in your strategy, and in your management system. Trust is hard to gain and all too easy to lose. If you are running Boeing, the market has trusted you for years to make long-term investments. If you betray that trust by approving a 737 MAX design that puts the front stairway in the wrong place just to satisfy Southwest Airlines, the trust built up over decades can evaporate in months.

One radical way of escaping the 90-Day Derby is to run a very simple business or set of businesses. When the accounting results are an accurate picture of performance, things get easier. If you manage a firm that takes orders for and manufactures high school sports trophies, there are clear measures of business performance and progress. Make ducting for climate control, not high-tech artificial intelligence systems for home automation.

Another way to get out of the spotlight of the 90-Day Derby is to go private. Here is Tesla's Elon Musk on the motivations to do this:

> As a public company, we are subject to wild swings in our stock price that can be a major distraction for everyone working at Tesla, all of whom are shareholders. Being public also subjects us to the quarterly earnings cycle that puts enormous pressure on Tesla to make decisions that may be right for a given quarter, but not necessarily right for the long-term. Finally, as the most shorted stock in the history of the stock market, being public means that there are *large numbers of people who have the incentive to attack the company.*
>
> I fundamentally believe that we are at our best when everyone is focused on executing, when we can remain focused on our long-term mission, and when there are not perverse incentives for people to try to harm what we're all trying to achieve.[12]

Many large companies do not need capital from the public markets. Their publicly traded stock is used as a way to create incentives and to acquire other companies without paying cash. However, for large companies, going private is a complex financial maneuver that requires either a very wealthy patron or a leveraged buyout that puts even greater pressure on short-term cash flow.

Many of the very successful entrepreneurs don't do it for the wealth. Yes, they like to be successful, and some spend extravagantly. But the prime motivation is dominance and winning, corporate value being a consequence. They want to create new products or new business models and to be admired as the alpha dogs in their fields. Of course, it helps to have a controlling interest in the company. And to have strategic insights.

Steve Jobs was famous for not worrying much about Apple's stock price. How did Steve Jobs manage Apple? He was not an engineer himself, yet he guided Apple into being one of the great engineering companies, in the true sense of what it means to "engineer." Competitors raced to be first to market or to include the most features in their products, but they tended to create products that were clunky and awkward in comparison to Apple's.

Many people and companies want to emulate Apple and study what the company has done. In trying to learn from Steve Jobs's

Apple, it is useful to pay attention to what he did not do. In compiling this short list, I have taken ideas and phrases in common use by managers, business writers, and consultants:

- He did not "drive business success by a relentless focus on performance metrics." Success came to Apple by having successful products and strategies, not by chasing metrics.
- He did not "motivate high performance by tying incentives to key strategic success factors." Apple did achieve high performance by pressuring individuals to deliver targeted accounting results.
- He did not have a strategy "built through participation by all levels to achieve a consensus that resolves key differences in perspectives and values." Strategy at Apple was mostly driven from the top.
- He did not waste time on the delicate distinctions among "missions," "visions," "goals," and "strategies."
- He did not use acquisitions to hit "strategic growth goals." Growth was the outcome of successful product development and accompanying business strategies.
- He did not seek to engineer higher margins by chasing Rust Belt concepts of "economies of scale." He left such moves to HP.
- He did not enter a horse into the 90-Day Derby.

Emulating Apple is not easy, but it is not impossible, either. We are all surrounded by expensively developed products that promise much more than they deliver. Remember Windows Vista. Remember the BlackBerry Playbook that tried to be a better iPad but didn't support BlackBerry email, the company's lead product. The engineers told CEO Balsillie that they couldn't put email on the PlayBook for security reasons. How do you think Steve Jobs would have responded to those engineers?

In 2017 Google introduced its Pixel 2 smartphone and its Pixel Buds. As a Pixel 1 owner, I watched the event and, like many others, was impressed when the presenter talked easily with Isabel, a Swedish speaker, using the Pixel 2 and the Pixel Buds. The conversation was natural and impressive. The audience clapped, oohed, and aahed. The presenter said that the new technology would let you have a natural conversation in forty languages. I travel a great deal and quickly ordered the new phone and the Pixel Buds.

The Pixel Buds were unimpressive in use. Not very comfortable, a bit of a bother to charge in their case, and the language translation didn't really work. Any kind of background noise confused the system. Trying to express an idea involved a lot of backtracking and correcting mistakes. The problem was that natural language translation is incredibly difficult, and coupling it with voice recognition tripled the complexity. As reviewer James Temperton wrote in *Wired*:

> Google's Pixel Buds are a badly-designed solution to a problem that doesn't exist. Want a decent pair of wireless headphones? Move on. Want a smart voice assistant in your ear? Nope. Want Silicon Valley's interpretation of a fictitious alien fish that performs instant translations between any languages? You'd be better off squishing a guppy into your ear and hoping for the best. Or just cut out the middle-man and use the Google Translate app on your phone.[13]

The secret to emulating Steve Jobs's Apple is not in pushing beyond the limits of technology. It is providing a truly excellent design that people will want to pay for—not just the prettiness of the box, not just the simplicity of the interface, but the whole sense that a product or service is the best it can be, for the moment, at what it does.

17

Strategic Planning

Hits and Misses, Uses and Misuses

Strategic planning, as a concept and process, grew out of US World War II activities. The military began to use the term in its overall plans, as did the many analysts who had been employed to plan and control civilian production for the war effort. George A. Steiner was one of these, planning production and distribution of metals and other goods during the war.[1] Later he became a recognized expert on planning and wrote a number of influential books on "long-range" and "strategic" and "top-management" planning. A gentle colleague of mine at UCLA, George was a painter in retirement, passing away in 2004 at age 102.

Over many lunches together, George told me how the "long-range" and "strategic planning" systems in industry were born in the utilities and resource-based industries. At AT&T, long-range planning started with the forecast of future demand for telephone calls and then worked back to the infrastructure necessary to satisfy that demand. Importantly, it was mainly about forecasting, as there was no competition. At electric power companies, the same kind of logic applied. There was no disruptive competition. In oil companies, things were more complex because of strong competition over discovering new sources of oil. Still, until the oil crisis of 1973, planning went on in much the same stolid way: forecast demand, forecast share, and plan the facilities needed to meet demand. Until deregulation, airlines proceeded in the same mechanical way: forecast demand, count on government-mandated airfares, and use the forecast to place orders for aircraft.

Long-range planning can be useful when the key flows and events can be forecast and when the organization has the grit to invest today for events whose timing and magnitude are uncertain. In many organizations, the demands of the immediate absorb the resources that might be committed to the future. The required grit is not there.

PANDEMICS

As I write this paragraph in the fall of 2020, I am holed up at home because of the COVID-19 pandemic. Here in Oregon, early in the pandemic, Oregon Health Authority director Patrick Allen told the state legislature that "without extraordinary efforts by the federal government, we are going to run out of needed protective gear for front-line health care workers." Similar alarms are being raised across the country, as local health bureaucrats realized that they had failed to plan for an *inevitable* national emergency.

Pandemics are not predictable, but they are inevitable. Like earthquakes, droughts, floods, and tsunamis, they strike without warning but are also bound to occur. During the past fifty years, the world has seen outbreaks of Ebola, SARS, swine flu, Zika, Marburg virus, dengue, West Nile, Powassan virus, and a host of HxNy flu-like viruses.[2] The outbreak of a virus like COVID-19 should not be a surprise; only the timing is unpredictable. Given global mobility, even more lethal pandemics are foreseeable. So why were we short of medical gear in Oregon?

One answer is that too many bureaucrats and citizens imagined that health was a federal responsibility. It is not. The US federal government sets policy and advises, but in the United States the actual administration of policy before and during a pandemic is a state and county responsibility. For example, as many are still surprised to learn, federal officials can advise about mask wearing, but the authority to require it or not lies with the states.

The more general answer is a failure of strategic planning and the grit to actually set aside that which the few plans called for. The 2005 US National Strategy for Pandemic Influenza and its accompanying Implementation Plan envisioned a flu-like virus spreading internationally. The virus would, it was (mistakenly) assumed, affect children most sharply, and it was (mistakenly) assumed that the epidemic would last six to eight weeks in "affected communities." It proposed a national stockpile of medical and nonmedical equipment. The strategy called on the federal government to "ensure that our national stockpile and stockpiles based in states and communities are properly configured."

The plan made no mention of testing as a useful countermeasure. The national stockpile was built but depleted to deal with the limited 2009 swine-flu epidemic, which shows how small it was. The materials used were never replaced. There was no oversight on whether the states, the true first line of action about health, had maintained readiness. As with so many strategic plans, the necessary grit to actually carry it forward was lacking at all levels.

In addition to plans, a number of nongovernmental bodies have carried out studies of possible pandemics. Only two years ago, the Center for Strategic and International Studies Risk and Foresight Group ran a scenario about a novel highly transmissible coronavirus. Their summary conclusions are both wise and foolish. Their wishful thinking is on display when they conclude that "establishing trust and cooperation domestically and internationally among governments, companies, workers and citizens is important before crisis strikes. . . . A critical ingredient for addressing pandemics is public order and obedience to protocols, rationing, and other measures that might be needed. . . . International cooperation is also key."

One problem with most "futurist" and "scenario" studies is that the outcome of the study is shaped by closely interested parties. Pandemic studies will all call for more research on virology, and international pandemic studies will call for more money from rich to poor nations. And despite the dismal subject, they remain strangely upbeat. Note that the quote above does not say that the United States or Oregon should stock up on masks, gloves, or drugs that we have been buying on just-in-time delivery from China and other foreign suppliers. An honest scenario analysis would not wax eloquent about global coordination but predict closed borders, restricted travel, and collapsing supply chains. It would not just mention "obedience to protocols." It would lay out the conditions that might warrant forced obedience versus those that permit a modicum of individual freedom. COVID-19's mortality rate for those under seventy is apparently less than 1 percent. What if the pandemic is truly horrific, with a 10 percent mortality rate, then what? And could anyone have predicted that the media and politicians would use the disease as a tool to bludgeon their rivals?

The big success in the United States with regard to the pandemic was not any long-range strategic plan but the highly crux-based strategic "Warp Speed" project. Before COVID-19, developing a vaccine was a long-term affair. The fastest prior vaccine development was for the mumps, which took four years. In March 2020, thirty-three-year-old Tom Cahill began to furiously research and network the problem. Having been a physician before becoming a venture capitalist, Cahill organized an influential group he called "Scientists to Stop Covid-19."[3]

The normal sequential process for drug development was of research, years of testing, FDA approval, then manufacture, then distribution. The group's memorandum called attention to the fact that new science allowed for the rapid creation of vaccines and advised that development, production, and distribution steps be done in parallel, coordinated by a special federal council. The *Wall Street Journal* compared the plan to the Manhattan Project. In essence, the team identified the crux of the problem as pushing aside the nation's profit-based, traditional step-by-step, cautious drug-development system. The team's contacts extended deep into the administration, and the plan gathered momentum. Congress agreed to fund it. Moncef Slaoui, a Moroccan scientist who had experience developing vaccines, became the federal coordinator. The FDA's initial refusal to fast-track a vaccine was overcome through direct executive authority. To the surprise of many scientists and most newspapers and TV stations, the vaccine was actually developed ahead of schedule and began distribution in early December 2020.

To see the value of this coherent strategy, compare this result with that obtained by the European Union. Rather than a Manhattan Project, Brussels approached the issue like any other government-contracting situation. The commission responsible constructed a committee of representative states to negotiate with potential producers, a very democratic structure that inevitably slowed action and dramatically facilitated extensive lobbying. The German-developed BioNTech vaccine, which came to the United States as the "Pfizer vaccine," was passed over because the company was not a major actor. The large pharmaceutical companies demanded protection against lawsuits, and the EU demurred. Production facilities were not created until the issue was resolved. There was only a rough schedule. Then the EU's two selected contractors each ran into trouble. French drug company Sanofi couldn't master the science and had to push the timeline for development to late 2021. The British AstraZeneca vaccine has been linked to a slight risk of blood clots, and many EU members have halted its use.

WATER

The Sultanate of Oman faces a very hot, arid climate, making water a scarce and valuable resource. For two thousand years, the traditional *aflaj* irrigation channels provided water to villages and small towns. These are subterranean tunnels and narrow channels carrying water from higher aquifer wells to villages. Key elements of the strategic plan for water have been the maintenance and refurbishment of these waterways and the construction of recharge dams (dams that collect water and channel it into underground passages to limit evaporation). With population growth, since the early 1990s there have been strategic plans aimed at water reclamation, desalinization, and saving agricultural lands from excess salinity. A major effort to build desalinization plants has been quite successful, with such plants supplying the drinking water in urban Muscat and other cities. A research project is seeking lower-cost desalinization techniques. The more difficult tasks are controlling the agricultural water uses, especially the overpumping of water for low-yield fields or crops. The government had taken ownership of all water in Oman and operates a permit system to control and redirect farmers' use of water, with subsidies for those who must cut their water consumption. All in all, Oman has successfully enacted a long-term strategic plan for dealing with its difficult water-resources challenges.

By contrast, California has no strategic water plan. In California, in 2015, a dry period was reaching its fourth year. Governor Jerry Brown said, "This is the new normal and we'll have to learn to cope with it." His pessimism was apparently driven by a belief that the dry period was due to global warming, although that process is actually predicted to be very gradual rather than abrupt. But his prognostication did not prove correct, and by early 2017 Brown was able to declare that the "new normal" drought was over. That fact was obvious to dwellers in the Central Valley, as Sierra snowpack hit record levels of depth, dams filled to bursting, and many orchards flooded. Lacking large reservoirs sized to the population, this extra water flowed into the sea.

The analysis of tree rings in California shows that "megadroughts" have occurred lasting up to fifty years, the last big one ending in the 1300s. Since then, the climate has varied with a cycle of perhaps twenty to one hundred years. The recent long cycle is one of the wettest. Thus, the population surge in California has occurred during a very wet cycle.

One response to the short-term variation could be more water storage. The legislature is not interested. The only sensible long-term strategies are either cheap desalinization, building underground water tunnels into the mountains with recharge dams as in Oman, or limits on either agriculture (which takes 80 percent of the water) or the population living in the region. With regard to living with the unpredictable yet inevitable cycles, the state is no more willing to plan than was Pharaoh when Joseph warned of "seven fat years followed by seven lean years."

It appears that when the issue is constant and evident to all, longer-term strategic planning can occur. When the problem varies in intensity, like pandemics and California water issues, governments are less likely to enact longer-term strategies.

MISSION STATEMENTS AND TURTLES

A currently popular approach to manufacturing "grit" is to create a sense of enduring meaningful purpose for a business or agency. According to this view, a leader is supposed to carefully craft a "vision statement," "mission statement," "statement of values," and "strategy statement" of the business and also work out its statement of "goals and objectives." Look into this on the Web, and a legion of wannabe consultants are happy to inform you of the delicate differences among visions, missions, values, strategies, objectives, and goals. You will be urged to create a mission statement because "if you lack a clear view of your mission, how can you create a strategy for its accomplishment?"

This short section aims to convince you that working with a cascade of "statements" about vision, mission, value, and strategy is a feckless activity, lacking a logical backbone, and having no evidence of being enduring. They cannot really guide strategy. Your commitment to basic values will be illuminated by your actions, not statements framed on the wall.

With regard to the abovementioned cascade of statements, I am reminded of an anecdote about an astronomer. After giving a talk explaining that the earth circles the sun, which, in turn, moves around the galactic center, an elderly woman approached the astronomer. She applauded his talk but argued that the earth actually rests on the back of a giant turtle. The astronomer raised his eyebrows and, believing he could easily refute her argument, said, "And, madam, on what does that turtle stand?" She replied with evident satisfaction: "It stands on another turtle. It's turtles all the way down."

The joke uses infinite regress to poke at the question of the existence of a prime mover. If A stands on, or is deduced from, B, then where did B come from? Similarly, if one needs a mission statement to derive a strategy, then from where does the mission statement come? The answer is that the mission statement comes from the "vision statement," which, perhaps, derives from the "statement of core values." Logically, this is like the turtles: "statements" all the way down.

According to Wikipedia, "Organizations normally do not change their mission statements over time, since they define their continuous, ongoing purpose and focus."[4] Are mission statements actually enduring? Consider Microsoft's 1990 mission: *A computer on every desk and in every home.* It was nice and clear but not much help in dealing with the rise of the Internet. After the world changed, with pads and smartphones and cloud computing, Microsoft's 2013 mission statement became this undecipherable pile of words: *To create a family of devices and services for individuals and businesses that empower people around the globe at home, at work and on the go, for the activities they value most.* Today, in 2021, that earlier statement has been compressed to the universal every-company mission: *To empower every person and every organization on the planet to achieve more.* That statement will be enduring because it doesn't really say anything about what Microsoft does or hopes to do.

In 1999 the Centers for Disease Control had this mission statement: *To promote health and quality of life by preventing and controlling disease, injury, and disability.* Today, in 2021, the notion of disease has expanded to include safety, security, obesity, gun violence, and more: *CDC works 24/7 to protect America from health, safety and security threats, both foreign and in the U.S. Whether diseases start at home or abroad, are chronic or acute, curable or preventable, human error or deliberate attack, CDC fights disease and supports communities and citizens to do the same.* The CDC's mission statement has been rewritten every few years to keep up with its continually expanding diversity of activity. It should be clear that this hodgepodge of responsibilities and purposes is of no use in devising any sort of strategy.

Back in 2012, Facebook's mission was *Making the world more open and connected.* Today, it is *Give people the power to build community and bring the world closer together.* Sony says its mission is *To be a company that inspires and fulfills your curiosity.* Like Facebook's, Sony's mission statement signals an aristocratic lack of concern with the grubby business of making money. Neither seems helpful in guiding a strategic response to COVID-19 or increased government scrutiny of anticompetitive actions.

Quite a few firms simply say that their mission is to maximize shareholder value. For example, Dean Foods was a national agglomeration of local dairy processors. In 2018 its mission statement was this: *The Company's primary objective is to maximize long-term stockholder value, while adhering to the laws of the jurisdictions in which it operates and at all times observing the highest ethical standards.* It did not work. One year later, the company's stock price went to zero in a bankruptcy.

Neither the high-sounding statements of global purpose nor the profit-oriented statements are of any use for the kind of problem-solving strategy being espoused in this book. If you accept that strategy is a form of problem solving, that it is a journey, and that it is a response to challenges, then mission statements are not helpful in strategy work. They are a waste of time and effort.

You don't need a vision or mission statement to lead a business. You decide and create your actual mission as you design and implement your strategic response to change and opportunity. Your publicly expressed mission is more advertising and social signaling than guidance; it will change with shifts in fashion and leadership.

My advice is to keep it to a motto. This is a maxim or dictum that evokes emotion and a sense of commitment.

There Is No Substitute	Porsche
Semper Fi	US Marine Corps

Faster, Higher, Stronger	Olympic Games
Blood and Fire	Salvation Army
Diamonds Are Forever	De Beers
Think Different	Apple
Non ducor, duco[5]	São Paulo, Brazil
We've Got You Covered	River Roofing (Bend, Oregon)
Unity, Integrity, Diligence	Rothschild family
That Others May Live	US Air Force Pararescue
Any Mission, Any Time, Any Place	Spetsnaz Guard Brigades (Russia)
Just Do It	Nike
Brutal Simplicity of Thought	M&C Saatchi

STRATEGIC PLANNING IN BUSINESS

Since the 1970s, most businesses have adopted the language of "strategic planning." Where the product or production life cycle extends over many years, or even decades, these strategic plans may have both content and great merit. Defense contractors, mining companies, petroleum companies, and many electric utilities have road maps of how demand and production are expected to evolve over the coming years.

For many businesses, however, strategic planning has been a disappointment. Most senior executives say their organization has a strategic-planning process. Yet the majority of these executives are unhappy with both the process and the outcomes. A 2006 McKinsey survey found that fewer than half of the eight hundred executives surveyed were satisfied with the strategic-planning process. More recently, in 2014, a Bain & Company partner, James Allen, noted: "In recent meetings with the CEOs of several large global companies . . . it became clear to me that many corporate leaders are fed up with their strategic planning processes. . . . [T]here was general agreement that 97 percent of these efforts are a waste of time and rob the organization of essential energy."[6]

One common complaint is that the plans don't work out. In 2009 I had a conversation with the CEO of Mattel, Robert Eckert. I asked him about strategy at Mattel. Smiling, he said, "We do a great job of strategic planning. The problem is implementation." Eckert's complaint is widespread. It expresses the unavoidable fact that plans cannot predict competitive outcomes. Or as Mike Tyson so eloquently put it: "Everyone has a plan until they get punched in the mouth."

The essential problem for most businesses is that their so-called strategic-planning exercises do not produce strategies. Rather, they are actually attempting to predict and control financial outcomes. Put simply, they are a form of budgeting. They do not address critical challenges. The process may glance at broader issues but quickly centers on financial goals, to be later followed by budget allocations.

To illustrate how too many business strategic-planning exercises work, consider the case of 'Royalfield.' It is a Fortune 500 company, and about twenty-five senior executives have gathered in a hotel ballroom. The first speaker is the CFO, who uses images from Marvel's *Thor* to dramatize his financial report.

The second speaker is the CEO, who uses a few PowerPoint slides to present what he calls the "strategic commitment" and the "Success Score Card." The "strategic commitment," he reminds the group, grew out of a key acquisition made three years earlier and defined the newly expanded scope of the business. It comprises a description of the market being served and the admonition that the company's products would "provide its customers with the most effective solutions to their needs." It would also aim to "provide a high level of service" for its products.

The "Success Score Card," for the whole of Royalfield, the SSC, is specified as a 15 percent annual growth in earnings with a 15 percent return on equity. These targets were somewhat higher than the recent financial record. He then shows the (negotiated) SSCs for each of the four business units. Each has agreed to targets on sales growth, profit rate, return on investment, and market share. He ends with a quote from nineteen-year-old Katie Ledecky, who has won five Olympic gold medals in swimming: "Set goals that, when you set them, you think they're impossible. But then every day you can work towards them, and anything is possible."[7]

During a break, uplifting music plays, and coffee mugs with the company logo are distributed. After lunch, each of the four business-unit managers presents their strategies for achieving their SSCs. There are references to key customers and improvements in certain products, but the basic language has been preset by the CEO: the language of financial performance. Their "strategies," therefore, boil down to promising to find new customers, somehow cutting costs, and keeping investment in check.

The CEO's system of defining the SSCs in largely financial performance terms shaped the options they considered and shifted strategic thinking away from technology, product, customer, and competition and toward tactics designed to achieve desired accounting results. There was no serious consideration of how the contradictory demands for increased sales and reduced costs would be reconciled.

One way of understanding Royalfield is that the CEO's almost daily experience was explaining the company's financial results to investors, Wall Street analysts, and pension and hedge funds and in reports to the board and Securities and Exchange Commission. The incentive package he was given was framed in terms of accounting results and stock-market returns. Thus, the world he inhabited had been engineered to make the SSCs his personal strategic problem.

Another way of understanding Royalfield is that the company leadership viewed their vague "strategic commitment" as having taken care of having a strategy. The mind-set was that strategy is a once-in-a-while fairly static issue. With strategy concerns apparently resolved by the "strategy commitment," the company's "strategy" retreat centered on what they saw as the "real work," the setting of financial performance targets.

Having interviewed two division executives in preparation for my talk, it seemed to me that some of Royalfield's strategic challenges were fairly evident. The company was still organized by regions, while the industry had become global. The technology they had invented and successfully deployed in the past had been equaled and in places surpassed by a competitor's inventions. The company's engineering group was competent but slow to act, responding to their own internal sensibilities rather than competitive issues. Other, less obvious, issues made it difficult to separate the important from the less important, the critical from the peripheral.

When, over drinks before dinner, I raised some of these issues with the CEO, he held out his hand, palm forward, asking me to stop. "I don't want to hear negative things about the team. I don't want them distracted from the SSCs."

I did not work with Royalfield again. In the years since that event, each of the company's competitors grew faster, and the share losses were greatest in Royalfield's core business. These losses were clearly due to the company not keeping pace with the technologies offered by competitors. Yes, Royalfield lowered expenses so that its net profit margin improved. But its growth rate fell behind that of its industry, and its market share dropped by 30 percent as competitors won sales by targeting key customer segments.

Royalfield had significant strategic issues that it should have faced in order to move forward. It did not do this because the company's leaders misunderstood the meaning and purpose of strategy itself. Part of this misunderstanding was evident in leadership's belief that they had taken care of most strategic issues by having a "strategic commitment" about where they would compete. The other part of the misunderstanding was their demand that each division create a "strategy" for achieving certain arbitrary financial outcomes. Absent solutions to their more fundamental challenges, higher margins came at the price of lost technical leadership and lower market share.

PART V

The Strategy Foundry

The Strategy Foundry is a process by which a small group of executives can do challenge-based strategy, discover the crux, and create a set of coherent actions for punching through those issues. It is quite different from strategic planning or other so-called strategy workshops, where the outcome is essentially a long-term budget.

18

Rumsfeld's Question

Earlier in my career, I tried to be a mini consulting firm—just me or sometimes just me and a few colleagues. I would work with a company on developing a strategy. Often, these clients had already been through an engagement with a top-tier consulting firm and were looking for something different.

There were a good number of satisfying engagements. My work with a number of companies contributed, I believe, to successful strategic actions. On the other hand, there were less successful efforts. It wasn't that the analysis wasn't done or that the recommendations were rejected. It was more like the difference between the warm-up routine and the starring show. Strategic analysis of the situation and recommendations for action were the warm-up routine—interesting but quickly forgotten. The starring show was the mainline annual "strategic plan."

One example of the latter was 'OKCo.' In 2002 OKCo was a significant manufacturer of home and business-office climate-control systems. The entire product line had fourteen different models. The problem, as they defined it, was low profitability and low growth. I worked with the vice president of strategy, who led a small team of analysts, and had periodic discussions with the CEO.

I gathered views of the situation from at least twenty different managers, engineers, and salespeople. There was both increasing competition and complexity in the business. What I saw was that the company's product line was stale and not up-to-date.

Competitors were bringing out systems that tied into the Ethernet or Wi-Fi. OKCo's systems, by contrast, had to be programmed by moving jumpers around on a printed circuit board. There were eight different circuit boards covering the fourteen models. Some competitors' systems were beginning to display multiple-zone information on a video screen on the wall or a laptop computer. The engineers who had designed OKCo's printed circuit-board systems had long since retired. To compensate for the decline in the product's performance, management had been lowering prices and increasing sales commissions. This was, in my view, not a good path to follow. It felt like working with the data-processing companies who stuck with old green-screen terminals until the Internet and PCs overwhelmed them.

The vice president of strategy and I did a thorough evaluation of the company's products and competitors' products and interviewed a good number of systems buyers and customers. OKCo was a widely recognized brand name. Large systems buyers liked the newer competitive designs, but also trusted OKCo because of its years in the business. Smaller buyers and contractors were split, with many installers preferring the older jumper system—it took about twice the time to install, and that meant twice the chargeable hours.

In addition to these product and marketing issues, the company's organization was sleepy and self-satisfied despite the slowly declining financial performance. Outsourcing the manufacturing of parts and assemblies to China had helped keep costs down.

The VP of strategy and I came up with a strategy to help build a better future for the company. The key was to invest in developing a microprocessor-based control system—we called it a "platform"—that could be adapted to work in all fourteen models. Taking a cue from the hand-calculator industry, we argued in favor of a platform that could do it all with certain features simply turned off for the less advanced products. To guide this investment, there would have to be some new blood, especially in engineering. As the product materialized, a cross-functional team drawn from training, manufacturing, marketing, and sales would work on bringing it to market. Again, we were taking a cue from history, in this case from Toyota's development of the Lexus using a "heavyweight" team, that is, a group that not only designed the car but also brought it to market. There were obviously organizational and personnel issues to be sorted out to make this idea work.

After presenting the field data, our analysis, and the strategy ideas to the CEO, I waited for the next step.

In the early fall, the CEO and CFO presented the company's "strategic plan." Despite the study work, the "strategic plan" did not address issues we had raised, nor did it even glance at the recommendations. Instead, it projected growing EBITDA and listed eight priorities:

customer satisfaction
unmatched brand awareness
supply-chain excellence
increased productivity and lower costs
pay down debt
build sales capability through active partnerships with key customers
margin improvement with advanced analytics
reduce greenhouse emissions by 15 percent

Pushing aside the obvious fluff, this plan essentially proposed paying down debt and trying to cozy up to key customers. The key customers were, of course, those whose needs most matched the company's existing product concept. The verbiage about "advanced analytics" was a sop to the new head of marketing who had just gotten a master's of science degree in "business analytics." There was no mention of the rising tide of new technology.

The problem at OKCo and many other companies was that the key challenge, already apparent to many, *was not owned* by the major policy makers. If a challenge is not owned, it cannot be surmounted. Good strategy can only flow from senior executives who own the critical challenge.

Three years later, I saw the news report about the decline in OKCo's value, triggering takeover bids. After the company was sold, the three top managers retired with hefty payment packages. Half of the employees were let go, since the acquirer seemed mostly interested in the OKCo brand name.

EXPERIENCES WITH OKCo and other organizations began to convince me that many organizations were sidestepping serious work on gnarly challenges because it was hard and potentially disruptive and because they had no method or system for doing it. Delegating it to the VP of strategy turned it into a sideshow. When the rubber met the road, when faced with an audience, too many top executives could not help falling back on the kind of positive-thinking "success theater" put on by Jeffrey Immelt at General Electric (see Chapter 8).

If delegating strategy to the VP of strategy or to a strategy consulting boutique doesn't reliably work, what can be done instead? It is natural to think that issues of great consequence should be considered by a small group of informed senior executives. Surely, rather than delegating the task, an informed discussion by the key actors would produce a better outcome. Surely, the sharing of information and the debate over what is both important and possible will be beneficial. And, yes, this is how some of the best strategies are generated.

Still, over the years, I have observed groups trying to do this and suffering more than a little confusion and dysfunction. There were a lot of smart executives and consultants looking at performance data and competition. Yet there was little overall focus on breaking through the complex web of issues and making progress—of concentrating on the games you can win. There was something wrong.

One popular theory about this malaise was inaugurated by Irving Janis with his well-known concept of *groupthink*. Examining the history of actual high-level policy-making cases, Janis concluded that choices were made without systematic data gathering or analysis. Group members (usually the president and close advisers in his examples) worked to preserve optimism rather than realism and seemed to work at minimizing controversy. He concluded that important information was not examined and alternative courses of action were pushed aside against the momentum of the group's quickly emerging consensus. Janis claimed that there was also great importance placed on a sense of cohesiveness and camaraderie. Group members softened their criticisms, even in their own thinking.

Janis's classic example of groupthink was President Kennedy's 1961 Bay of Pigs fiasco invasion of Cuba. It is clear that the advisory group did not examine very many alternatives. But another main element, not spotlighted in Janis's account, was the Central Intelligence Agency's double game. The CIA, led by World War II spy Allen Dulles, wanted to displace Cuba's Fidel Castro and also firmly believed that the invasion would not work unless US troops were involved. Kennedy did not want the political backlash that using US troops would produce. So there was actually a null set of feasible actions.

The CIA nevertheless continued to go forward because Dulles believed that "when the invasion actually occurred, the president would end up authorizing whatever was required for success, including overt U.S. military intervention if necessary, rather than allow the venture to fail."[1] In this high-stakes game of chicken, Kennedy did not budge, and the CIA didn't swerve. The invasion failed, and the political backlash was tremendous. One outcome was that Kennedy fired Allen Dulles and created the Defense Intelligence Agency under the secretary of defense as an alternative intelligence agency.

Irving Janis's general theory is that the purpose of a policy group is to make a rational choice. But one can only make a "rational" choice among known alternatives and using a single value metric. But most such groups faced gnarly challenges: there were competing ambitions, no given action alternatives, and the links between proposed actions and results were very tenuous. Unfortunately, the general advice offered in such situations is to establish a clear picture of the desired outcome—the overall "goals"—and then select the action most likely to get there. This way of thinking mixes up wishful thinking ("the desired outcome") with an inexplicable conversion of a gnarly challenge into a decision among known alternative actions. That conversion is the heart of the matter, not something to be blithely assumed. Laboring under this misconception about how to build an effective strategy, it should not be surprising when there is too early convergence on specific actions.

In my experience, it is not group process per se that causes too early convergence on action. It is the habits of viewing strategy as setting overall goals or as decision making among predetermined alternative actions. Observing a number of high-level decisions, and from discussions with senior government officials, it seems that most of the time the senior executive had a fixed opinion about the desired outcome, and that outcome was closely attached to only one or two conceivable actions. Given that starting point, the job of the group was to fine-tune the already-made choice and to design ways of explaining it to other parties, especially the press and the public, and to build confidence and solidarity among the group members. These predetermined purposes, not a defect in group process, made collective reflection impossible.

An uncomfortable example is the Second Iraq War. Its roots lie in an attempt to forge a new foreign policy. In 1997 twenty-five prominent conservatives signed on to the Project for the New American Century. The proposed policy was to build democracy around the world with specific attention to halting US support for dictators and, instead, actively opposing "regimes hostile to our interests and values." Among the signatories were future vice president Dick Cheney, future national security adviser Elliott Abrams, future secretary of defense Donald Rumsfeld, his future deputy Paul Wolfowitz, and several other future members of the George W. Bush administration.

For this group, the war in Afghanistan was a diversion. Early on in the Bush administration, attention focused on regime change in Iraq. Such an action would, advocates believed, show the world that the United States opposed dictators, could liberate people to democracy, and, importantly, show who was the alpha dog in the world. As an army colonel told me in 2002, just after the swift early victory in Afghanistan, "The lesson is . . . if you go against us, we will crush you like a bug."

When the United States previously forced Iraq out of Kuwait in 1991, a successfully hidden nuclear weapons program was discovered. Dismantled under UN supervision, the CIA remained embarrassed that it had been missed.[2] So, when in 1999, a single Iraqi informant, code-named "Curveball," began to claim that Saddam Hussein was again developing nuclear and biological weapons, it was taken as a casus belli for invasion. A more modest approach would have been to secretly drop some special forces troops on a supposed location and check out the claims. But the idea of full-scale invasion and regime change was predetermined.

The neoconservative group, led by Paul Wolfowitz and Dick Cheney, was convinced that the Middle East could be transformed. In a 2002 speech, Cheney was clear about the desired outcome:

> Regime change in Iraq would bring about a number of benefits to the region. When the gravest of threats are eliminated, the freedom-loving peoples of the region will have a chance to promote the values that can bring lasting peace. As for the reaction of the Arab "street," the Middle East expert Professor Fouad Ajami predicts that after liberation, the streets in Basra and Baghdad are "sure to erupt in joy in the same way the throngs in Kabul greeted the Americans." Extremists in the region would have to rethink their strategy of Jihad. Moderates throughout the region would take heart.[3]

I had the opportunity to interview then US secretary of defense Donald Rumsfeld in 2004. At that moment, he was trying to deal with a rising insurgency in Iraq. The invasion's outcome had been expected to be a popular celebration of democracy, not an insurgency. The interview topic was about how the Defense Department managed shifts in spending. Almost as an afterthought, I asked him about his view on strategy or policy creation. His reply remains fascinating.

Rumsfeld told me that as defense secretary, he had access to just about any expertise imaginable. "Do you want to know the various tribal histories, languages, customs, and intermarriage situations? We have people who know," he said. He described the wide variety of expertise on weather patterns in Iraq and internal politics. "Do you want to know who, in Turkey, blocked our access to a northern invasion and why did they do so? We have people who know. . . . The real problem," he said, was pulling all of this expertise together into a coherent strategy. Rumsfeld said that "each morsel of expertise came with an agenda attached. It came from a person or group with a perspective, an ax to grind, a budget to manage, a contract to renew, a career to push forward, and so on. Professor," he asked, "have you academics found a way to deal with this issue?"

Responding to his question, I thought for a minute and reflected briefly on what was systematically known about the policy process. I told him that I had to admit that our technology for these issues had not much improved from ancient times. I said, "We know a lot about what can go wrong, but very little about how to fix it. Basically, you put a *small* group of smart people in a room and see what they come up with."

WHAT IS KNOWN?

Rumsfeld's question illuminated two realities. First, when a strategy is described and promoted in terms of a fixed predetermined outcome (jubilation in the streets of Baghdad), there is great difficulty in dealing with information and advice that does not match that outcome. Second, and even more deeply, his question reinforced my concern that little was actually known about how a group should actually combine information to create a strategy. This lack was a professional embarrassment.

Techniques for analyzing business strategy, industries, the economy, competition, and the activities within a firm have advanced over the past half century. But the analysis of costs and competition, by itself, doesn't create good strategy any more than the analysis of paint colors creates fine art. Fundamental questions about process remain almost totally unresearched and unanswered.

Saying that there is almost no knowledge about the best process for creating good strategy is a very strong, sweeping claim. It will annoy many. Backing it up in detail would take another volume by itself. Here, in this section, I will look quickly at some of what has been studied and understood and at the limits of that knowledge.

The concept of *decision making* assumes that the issue is selecting the best action alternative. An elegant mathematical system, the problem with decision theory, whether economic or behavioral, is that it presumes someone has already cooked up a set of alternative actions to choose among. This is fine if you are trying to decide whether to buy or rent a forklift truck, but it is useless if you face the gnarly challenge of homelessness in San Francisco.

There has been a growing understanding about human cognitive biases and how they can affect decision making. Many of these are systematized and explained in Daniel Kahneman's fascinating book, *Thinking, Fast and Slow*.[4] For senior executives the most important seem to be optimism bias, confirmation bias, and the inside-view bias.

Optimism bias means that people tend to overestimate benefits and underestimate the costs of a plan or set of actions. This seems to be an inevitable outcome of basic "animal spirits." I recall asking then futurist Herman Kahn about how to get unbiased forecasts. He advised: "Hire forecasters who are clinically depressed."

Confirmation bias means we tend to favor information, news, and statements that confirm already-held beliefs and opinions. If management believes they have the best technology in spinal disc replacement, they will tend to discount news of a small firm having a better approach.

Inside-view bias occurs because there is a strong tendency to focus on our own experience. This common pattern tends to ignore two things: the general experiences of others in trying to do similar things and the probable actions and strength of the competition, particularly when we are pushing into new competitive areas. Logically, this bias is a close relative of the *winner's curse*—the statistical truth that someone who wins an auction is almost certain to have overvalued the item. (The "rational" cure is to bid so low that you very rarely win!)

For a strategist, the idea of biases in choice is important but misses the nerve center of strategy making. By skipping over the diagnosis of the challenge, these thinkers have biased their own thinking and writing. That conceptual bias is toward calculation and choice rather than problem identification and comprehension. And it is a bias away from the difficult judgment as to which ambitions and values to bring to bear in the situation.

Research on *problem solving* is even less helpful. Most research on "problem solving" has been done by educators who present students with puzzles rather than difficult, unstructured problems. That is because the researchers cannot evaluate their students' performances unless they know the solutions to the puzzles.

Work on groups is even muddier. Social psychologists have long believed that groups should outperform individuals. Nevertheless, decades of research, mostly on students, shows that skilled individuals frequently outperform groups in solving a commonly understood problem. (Almost none of this research deals with complex problems where different people have different pools of long-acquired expertise.)[5]

So two direct (negative) answers to Rumsfeld's question were: there is no known process for a group to create good strategy, especially when a particular outcome or action is a foregone conclusion, and you cannot create sound strategy or policy with a self-seeking, political, or disloyal team. As Dawn Farrell, CEO of energy company TransAlta, told me:

> I had to work to build an effective leadership team. There had to be less ego and more humility. The new rule was no more childish behavior. The message was clear: If you fool around with the data or the facts, I will fire you in a minute. Starting with a small cadre, we now have a group of forty at the top who can and do work together to identify what needs to be done and then help each other to get it done.

WHAT CAN BE DONE?

About the time Rumsfeld's question reignited my interest in the subject, I had been working with firms and some agencies on strategy as a speaker and consultant. Over time, I began to apply my own framework to what I saw. What was my diagnosis? That is, what were the sources of dysfunction? What made it hard to remedy? Was the problem politics or lack of knowledge? Was it optimism bias? Was it political infighting? Or was it simple foolishness? Of course, all of these are at work somewhere at some time. What I began to see as the crux was the general belief that strategy is in the service of preset goals or policy objectives.

What was needed was a way to break the habit of conflating strategy with marching along toward specific performance goals and to empower senior leaders to actually develop action plans for confronting critical problems. Also needed was a way to soften the influence of power and status in the discussion, defer decision until analysis has occurred, and help focus energy and action where they will have the most effect. These are the topics of the following chapter, which illustrates a process I call a Strategy Foundry.

19

A Foundry Walkthrough

'Joanna Walker' first contacted me by email. The CEO of 'FarmKor,' she was interested in a speaker for her annual strategy off-site. I agreed and, on a crisp fall day, gave a talk on ideas drawn from my previous book *Good Strategy/Bad Strategy*. Over dinner with the CFO and head of operations, we discussed a kind of intensive meeting I called a "Strategy Foundry."

Jeremy, the chief operating officer, wanted to know how it worked and what was the deliverable (that is business-speak for the kind of report being written). I told him that I had stopped doing "deliverables" several years ago. The problem most organizations had with strategy was not the lack of PowerPoints or reports. It was that most were not doing strategy in the first place. Most were drawn by social copying and financial markets pressures to framing strategy in terms of performance goals, especially financial targets. The point of a foundry was to break that frame and center instead on challenges.

I explained that the Strategy Foundry is challenge based. It centered on identifying the key challenge facing the organization. This set it apart from the vast literature and advice about "decision making" and "goal setting." By starting with the challenge, the group becomes responsible for designing a response rather than choosing among plans already advanced by members or others, or just filling in the blanks for a longer-term budget.

Joanna next asked how one prepared for a Strategy Foundry—and about the time commitment.

I explained that, in my experience, the Strategy Foundry should be a group of fewer than ten, preferably less than eight, senior leaders. It had to include the leader of the company or business division. And the group had to make a commitment to work with a challenge-based approach to strategy. The foundry worked best off-site and would usually take three consecutive days. There had been shorter sessions for smaller companies, and there had been longer foundries where we broke it into two sessions weeks apart.

I explained that the preparations were three steps. First, I had to get up to speed on the company, its competitive situation, and its past plans and performance. Second, I wanted to have a face-to-face interview of at least ninety minutes with each participant and, perhaps, other key personnel. Third, I would prepare written questions for each participant, and each would provide written responses, privately, to me. I would use portions of these responses, without attribution, during the workshop.

Paul, the CFO, asked about scheduling. The annual strategy off-site was normally held a month before the budgeting event. This is a key issue, and I worked to explain that the purpose of a foundry is to address the strategic issues. It will produce a set of critical challenges, guiding policy and action steps. However, the foundry is not a financial or accounting exercise. It is important that a Strategy Foundry be held separately from any budgeting process.

I could see that the idea of a foundry both interested and worried the group. I was asking for a change in the way things were done. Joanna felt that they had to break away from the model of listing all the cool things that would soon happen and really focus on key issues. So we set some preliminary dates and forged ahead.

THE INTERVIEWS AND QUESTIONS

The interviews resulted in these facts:

- In 2015 FarmKor produced and sold a line of hardware and software for use in agriculture and the first stages of food processing.
- FarmKor products tracked the weather and ground chemistry and tried to provide crops with just the right amount of water and nutrients.
- Their more recent products helped with early-stage processing of nuts and hard fruits.
- The company had equipment operating in ten countries and manufactured equipment in four locations around the world.
- Its origins were in flower growing in Denmark.
- Its software was developed both in the United States and in Denmark.
- The company had gone public in Europe in 1998 and then went through a management buyout in 2001.
- New investors were brought in, and debt holders added directors to the board. The company went public again in 2007, just in time to get whipsawed by the world financial crisis.
- The company's installations varied by location, crop, and acreage.
- As it expanded into France, Germany, and then the United States, its technology also developed.
- Originally, it could handle, for example, only a ten-acre orchard. By 2015 it worked with a US corporate customer who grew vegetables on eight thousand acres.
- FarmKor's systems were used for growing tree and vine fruits, nuts, soy, herbs, beans, and a variety of vegetables.

After reviewing the company's performance and its past strategic plans and presentations, I interviewed the eight executives selected to constitute the Strategy Foundry and about five other key managers.

The interviews were surprisingly informative. Most participants were fascinated by the process and seemed quite interested in expressing their views about the situation. One actually broke down crying in his office, explaining that he had devoted his life to the company only to see whole systems being eliminated to cut costs.

- The chief of human resources was enthusiastic about the ongoing process of harmonizing policies across different regions.
- The heads of region-based subsidiaries were privately incensed by this program, arguing that the California-based headquarters was ignorant of their differing situations.
- The CFO's point of view had been expressed openly. He believed that the company's P/E (price-to-earnings) ratio was too low. Other companies, he argued, with similar financial results, had higher P/E ratios, and therefore higher stock prices, because their brand names had worldwide recognition. FarmKor, by contrast, worked under different brands in different regions.
- The CEO's key concerns seemed to be her relationship with the board and the new vice president she had hired to take responsibility for all non-US and non-EU operations (called rest-of-world, or ROW). The company's fastest growth was happening abroad, she explained, but it was thus far unprofitable. She needed someone to treat the ROW as a day-to-day responsibility rather than a monthly report-and-review exercise.

THE WRITTEN QUESTIONS AND RESPONSES

After the interviews, I emailed each Strategy Foundry participant a list of questions to be answered in confidence directly back to me. The seven questions were similar to those I have asked in other complex corporate situations:

1. With regard to your industry, and taking a FarmKor perspective, and looking back over the past five years, what have been the important changes in technology, competition, and customer behavior? What has been the impact of these changes on FarmKor?

2. With regard to your industry, and taking a FarmKor perspective, and looking ahead over the coming three to five years, what do you expect to be the key changes in technology, regulation, competition, and buyer behavior? Which of these present problems for FarmKor? Which present opportunities?
3. What programs or projects undertaken by FarmKor in the past five years were, in your view, successful and worthy of pride? What were the difficulties faced in accomplishing these programs or projects? What, in your view, allowed FarmKor to successfully overcome these difficulties?
4. What programs or projects undertaken by FarmKor in the past five years were, in your view, unsuccessful? What were the difficulties that prevented success? What, in your view, might have been done differently?
5. In your view, what are the priority issues currently being addressed by FarmKor? What projects and programs currently underway at FarmKor are aimed at these priority issues?
6. A key to building a successful strategy is diagnosing the problems and difficulties that stand in the way of improvement. What, in your view, are the two critical challenges facing FarmKor? Note that a critical challenge is not a financial or other shortfall in itself, but is the underlying difficulty that makes improvement difficult. In addition to identifying these two challenges, please comment on the main difficulties blocking their resolution.
7. Can you identify issues and difficulties that arise from the structure or key policies of the company that deserve attention? Are any of these issues of sufficient magnitude to potentially block progress in resolving the key challenges you have identified in answer to question 6?

DAY ONE

The Strategy Foundry assembled at 8:00 a.m. on day one. Not surprisingly, the participants were curious as to what would happen.

The first subject was change. This is always a good topic to loosen up a group. What has happened over the past half decade, and what may happen in the future? The group enthusiastically dove into this topic. Everyone knew about what had changed, and everyone had an opinion about what might change in the future.

In general, competitive pressures had gotten stronger over the past five years. Automating agricultural processes had gained currency, and it had become easier to develop the required software. On the other hand, in the United States, the "organic" movement had caused a certain amount of confusion over what kinds of crop nutrients were acceptable. The views of the future ranged from "more of the same" to "we invent something new."

We then turned to examine what had worked and what had not worked in the past. The first part of this topic is usually invigorating, letting participants recall goals achieved and solid wins. The project most were proud of had been called "the Alpha Plan." It had identified the key cost divergences in service operations and brought interdisciplinary teams to bear on fixing the problems. A talented project leader and strong support from the top were cited as enablers.

One project that had not worked out, pushed by a former senior vice president, had been an effort to create a central group to handle large customer accounts. According to the participants, it was not implemented well, made a mess of customer relationships, and damaged hard-to-rebuild relationships.

After a coffee break, I handed out a list of strategic priorities. I had constructed this list from presentations to the board and all of their responses to question 5 on priorities. The list had twenty items:

- quality
- customer-service excellence
- supply-chain excellence
- low-cost manufacturing footprint
- increased efficiency and flexibility
- talent development
- organizational development and capability building

- new product and process technology offerings and capabilities
- improve debt rating
- culture of creativity, effective risk-taking, and entrepreneurship
- richer R&D pipeline
- better harmonization across districts and regions
- manufacturing technology: reduce variety, which is choking the system
- focus on nutrient variety and verified chemical composition
- build sales and marketing capability and performance
- enter new markets; create new products
- branding image positioning
- pursue active partnerships with key customers for new capability development
- strengthen research and competitive intelligence
- establish or strengthen presence in Mexico, Chile, Brazil, and Argentina

As the group finished studying this list, there was a pregnant silence. I asked: "Does this list mean we are done? Can we just send this to the printer?"

"The list is too long," offered one participant.

"These 'priorities' are too vague," said another.

"Yes," I agreed. "The title of this list purposefully misuses the term *priority*. The word *priority* means superiority in rank or privilege. At a stop-sign intersection, the cars on the through street have the priority. At an airport, the traffic controllers tell the pilots which aircraft has the priority. When we assign too many priorities, the concept loses its meaning. When senior leaders don't create crisp priorities, they leave it to everyone else to fight it out on the ground.

"This list is also mostly about what FarmKor would like to accomplish—about goals. This afternoon, after lunch, we will turn this around and work on what makes any of this difficult. That is, what are the key difficulties or challenges or obstacles that prevent you from just going ahead and doing some of these things?"

At this point it is useful to ensure that the group understands the value of strategy as a response to challenges and the importance of starting with challenges rather than goals. A short talk or reading should suffice.

The afternoon was focused on identifying challenges facing FarmKor. As they surfaced, I wrote a short description of each "challenge" on a five-by-eight-inch card and pinned it to a board. As we talked, some were taken down and others split into two or more challenges. As the participants discussed each, I would probe for detail and always ask, "What makes this important?" and "What makes this difficult?" What I avoided was a discussion of how these challenges could or should be met.

By the end of the day, there were ten five-by-eight cards. Discussion among Strategy Foundry participants had ended up with these ten challenges:

Diminished Advantage: Years ago, our ability to monitor and regulate an agrosystem was unique. Today, new digital technologies and wireless systems have made it much easier for others to develop good systems for tracking the weather, soil conditions, plant growth, and sunlight, and to program water and nutrients appropriately. Our advantages in clever control are evaporating. Everyone is advertising their clever systems, but the real revenue and work are more and more about mechanical devices, installation, and customer service. We have even seen competitors come and plug their control system into our physical system.

Big Players' R&D: There are big agrosystem operators that focus on the basic super-high-volume crops that feed the world: rice, wheat, and corn. These are the Deeres and BASFs of the world. They have, in the past five years or so, woken up to the opportunities in high-tech agriculture. They have the scale and scope to do development across the board—robotic apple picking to fully automated cattle-feed production. We simply cannot match their development budgets.

Founders: The company's founders still have a strong influence on the board of directors. As they have gotten older, their interests seem to be more and more slanted toward a steady, predictable payout of dividends. As we have grown, however, our profits have become more, rather than less, volatile.

Falling Revenue/Acre: We have gradually thinned out as we have grown. Revenue has risen, but profit margins have gone down. Revenue per acre has fallen 34 percent over the past decade. There has been a gradual reduction in the relative spending on customer service, installation, and R&D. Moving into bigger corporate farms has thinned the talent we can apply to any one situation.

Too Many Parts: There is too much variety in our equipment. There are 57 different valves, 142 different types of connectors, and so on. There should be some sort of scale economies as we grow, but it seems that increased complexity overwhelms that.

Precision Farming: For many years, big farming went in the direction of larger, ever-more-specialized machines. Instead of pulling a tiller with a tractor, companies developed giant specialized tilling machines. Our methods, by contrast, were developed in small-scale growing and expanded to deal with larger farms. Much of what we do is program pivot machines.[1] However, recently, really since 2003 or so, there has been a trend toward what is called "precision farming." This is the opposite of the "big-machine" trend. Instead, precision farming aims to use robotics and AI to make fleets of lightweight machines and aerial drones that can give individual attention to plants.

Regional Baronies: We grew through the efforts of a handful of entrepreneurial characters who loved both technology and growing things. Each of these people has made a lasting imprint on the region or district they developed. This has made harmonization difficult. Each region tends to have its own sales protocols, HR policies, and so on.

Less Talent/Acre: There is a lot of talent in the company. For almost any problem that arises in the field, there is someone who has the knowledge or experience to deal with it. But we are now at a size where we don't always know who has the know-how relevant to a particular problem. And, even if we do, are we supposed to fly them around the world?

Nutrient Substitutes: We make good margins on our specialized branded crop nutrients. Unfortunately, many local dealers are replacing them with cheaper substitutes over which we have no control.

High-Tech Start-Ups: There is a whole new set of agriculture-tech start-ups. Because of venture funding trends, anything that smacks of tech gets funded. There are so-called vertical-farming companies like Plenty and Bowery. There is even a company, City-Crop, selling tabletop city-farming devices to grow your own "organic" lettuce in your apartment. Is this an opportunity for us? A threat? Or never mind?

DAY TWO

The first day had produced a plethora of challenges. There had been good energy and interest in identifying these issues. But why had the company's responses been, thus far, so weak?

FarmKor had been an innovator in the application of software, sensors, and controllers to agriculture. But, today, FarmKor's style of agrotech was no longer a new thing. The application of sensors and software to agriculture had become fairly common, with many vendors offering roughly similar solutions. Still, there was no lack of opportunity, as evidenced by the development programs in robotics and precision farming by the majors and the clutch of new firms entering with vertical farming, hydroponics, rooftop farming, and fully controlled farming solutions.

I began the session with a brief review of what we had accomplished yesterday and summarized the ten challenges.

I then showed eight PowerPoint slides of quotes from my interviews. Each quote appeared alone on a slide, and we discussed each as it appeared. I kept the identities of all of the sources confidential. Six of these quotes are shown below:

> Much of the company has not really accepted that we have lost technological and cost leadership. Our own best abilities are not quickly brought to bear where needed.

> Our investment in the Versuchsstation [experimental station] has been considerable. It is a pretty show-off of new agrotech, but it has drained resources from our ability to create novel knowledge. We seem to be a "tech" company that is not investing in new tech.
>
> Our culture is to be collaborative, but this has also created a situation where every opinion counts as valid, even after decisions have been made. A different point of view after the decision has been made can stop the implementation.
>
> There is a lack of a real solutions-based approach. We do not deliver solutions to a customer; we sell products and systems. We need to ask about the problems faced by customers and potential customers and whether or not we have solved, or can solve, them. I am not sure we know how to make this transition.
>
> FarmKor is torn three ways: there are those who want to feed the world and save it from climate change, those who love technology for its own sake, and those who want to run a business.
>
> FarmKor's best growth opportunities are abroad. It does not, however, have a coordinated strategy for growth away from the regions it knows best.

These new observations were about internal disagreements and action disconnects. Not everyone agreed with them all, but they were the true confidential views of the people in the room plus a few key subordinates. Some participants were surprised that someone else in the leadership group held a particular opinion. These observations were uncomfortable, but they were a start on a real diagnosis. Yes, FarmKor has a very talented group of people. But somehow, that talent and energy were not creating the level of accomplishment that seemed possible. The company was capable of more.

After the midday break, the senior vice president of sales and marketing spoke first. "The problem," he said, "is a lack of focus. We are worried about twenty-odd problems and making headway on none."

"What is holding you back?" I queried.

"I am not really sure," he replied.

"Okay," I said, "let's try to find out. Of the ten issues we raised yesterday and today, are any of them impossible to confront if the company really focused on it?"

"It seems hard to create an advantage in the heavily competitive big flat-farm business. And the stuff about internal discord is not easy."

"None of these are impossible," offered the VP of operations.

"All right," I said, "which one of ten is the most important? Which one is critically important?"

"Our diminished advantage," the CEO said.

"The regional baronies," the head of HR offered.

"The thinning out—falling gross profit per acre served on the larger farms," said the CFO.

I took the three cards representing those challenges and put them in the center of the board and collected all the others. "Let's put aside all the challenges other than these three. Suppose we absolutely have to make good progress in dealing with at least one of them over the next eighteen months. It is simply *essential*, or we all lose our jobs and options. Which one would you pick, and what would be the action plan?"

I broke the participants into two groups. Each group was to come back with an action plan for dealing with at least one of these three most important challenges. Each had ninety minutes to do this and then report back after the coffee break.

The presentations and discussion that followed were the heart of this particular Strategy Foundry. The senior VP of sales and marketing's earlier comment on lack of focus being a root cause of difficulties had been essential. Being freed to concentrate on only the most important challenges seemed to clarify minds. Having this as a center post helped in making what I call the "audacious leap" from the gnarly problem to a potential action.

The discussion shifted between difficulties and actions. The three main action ideas were refocus the business on high-value crops, especially orchards, with the option of actually selling the large-farm portion of the business to one of the global majors; refocus research on the detailed chemistry of nutrients, developing the ability to customize liquid fertilizers to each crop, location, season, even time of day; and establish deep codevelopment relationships with one or two lead customers. No group chose to work directly on the issue of regional baronies.

By the end of the second day, the Strategy Foundry group had a sensible explanation of why they were in the doldrums and what to do about it. They had been pioneers in the field, but the technologies they had pioneered were now broadly known and more cheaply deployed. In expanding into larger farms and a more varied array of crops, they had come up against larger competitors and the more demanding economics of lower-value crops. The *crux of the challenge* was their expansion into lower-value crops combined with diminished differentiation from large global competitors.

If the company could refocus on higher-value crops, especially orchards and vines, it might be able to complement such a focus with the development of tailored nutrient treatments. Farmers with higher-value crops would afford more experimentation and afford to spend more on specialized sensors.

DAY THREE

The third day began with a surprise announcement by the CEO. She said that she had been in quiet discussions with the board for a month about selling one of the regional divisions. The division in question had been one of the most difficult to bring into coordination with the others. Selling it off would raise cash and be a political signal to the other regions.

The key policy adopted by the Strategy Foundry group was a shift toward serving high-value crops. Some of these were rapeseed (canola), gourmet mushrooms, saffron, nut trees, apple trees, plum trees, and high-end vineyards. The basic idea was that pivot irrigation of standard crops had been mostly automated and that competition in that area had become too fierce. The high-value crops, however, required a more nuanced approach.

The foundry group laid out specific actions to implement this new policy. They identified two particular customers that might act as lead collaborators on developing new technology for orchards and vineyards. The head of development agreed on creating a special team to work on new technological approaches to dealing with these farmers' problems. The time horizon for these actions was eighteen months.

In addition to the new guiding policy and specific actions, I tasked the group with making their key assumptions explicit. I explained:

> In devising this new direction, this strategy, you have made some key assumptions. That's absolutely necessary—that is how creativity and imagination work. For instance, you are assuming that you can develop tailored nutrients for different soil conditions, crops, weather, and so on. You have made some progress in this area already, but you are *assuming* continuing success in development. It is important to write down these assumptions. When you meet as a foundry group again, whether in five or eleven months, you need to look at whether these assumptions were correct. I call this process "strategic navigation." It is vital to be able to revise your actions when assumptions are not being borne out.

Sometimes in a Strategy Foundry, it is necessary to work on the public face of the chosen direction. Here, that seemed less of an issue. These new initiatives would change the direction of the company if they worked. If they did not, there was little gain in trumpeting them to the world.

The final step in the Strategy Foundry was a "swearing in." I explained that sometimes managers are of two minds about the new direction chosen. That is often the case. But the leadership group must have the discipline to act as a coherent whole, at least until the next Strategy Foundry. I had the eight members gather in a rough circle in the middle of the room.

This foundry, I said, has agreed on a specific guiding policy and several specific actions. For this to be successful, each member of the foundry team will support and act to implement these policies and decisions. Each will ask the others for aid when it is necessary, and that aid will be given. This foundry recognizes that these choices are not forever—that things may change. But for the next eighteen months, it will support and hold this course. Agreed?

20

Strategy Foundry Concepts and Tools

A Strategy Foundry is a methodology designed to help a leadership team break away from treating strategy as goal setting. It is designed to identify the key challenges facing the organization, diagnose their structures, identify the crux, and work out how it can be addressed. The result is clarity on what is critical and an outline of the action steps for dealing with it. Final attention is paid to the public face of the actions chosen.

FOUNDRY PRECONDITIONS FOR SUCCESS

For a foundry to work, the senior executive and key senior managers should be committed to using a challenge-based approach to strategy. If they are not interested or not willing to invest in this approach, the foundry will not work. If the group knows the absent senior will overrule their thinking, it will be limited. If the leader behaves as if he or she has the answer to all important questions, the foundry will not work.

The team constituting the foundry should understand and agree that the foundry is neither a financial or accounting exercise nor a standard exercise in setting budget-like performance goals.

It is not about setting overall performance goals. For this reason, it is important that a Strategy Foundry be held separately from any budgeting process. Periodic foundries should be divorced from the annual budget cycle. One could, for example, occur every eleven months, or every thirty-one months, or some other number of months not divisible by three, four, or twelve. This is to enforce the idea that a foundry is not a financial forecasting or budgeting exercise. If this discipline is not enforced, the foundry will decay into a standard exercise in setting budget-like performance goals.

A Strategy Foundry works best with a small number of senior executives. With too large a group, hierarchy takes over. There may be additional attendees to keep records.

The Strategy Foundry is best held off-site. Most I have conducted last two to five days, depending on the complexity of the situation. In simpler situations, two days may be sufficient. Occasionally, a foundry is split between two sessions some weeks apart.

I have been a facilitator at many Strategy Foundries, and I prepare for the foundry meeting by conducting interviews beforehand with each participant (and other selected persons). I hold this information in confidence and use it to guide and shape the discussion, allowing me to surface opinions that individuals may be hesitant to state openly.

You can conduct a Strategy Foundry with an internal facilitator if there is enough insulation from some of the politics and kickback associated with real strategy debate. My experience, however, is that people will talk more frankly to a trusted outsider. Other gains arise from an outsider's willingness to say things that others will not or cannot express. An outside facilitator is able to treat the boss as just another participant and enforce disciplines of focus and choice that an insider might find difficult. Conversely, an inside facilitator may be much more informed about the technicalities of the business.

Another of the facilitator's roles is to guide the group through the process of challenge identification, diagnosis, the generation of alternatives, and the creation of action steps. A third crucial role becomes important in the second half of the foundry—maintaining a pressure to focus on the critical, yet addressable, challenges and pushing through to action steps.

WHAT MAKES A FOUNDRY FAIL?

The foundry will fail if the senior executive cannot help dominating the discussion. Similarly, any participant who turns disagreement into outright hostility and aggression will damage the work of the foundry.

When participants cannot disconnect for the time needed, the foundry cannot work well. Sometimes, executives are so busy taking phone calls, texting, and leaving the room for various urgencies that sustained discussion cannot be achieved. In such cases, it is best to defer the foundry or change the participant list.

The foundry participants should have a good understanding of the basic functioning of the business or agency. If they are senior executives in a complex firm who only manage financial goals and budgets, the foundry may not work. For challenges to be identified and strategies created, there must be knowledge in the room about product, markets, competition, and technology.

One solution to the complex diversified firm problem is to do strategy at the business or division level where product and market expertise lies. I have had mixed results with this tactic. The division may eagerly develop a good strategy only to find that corporate support was not forthcoming. In a few cases, the corporation was looking for boilerplate cost, revenue, and performance forecasts, not strategy. Deviations from corporate objectives may not be acceptable. The solution is to include senior corporate leaders in the division-level foundry, or to first do a foundry at the corporate level and then work downward to the division.

KEY FOUNDRY TOOLS

Deferred Judgment

Deferred judgment helps avoid the problem of too early convergence on an answer, an issue Irving Janis pointed out in his analysis of groupthink. Convergence on action can be deferred by conscious attempts to focus instead on the identification of challenges and diagnosis of their inner logics.

Deferred judgment in the foundry has two meanings. The first, recognized by psychologists, is deferring judgments about good and bad or important and unimportant. Letting facts and information accumulate without putting them in these kinds of bins helps generate more information.

Deferred judgment in the foundry also means holding off on action plans until after judgments about which challenges are critical and which are actionable. My key role as a facilitator is to quickly develop norms of balanced discussion and avoid early convergence.

Exposed Beliefs, Observations, and Judgments

The confidential interviews I conduct help me get up to speed on the history of the organization and on the issues it faces. They also reveal ideas about what has worked well and what hasn't worked well in the past and provide insights on challenges and their potential resolution that executives may not be willing to address so bluntly in a group setting.

The content of each interview is confidential, but the insights are not. Presented without attribution to a specific person, these judgments can be powerful tools for opening new avenues of discussion as well as fueling debate. Having strong yet depersonalized ideas and opinions added to a discussion is a powerful check on everyone simply going along with an influential person.

Written Questions and Answers

I have found it extremely useful to instigate a written question-answer dialogue with the foundry participants and a few other relevant people. I have formalized this as sending each a list of five to eight questions and asking for written responses, emailed to me. The responses are kept confidential, although I reserve the right to present some of their comments to the foundry without personal attribution.

The standard questions I always ask are those shown for FarmKor in the previous chapter. They cover changes in recent years and those expected in the future. I ask about which projects and initiatives have worked and which have not and why. I ask about challenges facing the organization, what makes them hard, and what can be done about them. Beyond these standard questions, I tailor questions to the industry, business, or organizational situation. Useful questions have been about the impact of specific new technologies or particular competitor actions. Other questions may refer to internal issues.

When responses are too short, I will reply asking for more. When they lack detail, I will again respond with a request for clarification.

Attention to History

History is a great teacher, but only if you remember it and draw conclusions from it. One job of the facilitator is using interview results and group discussion to highlight the actions and projects that have worked well in the past. Critically, the group should try to articulate what conditions or actions led to success in these cases. Then, equally important is a review of projects and endeavors that have not worked out. Again, the group must try to articulate what led to these failures.

Important lessons from history are different in each organization. But the common themes are a lack of support from the top, having too broad a collection of initiatives, having an impossible goal, opposition from some powerful internal interests, insufficient resources, and too little understanding of the on-the-ground mechanics of action. Having this list, gleaned from one's own history, is invaluable when it comes to creating action plans for the chosen critical challenges.

Start with the Challenge

The single most important element of the Strategy Foundry is a focus on identifying and diagnosing the challenges facing the organization. Starting with the challenge defuses attempts to make favorite projects and goals the center of discussion. Starting with the challenge opens up minds to problem solving rather than the more traditional focus on attaining performance goals.

Think Again

One of the tests of reflective thinking is this question: "If it takes two machines two minutes to make two gizmos, how long would it take one hundred machines to make one hundred gizmos?" The answer many people give, even MIT students, is 100 minutes. You may have to "think again" to see that one hundred machines will make one hundred gizmos in two minutes. So, the answer is two minutes.

The only cure for such traps is the advice to "think again." That is, check your answer by coming at the question in a different way or by working out the implications of your first-impulse answer.

Think again can be a powerful tool. In strategy sessions it usually means restating the challenge in different terms, encouraging a shift in point of view. Or it means looking at the proposed actions and asking if there aren't other and more effective ways of acting. For example, when Apple introduced the iPhone, Jobs, as noted earlier, wanted to restrict the App Store to carrying only Apple-produced products—as always, his instinct was to control as much of the user experience as possible. But others challenged this plan, arguing that healthy competition among third-party apps would drive down the prices and make the phone more attractive.

Most executives, most of the time, have a quick intuitive sense of what to do about a problem or issue. With good experience and a sound intellect, these quick intuitions are the essence of expertise. As Gary Klein's study of firefighters found, commanders made decisions intuitively—"the ability to use experience to recognize situations and know how to handle them."[1] We could not get through life without this capacity.[2] At the same time, there are situations that are both very important and about which we have little experience. In such strategic situations, the costs of running with the first intuition can be very high. We would not want the commander of a nuclear submarine to jump to his first conclusion in a crisis. In a foundry, the hoped-for style of discussion and argument encourages skilled intuitions, but it also encourages mutual critique. With proper facilitation, groups can be much better at "think again" than can an individual.

The Time Viewer

I was working with French defense company Aérospatiale just before its 1999 merger with high-tech portions of Matra (an industrial conglomerate). I told the seven executives that I had the good fortune to know a scientist working on a time viewer. The previous night we had looked ahead seven years and obtained an image of *Fortune* magazine's cover. Unfortunately, the time viewer then imploded, and we could not get any other information. But we did have this . . . I then showed them a slightly singed *Fortune* cover dated 2005 featuring the story "Aérospatiale: Company of the Year."

"What could have happened to generate that cover story?" I asked. The executives broke into two small groups. Each came up with a narrative about how such a cover story might come to pass. The fascinating thing was that neither narrative had much to do with the defense business. Both envisioned applying the company's resources and know-how in totally new areas.

The cover-story process can also be applied to envision failure. The time viewer might produce a cover featuring a reworded version of Geoff Colvin's 2018 *Fortune* article titled "What the Hell Happened at GE?" This kind of looking ahead to possible failure had recently been named a premortem, following Gary Klein's 2007 article "Performing a Project Premortem."[3]

Another use of the time-viewer concept is retrospective. I ask the executives to imagine that we have a way to send a message to the company CEO's laptop *seven years ago*. There is only one message. It has to be short and cannot contain any specific information about the future. The time police forbid such messages. What would you send?

The trick about this exercise is that the message cannot seem to have knowledge of the future. Therefore, it has to be an insight based on data available seven years ago. At General Dynamics, some managers wanted to send back a message about IEDs blowing up vehicles in Afghanistan, but the time police did not allow that. At PricewaterhouseCoopers the 2018 advice was encouragement on rebuilding the consultancy practice. As the group discovers how hard this is, they gain a new appreciation for what they are trying to do in the foundry. And they cannot help wondering what a message like that, from seven years hence, would look like.

Instant Strategy

There are times when a group gets a little too "deep into the weeds" and has trouble narrowing focus to a few critical actions. This almost always happens with nonprofits, where strategy has, in the past, been taken to be long lists of "to-dos." In such situations a round of "instant strategy" can break through the fog. To carry out this exercise, I ask each participant to write down in one sentence their recommendation for action, not a vague strategy or a performance goal, but a focused action that has a good chance of being accomplished. They have two minutes to commit this to paper, fold it over, and dump it into a box (or a hat if you are being traditional).

I used this with XRSystems, whose story I described in Chapter 4. There the first four "instant" suggestions were R&D refocus only on wireless, phantom stock plan, reorganize sales, and more sales visits to nonclients. But the fifth, "automotive sensors," was a wild card that took the company in a new and profitable direction. Instant strategy may just repeat the obvious. When it doesn't, there is the chance of redirecting energy in an interesting new direction.

Forced Inward Analysis

The natural tendency when executives discuss strategy is to define challenges in terms of financial outcomes or competitive position. It may take an outside facilitator to lead the conversation to the challenges created by how the organization actually functions.

Working with a chemical company, I pressed the foundry group to explain, in some detail, the reasons for declining profits. The basic answers were competition forcing declining prices combined with the goal of running plants at full capacity.

"How are prices actually set?" I asked.

"By our reps in the field—they negotiate prices" was the answer.

"What tools do they have, and how are they trained?" I asked.

The fairly blank expressions I received in response were telling. The sales reps should have been equipped with tools showing how different chemical products would affect the cost and performance of each customer's products. Without this kind of information, the discussion with a customer turns into a pure price negotiation. They had neither these tools nor much training on selling itself. The discussion shifted from complaints about competition toward how the company was actually competing. There were more issues involved than just price, and the company reps were not prepared to use those points of leverage.

In my work with companies on strategy, I would estimate that in one-third of the cases, the true strategic challenge lay with the organization's structure or processes. Shedding light on that is not easy but should be rewarding.

Why Is That Hard?

Chapter 8 described the case of QuestKo and my question to the CEO: "What about all this is difficult?" This line of thinking is very helpful in evaluating and analyzing challenges.

Executives have a relatively easy time identifying challenges. But addressability is more complicated. The question that often breaks this into pieces small enough to think about is "Why is this hard?" That is, what are the obstacles to dealing with this challenge?

Sometimes, as in the case of QuestKo, the obstacles had become unmentionable. The lack of divisional coordination was glossed over, the issues of customer ratings were shunted aside, and senior discussions focused on success rather than issues. Instead, more effort had been spent in unhelpful directions. In other cases, the obstacles are so great that the challenge is simply not addressable.

More commonly, an obstacle can be overcome if there is focused effort on doing so. Many times, management has been encouraging a direct assault on metrics rather than obstacles. Once detailed, listed, and given priority, an obstacle can be overcome.

Red Team

A "red team" is a term of art taken from the military. In US and NATO war games, the red team is the enemy. The game works by assigning talented people to the red team and having them devise tactics and strategies for winning against the opposing blue team.

In recent years, red-team exercises have proliferated in the cyber world among companies like Microsoft and organizations like the National Security Agency. There the issue is cyber attacks on networks and cloud-based server farms. By having the same people who design protection methods then work on breaking through them, improvements are speeded.

Sometimes a red-team exercise is as simple as having a particular member of the group role play a competitor or other outside party. How would the company's plans look from that point of view? Would moves be misinterpreted?

When creating a strategy, a red-team exercise forces the group to evaluate "frame risk"—the chance that the way they think about the world and competition is wrong or critically incomplete. The trick about frame risk is that our frames cannot tell us if they are wrong; we have to do that with human judgment. If our frame of the situation was obviously wrong, we would not be using it. The only way to see what is wrong with our current "best" model is to have a group shift points of view, attack it, and try to take it down.

The red team is one way of adjusting for currently unanticipated contingencies. It tries to uncover "black swans," unanticipated weaknesses, or failure modes. The red team knows the broad outline of our ways of doing business and tries to outwit them, even turning our strengths against us.

Find the ASCs

Two words frequently used in discussions of strategy are "important" and "focus." By definition strategy is about what is important. The role of focus is less obvious because modern models of firms, people, and competition give scant attention to the costs of complexity. It is not that one cannot do everything at once. It is, rather, that each initiative draws attention and cognitive space from others and that multiple initiatives are each blunted to accommodate one another.

One of the most powerful foundry tools is boiling the situation down to a few addressable strategic challenges, or ASCs. The crux of the situation will normally reside there. Searching for the few limited challenges that are both very important and that can be overcome is the core of the Strategy Foundry. One approach, detailed in the Intel exercise described in Chapter 4, is to formally evaluate both the importance and the addressability of each of a number of challenges.

A second approach is to "take things off the table." At one government agency, the group had developed a list of twenty-six "key" challenges. Each was noted on a five-by-eight-inch index card on the conference table. I told the group that we had to simplify down to five by physically taking twenty-one "off the table."

No one volunteered to remove any of the "key" challenges. I turned to the director and said, "This is where you earn your pay. It is up to you to pick the five most important."

He did so, playing it as an exercise. As we focused in on the most important of the five, an hour of discussion broke it down into four components, so we now had nine important challenges back on the table. I again insisted on just five.

One important result of this focusing is going more deeply into each challenge. As that happens, people realize how complex it is and the many subproblems it exposes. With that increase in complexity comes the need to once again focus on the parts that are critical and doable.

Focus on One or Two Proximate Objectives

There is a sense in which strategy is almost always about some sort of focus. Absent a crisis or very competent strategic leadership, most organizations gradually defocus. They try to do fifty different good-sounding things and do none of them well. One of the most important functions of the Strategy Foundry is to focus energy and resources on adroitly resolving the most important challenges.

One powerful tool for accomplishing this is the proximate objective. By this I mean a task, not a performance goal, that has a reasonable chance of being successfully accomplished within a short period of time. The task, or objective, is *proximate* in that it can be done and can be done fairly soon.

There is nothing that motivates an army or company better than winning. By tackling an important objective and overcoming it, leadership sets the stage for the next battle. Think of strategy as a series of proximate objectives rather than a long-term vision.

Time Horizon

A second advantage of creating tasks that are proximate is that it facilitates an emphasis on action. A good strategy evolves out of focused attention on those important issues that can be addressed in the near future. I often suggest an eighteen-month horizon. The period can be longer, of course, for issues where current actions take much longer to reach fruition.

A shorter time horizon also helps with achieving agreement. Groups are hesitant to "take things off the table" because each challenge is often connected to favorite projects and initiatives. Taking it off the table means saying no to that project or at least to its full funding and attention. This is the reason so many strategy exercises wind up being laundry lists of all the things all those involved want to do. Behind closed doors, managers have engaged in political log-rolling where support for projects is negotiated and traded.

Having a shorter time horizon is one way around this common impasse. If, for example, the policies and actions to be adopted are aimed at accomplishments over the coming eighteen months, then there will soon be another chance to put a project or interest back on the table. Seeing strategy work as a fairly fast-paced cycle takes the sting out of not having one's pet interest at the top of the list. On the other hand, seeing strategy as a long-term commitment turns the selection of priorities into a life-or-death struggle. Keeping the time horizon short facilitates agreement on priorities because they are not forever.

Reference Classes

A common bias is thinking that one's case or situation is special. This is equivalent to the optimism bias or what researchers Kahneman and Lovallo call "competitor neglect."[4] It happens when I think that the statistics on auto accidents don't apply to me because "I'm different." The problem is that everybody thinks that they are different, and the statistics come from us all.

A reference class is a group of comparable situations or companies or challenges. An excellent use of professional consultants is the collection of information on a useful reference group: companies that have entered the Chinese market for consumer goods, companies that have technologies go off-patent, and so on. McKinsey consultants Bradley, Hirt, and Smit's book *Strategy Beyond the Hockey Stick* does a nice job of describing the issues. They note that the large documents often prepared for strategy making "provide detail, but no reference data with predictive power. Interestingly, the more detailed the information you have, the more you lead yourself to believe that you know; and the more your confidence grows, the higher the risk of arriving at the wrong conclusions."[5]

An interesting example of this bias at work appears in the Rand Corporation's study of forty new-process chemical plants. The early cost estimates, the ones used to justify the projects, averaged 49 percent of the ultimate cost. The early estimates ranged (one standard deviation) from 27 to 72 percent of the ultimate cost. One of Rand's summary observations was this:

> We can detect no trend of improvement in cost estimating over the 12 years or so covered by plants in our data base, nor can we discern any change in expectations about plant performance. The persistence of underestimation of costs and over-optimistic assumptions about performance raises questions about why industry has not been able to adjust its expectations over the years.[6]

One simple answer is that industries don't think; people do. In several Strategic Foundries, the group has recessed so that further work would be done before reaching conclusive decisions. Some of that work has been to collect information on similar situations faced by others—to build a reference class.

Strategic Navigation

The key to survival in difficult times is adapting to changing circumstances. As argued in Chapter 3, strategy is an ongoing journey. To bring that concept to life, executives should take the time to write down the key assumptions underlying their strategy. The heart of moving from difficulty to action is making assumptions. Unfortunately, some of these may be wrong. Unless we commit to making them explicit, and checking their accuracy as events unfold, it becomes very hard to adapt. Strategic navigation is the process of making assumptions explicit and then checking them as events unfold.

Swearing In

The 'National Agency' is a large organization whose purpose has been to provide critical services to local governments. After holding a Strategy Foundry, I revisited the National Agency two months later. To my dismay, the key guiding policies the group had adopted were being ignored. The director explained that two members of top management had "turned coat" and begun to bad-mouth the proposed actions soon after the foundry exercise. Although they had gone along with the ideas during the foundry, afterward they had begun to tell their subordinates and associates to resist these initiatives.

This kind of behavior is endemic in public organizations because the senior executives inherit the key personnel and structure, rarely holding office long enough to form a more cohesive group.

The basic cure for this kind of Machiavellian politicking is to not permit two-faced managers. Executives who say one thing to the boss and another to subordinates should be sent back to junior high school.

One step that can help instill some moral spine about such behavior is "swearing in." When it seems appropriate, I will ask the members of the foundry to gather in the center of the room in a circle. I then say:

> As a group, you have looked deeply into the challenges you face. You have agreed on a few tasks to be undertaken in order to overcome the most important challenges. You have knowingly put aside many other concerns to focus on these tasks. I ask you to affirm, to yourselves and to each other, that these choices are binding until the next foundry. I ask you to affirm that you will not disparage these decisions to others, that you will not seek to undermine them, and that you will provide aid and support to one another in accomplishing them.

They should each acknowledge agreement, by word or gesture. In some cases, they have pressed fists together in the center of the circle.

Public Face

Some years back I worked a foundry with a large international manufacturing company. We had a four-and-a-half-day foundry during which basic guiding policies were hard fought and developed after flying in key experts on day three. As we began to conclude, I had the three key tasks we had developed described on large paper easels in the front of the room. One of the participants then asked, "But where is the strategy?"

"What do you mean?" I questioned back.

"Well, three years ago we had a strategy that was distributed to everyone and covered a lot more detail about what we wanted to do."

"You mean this?" I asked, pointing to the paper document that was the three-year-old "strategy" pinned to the wall.

"Yes, that," he said.

I moved over to the document with my red marker in hand. I read each of the ten lines aloud and asked the group whether that objective had been met.

"Did you continue to lead the industry, as it says on line one?" I asked. The answer was no because market share had been lost. I put a red *X* next to the line.

"Did you maintain the highest safety standards?" Yes, checkmark.

"Did you increase profitability?" No, a red *X*.

"Did you penetrate the Chinese market?" Not really, a reddish *X*.

"Did you maintain high employee morale and confidence?" Well, with 15 percent layoffs, that was an interesting question. Red *X*.

"Did you dramatically reduce carbon-based energy usage?" Keeping it level is not a reduction. Red *X*.

When I stopped, there were eight red *X*'s.

"Is this the kind of strategy you want to again publish?" I asked. "A document full of pious objectives few of which will be met in the next three years?"

For too many executives, "strategy" is all about the public face. That is, it is about the shape and substance of a public statement of purpose and priorities. Employees and investors have come to expect a public statement of "strategy" that describes the organization's basic activities, values, and priorities.

To deal with this demand, it is important for the foundry to spend time and effort on the public face of the chosen policies and actions. In constructing a public face of the strategy, it is best to avoid goals and objectives and instead speak to a few key priorities. (Having more than three priorities stretches the meaning of the word!) You do not want to create the sense that a strategy document is mentioning everything that is important, that it has a present under the Christmas tree for each interested party. This may be a break with tradition, but it is a necessary break. Good strategy is about focus, not about everything that everybody does.

ACKNOWLEDGMENTS

I could not have written this book without the daily support of my wife, Kate. A former professor of strategy, she listened to me about each conundrum I encountered and always suggested a way around. She read each chapter as it appeared and suggested changes, up to and including dropping the chapter entirely. Dan Lovallo, a professor at the University of Sydney, also read many chapters as they appeared and gave immensely helpful comments. I am also grateful to Steven Lippman, Pete Cummings, and Norman Toy who read early versions of chapters and provided insightful feedback.

At Hachette Book Group's PublicAffairs, I thank John Mahaney, whose contribution went beyond being an editor. He saw the central message of the book and gently helped me hone and shape it. I asked Michael V. Carlisle, a cofounder of Inkwell Management, to be my literary agent for this book. He saw the early manuscript and gave me needed encouragement. I thank him sincerely for his wise counsel on the shape of the book's central message and its title, all in addition to being a fine agent.

NOTES

INTRODUCTION: THE ROOF OF THE DOG'S ASS

1. The short climb is rated 7A on the Fontainebleau system, a difficulty first mastered in the mid-1950s. Today, in 2021, the scale tops out at 8C, with only a very few climbers in the world claiming boulder routes at that level.

2. Much later, I asked Asya about that move in Figure 1. What is the crux? She said, "Yes, for me [that] is probably the crux, although others might say it's the next move."

CHAPTER 1. CAROLYN'S DILEMMA: HOW DO I CREATE A STRATEGY?

1. Gary Hamel, "Killer Strategies That Make Shareholders Rich," *Fortune*, June 23, 1997, 70.

2. Jack Kavanagh, "Has the Netflix vs Disney Streaming War Already Been Won?," *Little White Lies: Truth and Movies*, March 17, 2018.

3. Garth Saloner, Andrea Shepard, and Joel Podolny, *Strategic Management* (New York: John Wiley & Sons, 2001), 20.

CHAPTER 2. UNTANGLING THE CHALLENGE: FINDING AND USING THE CRUX

1. Kees Dorst, "The Core of 'Design Thinking' and Its Application," *Design Studies* 32, no. 6 (2011): 527.

2. Here and hereafter disguised company and personal names will be first enclosed in single quotes.

3. Michael Porter would have never approached an actual company strategy this way. His categories were broad descriptions of whole collections of strategies, not the strategies themselves.

4. Herbert A. Simon, *The Sciences of the Artificial* (Cambridge, MA: MIT Press, 2019), 111.

5. A tensor is a multidimensional array that transforms according to different laws for each dimension or index.

6. This description has evolved from the original description of "unstructured problems" in Richard M. Cyert, Herbert A. Simon, and Donald B. Trow, "Observation of a Business Decision," *Journal of Business* 29, no. 4 (1956): 237–248.

7. John Kounios and Mark Beeman, "The Cognitive Neuroscience of Insight," *Annual Review of Psychology* 65 (2014): 88.

8. Michael C. Lens, "Subsidized Housing and Crime: Theory, Mechanisms, and Evidence" (UCLA Luskin School of Public Affairs, 2013), https://luskin.ucla.edu/sites/default/files/Lens%204%20JPL.pdf.

9. Kounios and Beeman, op. cit., 80.

10. Charles Darwin, *The Autobiography of Charles Darwin* (Amherst, NY: Prometheus Books, 2010), 42.

11. John Dewey, *How We Think* (Lexington, MA: D. C. Heath, 1910), chap. 3.

12. It is usually best to retrace your steps, even if that means climbing back up a bit. If you have to spend the night, worry about warmth and water. Don't waste energy looking for food. Unless you are hurt or freezing, you have days to work it out.

13. Merim Bilalić, Peter McLeod, and Fernand Gobet, "Inflexibility of Experts—Reality or Myth? Quantifying the Einstellung Effect in Chess Masters," *Cognitive Psychology* 56, no. 2 (2008): 73–102.

14. In 2002 Overture filed a patent infringement suit against Google that was settled in 2003 for a payment of $350 million in Google shares. Overture's basic claim was for "a method of generating a search result list . . . [and] ordering the identified search listings into a search result list in accordance with the value of the respective bid amounts." Since Google did not use bids to order its search results, Overture's patent may or may not have had relevance to Google.

15. With the rise of mobile search, Google moved paid ads to the top of the search results, somewhat fogging the issue. Today, in 2021, Google has unfortunately further blurred the line between organic search results and paid advertising with formatting changes that make it hard to tell the difference.

CHAPTER 3. STRATEGY IS A JOURNEY

1. "Mid-market CRM Total Cost of Ownership" (Yankee Group, July 2001).

2. Marc R. Benioff and Carlye Adler, *Behind the Cloud: The Untold Story of How Salesforce.com Went from Idea to Billion-Dollar Company—and Revolutionized an Industry* (San Francisco: Jossey-Bass, 2009), 134.

3. Ben McCarthy, "A Brief History of Salesforce.Com, 1999–2020," November 14, 2016, www.salesforceben.com/brief-history-salesforce-com.

4. Marc Benioff, comments at Dreamforce 7, November 18, 2009.

5. "Telegraph Travel," *Telegraph*, September 28, 2016.

6. "Telegraph Travel"; Michael Hogan, "Michael O'Leary's 33 Daftest Quotes," *Guardian*, November 8, 2013.

7. Siddharth Vikram Philip, Matthew Miller, and Charlotte Ryan, "Ryanair Cuts 3,000 Jobs, Challenges $33 Billion in State Aid," *Bloomberg*, April 30, 2020.

CHAPTER 4. WHERE YOU CAN WIN: THE ASC

1. Louis Morton, "Germany First: The Basic Allied Concept of Strategy in World War II" (US Army Center of Military History, 1990); emphasis in the original.

2. Joseph A. Califano, *The Triumph and Tragedy of Lyndon Johnson: The White House Years* (New York: Simon and Schuster, 2015), 326.

3. Bethany McLean, "The Empire Reboots," *Vanity Fair*, November 14, 2014.

4. John F. Crowell, "Business Strategy in National and International Policy," *Scientific Monthly* 18, no. 6 (1924): 596–604.

5. All the information was drawn from public sources. No Intel employee or executive was interviewed or consulted.

6. Shawn Knight, "Intel Internal Memo Reveals That Even Intel Is Impressed by AMD's Progress," Techspot, June 26, 2019, www.techspot.com/news.

7. Leo Sun, "Intel's Chip Issues Are Hurting These 3 Tech Giants," *Motley Fool*, April 8, 2019.

8. Charlie Demerjian, "Why Did Intel Kill Off Their Modem Program?," *SemiAccurate* (blog), April 18, 2019, www.semiaccurate.com/2019/04/18/why-did-intel-kill-of-their-modem-program.

9. Don Clark, "Intel's Culture Needed Fixing. Its C.E.O. Is Shaking Things Up," *New York Times*, March 1, 2020.

CHAPTER 5. THE CHALLENGE OF GROWTH

1. The S&P 1500 is a group of firms compiled by Standard & Poor's, which accounts for about 90 percent of the total value of US stocks.

2. Jon Peddie Research is a technically oriented marketing and management consulting firm specializing in graphics and multimedia.

3. Frederick Kempe, "Davos Special Edition: China Seizing AI Lead?," Atlantic Council, January 26, 2019, www.atlanticcouncil.org/content-series/inflection-points/davos-special-edition-china-seizing-ai-lead.

4. David Trainer, "Perverse Incentives Produce Deals That Shred Shareholder Value," *Forbes*, May 2, 2016, www.forbes.com/sites/greatspeculations/2016/05/02/perverse-incentives-produce-deals-that-shred-shareholder-value.

5. F. Homberg, K. Rost, and M. Osterloh, "Do Synergies Exist in Related Acquisitions? A Meta-analysis of Acquisition Studies," *Review of Managerial Science* 3, no. 2 (2009): 100.

6. Colin Camerer and Dan Lovallo, "Overconfidence and Excess Entry: An Experimental Approach," *American Economic Review* 89, no. 1 (1999): 306–318.

7. D. Fisher, "Accounting Tricks Catch Up with GE," *Forbes*, November 22, 2019.

8. J. R. Graham, C. R. Harvey, and S. Rajgopal, "The Economic Implications of Corporate Financial Reporting," *Journal of Accounting and Economics* 40 (2005): 3–73.

9. Ilia Dichev et al., "The Misrepresentation of Earnings," *Financial Analysts Journal* 72, no. 1 (2016): 22–35.

10. Justin Fox, "Learn to Play the Earnings Game (and Wall Street Will Love You)," *CNN Money*, March 31, 1997.

11. Changling Chen, Jeong-Bon Kim, and Li Yao, "Earnings Smoothing: Does It Exacerbate or Constrain Stock Price Crash Risk?," *Journal of Corporate Finance* 42 (2017): 36–54. "Crashes" were measured by the number of three standard-deviation down quarters less the number of three standard-deviation up quarters in their stock prices.

12. John McInnis, "Earnings Smoothness, Average Returns, and Implied Cost of Equity Capital," *Accounting Review* 85, no. 1 (2010): 315–341.

CHAPTER 7. CREATING COHERENT ACTION

1. Nancy Bouchard, "Matter of Gravity, Petzl Turns the Vertical Environment into Bold Opportunity," SGB Media, August 1, 2008.

2. A. G. Lafley and Roger L. Martin, *Playing to Win: How Strategy Really Works* (Boston: Harvard Business Review Press, 2013).

3. "Cost-Benefit Analysis Used in Support of the Space Shuttle Program," National Aeronautics and Space Administration, June 2, 1972, http://archive.gao.gov/f0302/096542.pdf.

4. The ideas for the shuttle originated in the US Air Force Dyna-Soar project that ran from 1957 through 1963. Neil Armstrong was originally attached to this project as a pilot. The concept was a piloted spacecraft that could carry weapons anywhere in the world on short notice and land like an aircraft. Its antecedent was the 1942 Nazi Amerika Bomber project that examined multiple options for bombing the Americas from Europe.

5. Two failures in 135 launches is a 1.5 percent rate of failure. The "O"-ring failure on *Challenger* was indirectly due to the difficulty of coupling two solid-fuel rockets. The heat-shield failure on *Columbia* was due to a piece of a solid-fuel tank breaking off and damaging a tile.

6. Jean Edward Smith, *Eisenhower: In War and Peace* (New York: Random House, 2012), 278.

7. Maurice Matloff and Edwin Marion Snell, *Strategic Planning for Coalition Warfare, 1941–1942 [1943–1944]* (Office of the Chief of Military History, Department of the Army, 1953), 3:219.

8. "President Bush Visits with Troops in Afghanistan at Bagram Air Base," White House press release, https://georgewbush-whitehouse.archives.gov/news/releases/2008/12/20081215-1.html.

9. Craig Whitlock, "At War with the Truth," *Washington Post*, December 9, 2019.

CHAPTER 8. WHAT IS THE PROBLEM? DIAGNOSING THROUGH REFRAMING AND ANALOGY

1. Thomas Gryta, Joann S. Lublin, and David Benoit, "How Jeffrey Immelt's 'Success Theater' Masked the Rot at GE," *Wall Street Journal*, February 21, 2018.

2. Brian Merchant, "The Secret Origin Story of the iPhone," *Verge*, June 13, 2017.

3. Walter Isaacson, *Steve Jobs* (New York: Simon & Schuster, 2011), 246.

4. David Lieberman, "Microsoft's Ballmer Having a 'Great Time,'" *USA Today*, April 29, 2007.

5. John C. Dvorak, "Apple Should Pull the Plug on the iPhone," March 28, 2007, republished on *MarketWatch*, www.marketwatch.com/story/guid/3289e5e2-e67c-4395-8a8e-b94c1b480d4a.

6. Translated from www.handelsblatt.com/unternehmen/industrie/produktentwicklung-nokia-uebt-sich-in-selbstkritik;2490362.

7. *New York Times*, June 19, 1986.

8. "Assessment of Weapons and Tactics Used in the October 1973 Mideast War," *Weapons System Analysis Report 249*, Department of Defense, October 1974, www.cia.gov/library/readingroom/docs/LOC-HAK-480-3-1-4.pdf.

9. NATO Force Structure (declassified), www.nato.int/cps/fr/natohq/declassified_138256.htm.

10. "Sensitive New Information on Soviet War Planning and Warsaw Pact Force Strengths," CIA Plans Division, August 10, 1973, 7, www.cia.gov/library/readingroom/docs/1973-08-10.pdf. See also "Warsaw Pact War Plan for Central Region of Europe," CIA Directorate of Intelligence, June 1968, www.cia.gov/library/readingroom/docs/1968-06-01.pdf.

11. Romie L. Brownlee and William J. Mullen III, "Changing an Army: An Oral History of General William E. DePuy, U.S.A. Retired," United States Center of Military History, n.d., 43, https://history.army.mil/html/books/070/70-23/CMH_Pub_70-23.pdf.

12. Alexander Haig to William DePuy, September 10, 1976, as quoted in Major Paul Herbert, *Deciding What Has to Be Done: General William E. DePuy and the 1976 Edition of FM-100-5, Operations* (Leavenworth Papers, no. 16, 1988), 96.

CHAPTER 9. DIAGNOSE VIA COMPARISON AND FRAMEWORKS

1. Brian Rosenthal, "The Most Expensive Mile of Subway Track on Earth," *New York Times*, December 28, 2017.

2. Greg Knowler, "Maersk CEO Charts Course Toward Integrated Offering," March 7, 2019, www.joc.com/maritime-news/container-lines/maersk-line/maersk-ceo-charts-course-toward-integrated-offering_20190307.html.

3. Richard P. Rumelt, "How Much Does Industry Matter?," *Strategic Management Journal* 12 (1991): 167–185.

CHAPTER 10. USE SHARP ANALYTICAL TOOLS WITH CARE

1. Technically, Bradley faced a convex payoff, shaped like a call option. Thus, he benefited from increases, rather than decreases, in risk.

2. Alan Zakon's original definitions of the quadrants were analogies to financial instruments: Savings, Bond, Mortgage, and Question. Wommack coined the "Cow" label and was subsequently a bit annoyed when it went public.

3. Joseph L. Bower and Clayton M. Christensen, "Disruptive Technologies: Catching the Wave," *Harvard Business Review* (January–February 1995): 43.

4. Jill Lepore, "What the Gospel of Innovation Gets Wrong," *New Yorker*, June 16, 2014, www.newyorker.com/magazine/2014/06/23/the-disruption-machine.

5. Mitsuru Igami, "Estimating the Innovator's Dilemma: Structural Analysis of Creative Destruction in the Hard Disk Drive Industry, 1981–1998," *Journal of Political Economy* 125, no. 3 (2017): 48.

6. Josh Lerner, "An Empirical Exploration of a Technology Race," *Rand Journal of Economics* (1997): 228–247.

CHAPTER 11. SEEK AN EDGE

1. Karl Popper, "Natural Selection and the Emergence of Mind," speech delivered at Darwin College, November 8, 1977.

2. Thomas McCraw, *American Business, 1920–2000: How It Worked* (Wheeling, IL: Harlan Davidson, 2000), 51.

3. "How Intuit Reinvents Itself," part of "The Future 50," *Fortune.com*, November 1, 2017, 81.

4. Karel Williams et al., "The Myth of the Line: Ford's Production of the Model T at Highland Park, 1909–16," *Business History* 35, no. 3 (1993): 66–87.

5. Armen Alchian, "Reliability of Progress Curves in Airframe Production," *Econometrica* 31 (1963): 679–694.

6. Grace Dobush, "How Etsy Alienated Its Crafters and Lost Its Soul," *Wired*, February 19, 2015, www.wired.com/2015/02/etsy-not-good-for-crafters/.

CHAPTER 12. INNOVATING

1. Mark A. Lemley, "The Myth of the Sole Inventor," *Michigan Law Review* (2012): 709–760.

2. www.sleuthsayers.org/2013/06/the-3500-shirt-history-lesson-in.html.

3. Bernardo Montes de Oca, Zoom Company Story, slidebean.com, April 9, 2020.

4. Jon Sarlin, "Everyone You Know Uses Zoom. That Wasn't the Plan," CNN Business, November 29, 2020.

5. David J. Teece, "Profiting from Technological Innovation: Implications for Integration, Collaboration, Licensing and Public Policy," *Research Policy* 15, no. 6 (1986): 285–305.

CHAPTER 13. THE CHALLENGE OF ORGANIZATION DYSFUNCTION

1. Maryann Keller, *Rude Awakening: The Rise, Fall, and Struggle for Recovery of General Motors* (New York: HarperPerennial, 1990), 107.

2. Anton R. Valukas, "Report to Board of Directors of General Motors Company Regarding Ignition Switch Recalls," Jenner & Block, May 29, 2014, 252, 253.

3. James Surowiecki, "Where Nokia Went Wrong," *New Yorker*. September 3, 2013, www.newyorker.com/business/currency/where-nokia-went-wrong.

4. Yves Doz and Keeley Wilson, *Ringtone: Exploring the Rise and Fall of Nokia in Mobile Phones* (Oxford: Oxford University Press, 2017).

5. Juha-Antti Lamberg et al., "The Curse of Agility: Nokia Corporation and the Loss of Market Dominance, 2003–2013," Industry Studies Conference, 2016.

6. Timo O. Vuori and Quy N. Huy, "Distributed Attention and Shared Emotions in the Innovation Process: How Nokia Lost the Smartphone Battle," *Administrative Science Quarterly* 61, no. 1 (2016): 22.

7. Vuori and Huy, op. cit., 24.

8. Daniel Quinn Mills and G. Bruce Friesen, *Broken Promises: An Unconventional View of What Went Wrong at IBM* (New York: McGraw-Hill, 1996), 43, 45.

9. Paul Carroll, *Big Blues: The Unmaking of IBM* (New York: Crown, 1994), 24.

10. Lynda M. Applegate, Robert Austin, and Elizabeth Collins, "IBM's Decade of Transformation: Turnaround to Growth" (Harvard Business School Case 9-805-130, 2009).

11. Lou Gerstner, "The Customer Drives Everything," *Maclean's*, December 16, 2002, https://archive.macleans.ca/article/2002/12/16/the-customer-drives-everything.

12. Louis V. Gerstner, *Who Says Elephants Can't Dance? Inside IBM's Historic Turnaround* (New York: HarperInformation, 2002), 187.

13. Applegate, Austin, and Collins, "IBM's Decade of Transformation," 6.

CHAPTER 14. DON'T START WITH GOALS

1. Richard P. Rumelt, *Strategy, Structure, and Economic Performance* (Cambridge, MA: Harvard Business School Press, 1974).

2. John B. Hege, *The Wankel Rotary Engine: A History* (Jefferson, NC: McFarland, 2006), 115.

3. Total value is the value of all stock plus the value of all debt, summing the interests of stockholders and debt holders.

4. Dean Foods Company Overview, PowerPoint slides, 2015.

CHAPTER 15. DON'T CONFUSE STRATEGY WITH MANAGEMENT

1. Apparently, this was one of his standard pronouncements. Arthur Schlesinger Jr. reported a very similar statement in 1964. Papers of Robert S. McNamara, Library of Congress, Part L, folder 110, interview with Arthur M. Schlesinger Jr., April 4, 1964, 16.

2. Robert McNamara, *In Retrospect: The Tragedy and Lessons of Vietnam* (New York: Times Books, 1995), 203.

3. Clark Clifford with Richard Holbrooke, *Counsel to the President: A Memoir* (New York, Random House, 1991), 460.

4. Rosabeth Moss Kanter, "Smart Leaders Focus on Execution First and Strategy Second," *Harvard Business Review* (November 6, 2017).

5. Alfred D. Chandler, *Strategy and Structure: Chapters in the History of the Industrial Enterprise* (Cambridge, MA: MIT Press, 1961), 22.

6. Robert S. Kaplan and D. P. Norton, *The Balanced Scorecard: Translating Strategy into Action* (Cambridge, MA: Harvard Business School Press, 1996).

7. Robert S. Kaplan and David P. Norton, "Focus Your Organization on Strategy—with the Balanced Scorecard," *Harvard Business Review* (2005): 1–74.

CHAPTER 16. DON'T CONFUSE CURRENT FINANCIAL RESULTS WITH STRATEGY

1. Justin Fox and Rajiv Rao, "Learn to Play the Earnings Game," *Fortune*, March 31, 1997.

2. Jerry Useem, "The Long-Forgotten Flight That Sent Boeing Off Course," *Atlantic*, November 20, 1999.

3. Fischer Black and Myron Scholes, "The Pricing of Options and Corporate Liabilities," *Journal of Political Economy* 81, no. 3 (1973): 637–654. Fischer Black died in 1995 at only fifty-seven. Had he lived, he would have received the Nobel Prize in 1997 along with Merton and Scholes.

4. Warren E. Buffett and Jamie Dimon, "Short-Termism Is Harming the Economy," *Wall Street Journal*, June 7, 2018.

5. M. C. Jensen, "Agency Costs of Free Cash Flow, Corporate Finance, and Takeovers," *American Economic Review* 76, no. 2 (1986): 323–329.

6. "CEO and Executive Compensation Practices: 2019 Edition," Conference Board, 17.

7. K. H. Hammonds, "The Secret Life of the CEO: Do They Even Know Right from Wrong?," *Fast Company*, September 30, 2002, www.fastcompany.com/45400/secret-life-ceo-do-they-even-know-right-wrong.

8. https://cio-wiki.org/wiki/Shareholder_Value.

9. ExxonMobil, "Notice of 2011 Annual Meeting and Proxy Statement," April 13, 2011.

10. Brian J. Bushee, "Do Institutional Investors Prefer Near-Term Earnings over Long-Run Value?," *Contemporary Accounting Research* 18, no. 2 (2001): 207–246.

11. Kim, Yongtae, Lixin (Nancy) Su, and Xindong (Kevin) Zhu. "Does the Cessation of Quarterly Earnings Guidance Reduce Investors' Short-Termism?" *Review of Accounting Studies* 22, no. 2 (June 1, 2017): 715–52.

12. Lucinda Shen, "The Most Shorted Stock in the History of the Stock Market," *Fortune*, August 7, 2018 (emphasis added).

13. James Temperton, "Google's Pixel Buds Aren't Just Bad, They're Utterly Pointless," *Wired*, December 7, 2017.

CHAPTER 17. STRATEGIC PLANNING: HITS AND MISSES, USES AND MISUSES

1. George Albert Steiner, *Top Management Planning* (New York: Macmillan, 1969).

2. There are nine kinds of neuraminidase from N1 to N9 and seventeen types of hemagglutinin, from H1 to H17. The 1918 flu was H1N1, and COVID-19 is H7N9.

3. https://s.wsj.net/public/resources/documents/Scientists_to_Stop_COVID19_2020_04_23_FINAL.pdf.

4. https://en.wikipedia.org/wiki/Mission_statement.

5. "Not led, I lead."

6. James Allen, "Why 97% of Strategic Planning Is a Waste of Time," *Bain & Company Founder's Mentality* (blog), 2014, www.bain.com/insights/why-97-percent-of-strategic-planning-is-a-waste-of-time-fm-blog/.

7. www.brainyquote.com/quotes/katie_ledecky_770988.

CHAPTER 18. RUMSFELD'S QUESTION

1. Lucien S. Vandenbroucke, "Anatomy of a Failure: The Decision to Land at the Bay of Pigs," *Political Science Quarterly* 99, no. 3 (1984): 479. Their reference was (CIA director) Allen Dulles, handwritten notes, box 244, Allen W. Dulles Papers, Seeley Mudd Manuscript Library, Princeton University, Princeton, NJ.

2. According to the *New York Times*, October 20, 1991, "The startling revelations by United Nations inspectors about Iraq's nuclear weapons program are both exhilarating and embarrassing for the American intelligence agencies—exhilarating because they provide a flood of reliable data about the country's ambitious quest for nuclear bombs, embarrassing because they illustrate just how little the United States knew about the program. In the months since United Nations teams began their search-and-destroy mission against Iraq's weapons of mass destruction, they have uncovered a nuclear program far grander in scope, more sophisticated in design and much further along than was suspected in Washington."

3. Vice President Dick Cheney, speech to the Veterans of Foreign Wars national convention, August 2002. Cheney did not always think this way. In the early 1990s, after Bush Senior pushed Iraq out of Kuwait but refused to march on Baghdad, Cheney said, "If you can take down the central government of Iraq, you can easily see pieces of Iraq fly off. Part of it the Syrians would like to have in the West. Part of Eastern Iraq the Iranians would like

to claim—fought over for eight years. In the North you have the Kurds, and if the Kurds spin loose and join with the Kurds in Turkey, then you threaten the territorial integrity of Turkey. It's a quagmire if you go that far and try to take over Iraq." *ABC News* interview, 1994, youtu.be/YENbElb5-xY.

4. Daniel Kahneman, *Thinking, Fast and Slow* (New York: Macmillan, 2011).

5. Hill's exhaustive review of the experimental results on group performance concluded, "For easy tasks, performance was often determined by one competent member." On more complex tasks, "group productivity seemed to be determined by the most competent group member, plus 'assembly bonus effects,' minus losses due to faulty group process." An unpopular conclusion, this line of research has been superseded by investigations into the benefits of diversity in group membership. G. W. Hill, "Group Versus Individual Performance: Are *N* + 1 Heads Better Than One?," *Psychological Bulletin* 91, no. 3 (1982): 535.

CHAPTER 19. A FOUNDRY WALKTHROUGH

1. A pivot machine is a watering system that rolls around a central pivot. The term is also used for watering machines that roll horizontally across the planted acreage.

CHAPTER 20. STRATEGY FOUNDRY CONCEPTS AND TOOLS

1. Gary A. Klein, *Sources of Power: How People Make Decisions* (Cambridge, MA: MIT Press, 2017), 58.

2. This is the core of the argument made by Daniel Kahneman in *Thinking, Fast and Slow* (New York: Macmillan, 2011).

3. Gary Klein, "Performing a Project Premortem," *Harvard Business Review* 85, no. 9 (2007): 18–19.

4. D. Kahneman and D. Lovallo, "Timid Choices and Bold Forecasts: A Cognitive Perspective on Risk Taking," *Management Science* 39, no. 1 (1993): 17–31.

5. Chris Bradley, Martin Hirt, and Sven Smit, *Strategy Beyond the Hockey Stick: People, Probabilities, and Big Moves to Beat the Odds* (Hoboken, NJ: John Wiley & Sons, 2018), 6.

6. Edward W. Merrow, Kenneth Phillips, and Christopher W. Myers, *Understanding Cost Growth and Performance Shortfalls in Pioneer Process Plants* (Santa Monica, CA: Rand Corporation, 1981), 88.

INDEX

Photo credit: Cathy Maier Callahan

Richard P. Rumelt is one of the world's most influential thinkers on strategy and management. *McKinsey Quarterly* described him as "strategy's strategist" and "a giant in the field of strategy." He is the author of *Good Strategy/Bad Strategy: The Difference and Why It Matters*, reviewed by the *Financial Times* as "the most interesting business book of 2011" and by *Strategy + Business* as "the year's best and most original addition to the strategy bookshelf." Dr. Rumelt received his doctoral degree from Harvard Business School and is Professor Emeritus at the UCLA Anderson School of Management.

PublicAffairs is a publishing house founded in 1997. It is a tribute to the standards, values, and flair of three persons who have served as mentors to countless reporters, writers, editors, and book people of all kinds, including me.

I. F. Stone, proprietor of *I. F. Stone's Weekly*, combined a commitment to the First Amendment with entrepreneurial zeal and reporting skill and became one of the great independent journalists in American history. At the age of eighty, Izzy published *The Trial of Socrates*, which was a national bestseller. He wrote the book after he taught himself ancient Greek.

Benjamin C. Bradlee was for nearly thirty years the charismatic editorial leader of *The Washington Post*. It was Ben who gave the *Post* the range and courage to pursue such historic issues as Watergate. He supported his reporters with a tenacity that made them fearless and it is no accident that so many became authors of influential, best-selling books.

Robert L. Bernstein, the chief executive of Random House for more than a quarter century, guided one of the nation's premier publishing houses. Bob was personally responsible for many books of political dissent and argument that challenged tyranny around the globe. He is also the founder and longtime chair of Human Rights Watch, one of the most respected human rights organizations in the world.

• • •

For fifty years, the banner of Public Affairs Press was carried by its owner Morris B. Schnapper, who published Gandhi, Nasser, Toynbee, Truman, and about 1,500 other authors. In 1983, Schnapper was described by *The Washington Post* as "a redoubtable gadfly." His legacy will endure in the books to come.

Peter Osnos, *Founder*